A Long Day in Venice

A Long Day in Venice

ABEL POSSE
GEORGE HENSON (TRANSLATOR)

First published in the English language in Dublin, Ireland, in 2022
by Betimes Books CLG

www.betimesbooks.com

Originally published in Spanish (Argentina) as *Vivir Venecia* by Emece in
2016

Work published within the framework of "Sur" Translation Support Program
of the Ministry of Foreign Affairs and Worship of the Argentine Republic

Obra editada en el marco del Programa "Sur" de Apoyo a las Traducciones del
Ministerio de Relaciones Exteriores y Culto de la República Argentina

ISBN 978-1-9161565-3-1

Cover image © Svetlana Pironko

Cover design by JT Lindroos

TRANSLATOR'S NOTE

When Betimes Books approached me about translating *Vivir Venecia*, Abel Posse's Venetian memoir, I eagerly accepted, for a multiplicity of reasons. First and foremost, Posse's literary reputation preceded the invitation. His novel *Los perros del paraíso*, translated as *The Dogs of Paradise* by the late Margaret Sayers Peden, had been required reading as a graduate student, a novel that earned the author the prestigious Rómulo Gallegos International Novel Prize, a distinction he shares with his contemporary Elena Poniatowska, whom I have also translated. I was also attracted to the fact that Posse's life paralleled in many ways that of Sergio Pitol, whose seventh book I was translating at the time. Not only are Posse and Pitol contemporaries, but they also share similar biographies: both are descendants of Italian immigrants, studied law, were career diplomats, and, finally, shared a deep connection to and admiration for Venice.

Despite these parallels, however, their prose could not be more dissimilar. Where Pitol employs long, complex sentences, with interrupting parentheticals, Posse's syntax is shorter, more linear. This does not mean, however, that Posse's prose was easier to translate. On the contrary, his use of playful language, metaphor, and colloquialisms presented unique challenges. As a rule, I favor a foreignizing approach to translation. By this, I mean that I resist the temptation to erase the foreign from the text. Instead, I allow the text's foreignness—linguistic and syntactic—to shine through.

As for the text's lexical challenges, Rioplatense Spanish notwithstanding, Posse employs words in both Italian and Venetian—I refuse to refer to it as dialect—throughout the text to refer to various aspects of Venice and Venetian life (e.g., *rio, canaletto, palazzo, piazza, vaporetto,* etc.). These words will appear in italics; a translation or equivalent will appear in a glossary at the end of the text. Often, after the first occurrence of the Italian word, the author defaults to the Spanish equivalent of these words (palacio, plaza, etc.). Rather than surrendering to the temptation to recur to English, and because the Italian cognates are easily understood by a general readership, I have expanded the use of these and other Italian words. Likewise, the names of buildings, institutions, monuments, etc. will appear in Italian rather than in English translation.

Syntax and lexis aside, other immediate challenges in translating this memoir were the abundant cultural and historical references specific to Venice. In short, one who has not been to Venice would find it very difficult to write—and by extension translate—about *La Serenissima* without betraying a certain ignorance. Equally numerous were the many political references to Italy and Argentina during the 1970s, a chaotic decade for both countries. While footnotes in literary translation are (rightfully) viewed with scorn, their use in nonfiction can play an important role. My rule of thumb is simple: if the text lends itself to footnotes in the original, footnotes are permissible in the translation, but only when the references in the text—historical, cultural, political, literary—would be lost on the contemporary English-language reader. Similarly, rather than relying on interlinear explication to define or explain some words or metaphors, I provide translations in footnotes. I have also employed footnotes for other explanatory reasons.

Also like Pitol, Posse employs, to great effect, a large number of quotations, from a variety of languages—English, Italian, German, French—which have been translated into Spanish. And like Pitol, the sources of some of these quotations were, at times, difficult to locate. Wherever possible, I will use existing English translations throughout the text; where none exists, however, I will provide my own translation. When the original text or existing translation deviates significantly from the original version, I have explained the differences in footnotes.

As you read *A Long Day in Venice*, the title I have chosen, you will discover it to be more than a mere memoir, but an important cultural and literary artifact that chronicles not only the life of one of Argentina's most important literary figures, Abel Posse, during his consulship in Venice, but also the political and cultural histories of two countries, Italy and Argentina, during the turbulent decade of the 1970s. As a member of the Argentine diplomatic corps, serving in Venice, Posse provides a unique perspective from which to understand this complex and often chaotic time. As consul to one of the most culturally significant cities in the world, through which passed such literary luminaries as Byron, Mann, James, Hemingway, Posse provides a snapshot of the lives of some of the Latin American literary titans who visited Venice during his consulship—Borges, Sabato, Carpentier—as well as numerous Argentine cultural figures from the period.

Finally, as much as the figure of the solitary translator has permeated popular culture, there are many more people involved in the translation of a literary work than its readers may know, all of whom deserve thanks. First and foremost, I am indebted to Svetlana Pironko, the publisher of Betimes Books, for having asked me to translate this book, for her constancy, her thoughtful reading of my translation, and her always helpful suggestions. Many thanks are also due Lawrence Schimel, an always collegial translator, who referred me to the publisher. I also owe a debt to the Tulsa Artist Fellowships, where I am a translation fellow, for providing a stipend that allowed me to hire Michelle Mirabella, a former student and emerging literary translator, who provided invaluable assistance during the research and revision process. Lastly, and most importantly, I owe an immeasurable debt to the author, Abel Posse, for entrusting his memories to me. I hope I have done them the justice they deserve.

George Henson, May 2022

CONTENTS

1

VENICE, A RADIANT midday in April. The water taxi parted the motionless silk of the Grand Canal. We entered through a narrow *rio* toward the Hotel Malibran, which the people at the consulate had reserved for us until we were able to settle into the Palazzo Mangilli Valmarana, on the verge of ruins, ramshackle, nostalgic, with the smell of cats and that deep-scented basil that Lisetta, the caretaker, was growing in planters in the courtyard.

The water taxi left us a couple of hundred meters from the hotel, a distance we must negotiate, carrying valises and other oversized bags from the small stone bridge, guided by Rega and Milossi, the consulate employees. Sabine and Iván, and Delia our maid, behind them, in tow.

The bells of the church of Santa Maria dei Miracoli are ringing. A flock of schoolchildren run about, shouting their joy at being free in the street. They run to the bridge because a wedding gondola passes by, festooned in tulle and balloons. The bride waves with her bouquet of mistletoe and lilacs. A Japanese couple pushes and shoves to take the indispensable photograph. The gondolier shouts. There, in that intimacy of alleyways, Venice is more Middle Ages than Renaissance. Hammering, shouting, employees stopping for an aperitif in a bar as they pass by. The fair-like clamor.

The banality of life just for the sake of it. (All obligations renounceable, replaceable.) We make signs to each other so as not to get lost in the labyrinth's corners.

Venice welcomes us into her intimacy—Mediterranean, Levantine, bordering on Moorish. Further ahead I spy domes. That is where Byzantium must begin. Venice greets us in her raucous, protesting expanse. An eternal schoolyard bustle when ranks are broken. It's twelve o'clock.

I slipped away from the chores of arrival. I went up to the reserved room. I half-opened the blinds and lay down on the coolness of the bed with its canopy of ducal aspiration, but barely three stars. A bed with faded golden columns where surely the indifferent Casanova, in the age of decadence, spent the night with an actress from the old Teatro Malibran that still lent its prestige to the neighborhood and the hotel.

The grace of a moment of peace and harmony. It was as if it had floated through the window to save me from the hubbub of the spring midday.

Happiness to be. Happiness just because, "like the pointless music of the cricket."[1] Like happiness that suddenly falls...And the intimate postcard of that instant will remain for many years at the bottom of the drawer without taking on the sepia tones of age.

We were in that unique city, defended since her birth by her walls of water, inaccessible in many ways, unrepeatable. We would live there for a long day that lasted six years. A circular sexennial, without a before and an after. A continuum. The blurred signs that destiny sends us will

---

1   From the sonnet "El grillo" [The cricket] by the Argentine writer and humorist Conrado Nalé Roxlo.

go about appearing, as if to play with our will, innocent of certainties and plans. I will remember Venice from my Blue Age. That time that invites us not to fear death and misfortune as much as to value the moments of grace. Strumming mists of oblivion, a celebration of having existed during a cycle in Venice. A last time among all her times.

2

IMAGINING VENICE, remembering Venice. Floating with Venice among her *palazzi*, driftless and immobile. The most profound features and nuances appear after two or three weeks of enchanted exaltation, when the astonished traveler passes to the serene reflection of the resident. And becomes even more perplexed!

During one of those first sleepless nights, I went out for a stroll on the long Strada Nova, in the direction of the neighboring palace of the Ca' d'Oro, the greatest expression of Venetian Gothic.

Before arriving there, it occurred to me to slip into the *vicolo*, the tiny street, that leads to the gondola station. There was no one, either there or in the streets. The boats were docked between *paline*, some of them painted in a two-color spiral. They swayed gently in the current of the *Canalazzo*, the Grand Canal, the most splendid avenue in the world. I had the bright idea to try to find the creature that Delia, little Iván, and I had seen that morning, a young female cat raised by gondoliers, which we would christen Ada. The caretakers insisted that in Venice a cat is a necessity in every house. Cats are the masters of the Venetian night, and perhaps so are rats. As I walked onto the gondola dock I saw the eight or ten cats of the colony there waiting in silence. Some of them had surely seen me that morning. But now they were motionless, as if attentive to my footsteps that echoed through the alley that led to the dockyard. They seemed to be watching me, studying me. They'd surely interrupted their brawling and coupling at the arrival of a nocturnal biped, knowing that it is precisely at night when those of their species are most dangerous. It was as if they were looking for a reassuring gesture from me so as not to disband at my intrusion. Cats have a clear distrust of humans; they carry it by experience in their DNA. Human stupidity declared them incarnations of the devil during several centuries of medieval holocaust. In Egypt, however, they'd been declared gods, condemned to a life without freedom among pharaohs or in the silence of the temples. They were included in hieratic hieroglyphs, their flattened profiles alongside humans in scenes sculpted millennia ago in tombs.

I crossed the gondolas' *campiello* and turned back. The cats remained still. The silence seemed false and excessive, like that of a classroom when the teacher walks in. In the half-light their colors were hardly distinguishable, except for a white one and one with a light golden coat. Tabbies and the heirs to panthers prevailed. It didn't take me long to recognize Ada, who was small, nervous, svelte, and whose coat shone bluish black in the moonlit night. Surely a generous god created that species to give humans a chance to pet tigers and absorb a bit of that cosmic calm that is so unreachable to us.

I crouched down to instill confidence in the skeptical and distrustful audience and called out several times to Ada, snapping my fingers. I tried to get closer; Ada didn't move. I was careful not to trespass. She held my gaze, or at least I thought she did, for a moment. I received silence, if not approving, at least accepting, in response. After a moment Ada stepped back and climbed onto the back of the gondoliers' bench.

It seemed right to allow them to return to their trysts, hunts, and territorial skirmishes. I sensed that with Ada we would inaugurate a long friendship in the Valmarana Palace.

Then I walked to the edge of the canal. I looked toward the curve of the Rialto and continued along the opposite bank toward the medieval arches of the *Pescheria* market and beyond, toward the marble masses of Palazzo Corner and the Ca' Pesaro, in the waning moonlight. Stone masses born of lives of power, wanton luxury, vitalism.

The purest water is that of the night tide. Black water, shimmering, with a faint rustle as it laps against the stone steps that descend into the canal. Waters that follow the longing of the tide that begins to retreat to the sea after purifying the marshy silt with salt. Produced there was the satori of the beauty that is power, empire, the surmounting of all that is human taken to the extreme of what is possible. Venice *la abnorme*. Venice on another of her nights. Venice at the dawn of another of her days.

And it was from that dawn that the city wrapped me in her cape of water and marble. I was there, before her majesty, an astonished witness to the lost passion of our residual "Western civilization." Venice had been politically defeated since that fateful 1797, waiting to become sunken like the last Atlantis. Yet it was more West than ever; it was the dignity and pride of being, the greatness of being. A cruel mirror reflecting the present decadence, in the night's lofty silence. It was Tiziano, Michelangelo, and the admirals who at Lepanto courageously defended the injustice against their civilization. Now, I was yet one more. Venice, with her palatial stole and her dead sailors floating among her waters, waxing and waning with the slowness of seaweed.

I must have remained more than an hour in that ecstasy. When I returned, the cats were gone. Day was breaking. I opened the palace gate and crossed the gatehouse courtyard. There was a pungent scent of jasmine. I remembered then the irony of my colleague Enrique Ros, who upon learning that I'd agreed to "be buried" in Venice said to me: "It's incomprehensible that you'd accept a post with the smell of cat piss."

3

BUT HOW HAD I arrived in Venice, which would live within me forever? It began six months before, at the end of November. A change of government was imminent, another storm was brewing in Argentina's rancorous political landscape. By the early seventies in Argentina, a shadow of death foretold a truly unspeakable decade. The unspeakable decade of a child lost to counter-history. A halfwit who discovers a loaded gun.

I recall: the Directorate-General for Political Affairs under the charge of Ambassador Guillermo De la Plaza. It was a sweltering afternoon, and we were in the gallery of the Palacio San Martín that faced Basavilbaso Street. There was a discussion about who should be assigned to what post. We were asked to specify where we'd like to go. Ceustermans was our immediate boss, and he gave each of us the form. I sat at my desk. Medus was laughing. He put down New York, Paris, Rome. We all had our own ideas. I was coming from Russia and Peru, and I thought it was reasonable that I be considered as a second secretary for a minor post in an important political or cultural spot. I put "Delegation to UNESCO, Embassy in Madrid, Consulate in Venice." I added Venice after shouting at the other desks,

"What consulate is available where a secretary can be the chief officer?" Bianculli was the only one who answered me: "Put down Venice, it's Italy .... The Basque, Zubiaurre, who's consul there, has been asking for a transfer for two years. He can't take it anymore." Without saying a word, I filled in the box, and it seemed unbelievable to me that someone might be unhappy in Venice ... and that someone else would put in for a "Second Rate Consulate."

We sought respite from the December heat, nearly every Thursday through Tuesday, in that other Venice, wild and subtropical, which is the Tigre Delta, Buenos Aires's solace and most breathless jewel. We'd rented La Dianita, a run-down house on piles, with no electricity and a water pump, on the Capitán River, close to the Paraná. We'd spend infinite hot mornings in a hammock tied between two casuarina trees. From time to time I'd go to the wobbly pier and swim with Iván and his friend Martín Imaz, both from the secret family of Enoch, who would spend hours on a tiny beach next to the dock's pilings waiting for "the waves" when a passenger boat would motor by. They'd gather the brown water in their hands and toss each other silver coins that glittered ephemerally in the sun.

On the morning of January 9, the boat that runs between the islands bringing ice and newspapers forced me to leave the hammock and go to the dock to collect the block of ice that would burn your hands until you deposited it in the zinc icebox. The newspapers were tied to a stick and thrown without the boat stopping at the moorings. I grabbed them and stretched out in the hammock, where I happened upon the news from the Foreign Ministry. The decree had been signed, and I was being sent to Venice.

There was great rejoicing among our small family. That evening, Sabine and I drank a bottle of Bragagnolo wine, the one the grocery boat sold as a delicacy for gourmets.

I went to the Ministry to report and inquire about the conditions. No one was clear about the consular premises or housing. I was referred to the archive that was located on Diagonal Sur. In the most forgotten corridor of the labyrinth of old desks and employees, which they called La Siberia for good reason, was Sr. Márquez, a clerk who could no longer muster the strength for meaningless formalities. I told him that I was being sent to Venice. It sounded strange when I said it. In the seventeenth century, it would have been like a transfer to London or Vienna.

"Venice? I thought they'd closed that consulate. I saw it once on a list of proposed closings…"

Márquez went to work as well as his arthritis would allow. He'd joined the Foreign Ministry half a century ago, at the end of Alvear's presidency.

"The letter V is up there…," he said. He took down a brown manila envelope. "The last person to see this must have been Minister Zubiaurre when he was sent there during Onganía's term. Is he still there?"

"Yes. I'm going to relieve him in the post."

He opened the envelope and took out a yellowed typed inventory list and allowed me to glimpse at black and white photos in a tone that wasn't sepia, but the brown of old age and humidity.

"You see what I mean? Look at this marble staircase that descends into the water, look at the broken steps…" I saw gay white and blue pilings as if for mooring boats, crowned by a seagull in pose. Márquez was miserly about showing the photos, as if they were pornographic, or he didn't want to displease me too much. The envelope read "Consulate in Venice, Palazzo Mangilli-Valmarana. Lease." I saw faded Pompeian murals, with griffons and garlands of imaginary fruits; a gilding in the furniture designed by a certain Vicentini, dulled over the course of three centuries; a descent from the Cross from the workshop of a certain Tiziano ....

"That's how it is here, the well-connected always get the best posts. As things stand, Secretary, it would be better for you, if I may, to stay a couple of years in Venice and work toward a serious assignment, like you deserve," said Márquez.

I thanked him for the sensible advice and asked him to leave the envelope with me for a few days so I could examine the details.

"Of course. But keep in mind that there's no duplicate ... "

I realized that I was receiving a wonderful life moment. I rushed home in a taxi and refrained from leafing through the photos Márquez had just shown me so as not to be disappointed.

Amazed, Sabine and I went about removing Venice from the envelope. Then Palazzo Mangilli Valmarana appeared on the Grand Canal, with a morning sun delicately veiled in the pictures overshadowed by three decades of bureaucratic oblivion. Someone, an old consul, surely now retired, or worse, seemed to wave from the *piano nobile*. The photos of the grand salon with its withered stuccoes, the Pompeian drawings, even the marble staircase and the shadow of an almost ghostly gondola passing by. Every object, every door, and even every piece of furniture was all Venice.

We toasted with wine. Sometimes it's good to take a step backwards ... to Venice!

4

VENICE WAS INSINUATING itself into our destiny. Every intense trip, of a long and deep relationship with another reality leaves a mark on us. I sensed that Venice would be more than a professional transfer; it would mean becoming close to and part of the past of a people who prefer to be on the margins of history, as if offended, displaced, or wronged. We would soon know that Venice has her own relevance, it submits us to tests, reflections, and a transformation in the face of what we think is real, of the world as it is. Behind the curtain of tourism, I sensed the message of her glory in such gray times.

We had left the Malibran and settled as best we could into the *mezzanino*, the entresol of the consulate. Our furniture was yet to arrive, crossing the Atlantic on some melancholy Greek freighter. I signed my personal contract with Dr. Chiesa, representative of Count Cini, owner of the Palazzo Mangilli Valmarana.

I slowly grew accustomed to the rumbling bellow of the *vaporetti* at night. I suffered from insomnia and unfamiliar feeling of insecurity. I'd try to read before dawn, but without being able to concentrate. I'd listen, after the passing of some boat, to the churning "waters dark as oil but brought to life by salt and pure sea." The wakes, already fading, died out between the broken marble steps, the ones the archivist Márquez had shown me in the photos. But the reservations of the first weeks were irrational: the fear of getting sick, an ineffable sensation of instability. One night I thought that we'd actually left the world of real appearances. We'd entered the nineteenth century and perhaps further back.

In those early days I fulfilled the professional obligation to visit functionaries, starting with the prefect, the mayor of the city, and colleagues from the consular corps. The most receptive and effusive seemed to me to be the Honorary Consul of Mexico, Dr. Giavi, an extremely wealthy international coal trader. His luxury office was above Harry's Bar, with a spectacular view of San Marco and the Giudecca. He was slim, aristocratic, and spoke Castilian free of any sort of fake Mexicanisms. During our long conversation, it occurred to me to confide my nighttime fears to him; Giavi was aware of the apparently quite frequent subject.

"It's quite common. There are people who suffer from what one might call a hypochondria syndrome. People who experience the irrational fear of having left the habitat of normality, and must circulate on water streets, among floating marble palaces. Many newly arrived colleagues make doctor's appointments for some imaginary illness; in reality it's an incompatibility with an abnormal aquatic world. Without saying more, your predecessor, Zubiaurre, believed he had major gastric problems. He had a complete checkup in Padua. But they found nothing. And he was not reassured! Venice unsettles, disturbs, until you surrender or she tames you. Venice has the strength of those who've already lost. The attraction of the defeated or the agonist. She seduces, not surprisingly ... with her irresistible beauty."

Symbol of the other West. Always in danger of non-existence, Venice faces the threat of another death, this time perhaps from that sea that launched her into the frenzy of her centuries of greatness, triumphs, adventures, and riches.

That same morning, I was received by the Cardinal Patriarch. I merely had to cross from Giavi's office, beneath the light of an already torrid summer, the incredible piazza, in the direction of the Basilica di San Marco, with its splendid chariot of bronze horses, while the giants of the Clock Tower struck the eleventh hour, to the astonishment and even the applause of a motley throng of tourists. I entered the Building of the Patriarchate for my protocolary visit to the Cardinal.

The ceremonial rooms were closed. I was ushered into the office area. The Cardinal received me without the slightest sign of his high investiture; he was wearing a working cassock and we sat around his desk. He spoke to me generously about the welcoming reception Argentina had given to émigrés from Friuli and Veneto, especially during difficult times for Italy. His tone was soft, his voice impeccable, his gaze attentive and warm. I communicated the goodwill of our consulate. Patriarch Luciani was the "priest son" of a family of humble peasants from the Veneto. The Venetians paid him little attention. They couldn't imagine the power and the glory that destiny would afford that great man from Canale d'Agordo,[2] of the almost shiny cassock of a poor priest. The history of Venice was made with patriarchs who arose from the Venetian aristocracy; they'd thus defended themselves from the papacy and its policy of domination.

---

2   A town and commune in the province of Belluno in the Veneto region, birthplace of Pope John Paul I.

They had the ability to impose their cardinals on Rome and to manage even their own inquisition. They'd thus moderated for centuries the power of the Vatican. Venice was a territory reasonably free of religious repression. It was tolerant of religions and races. It gave temporary refuge to Giordano Bruno and other occultists and heterodox. It was the vanguard of a new sexual conduct and assumed the role of libertine. But that *Serenissima* no longer existed either as an empire or as a power in Italy itself. It was more important: it existed as a mystery and a challenge.

The patriarch, with his calm voice, referred to the new decadence, to the new danger of a kind of "beach paganism" that imposed itself as a globalized and youthful fashion. Modernity. He gestured to a file. It was a report of his dioceses, especially those of the seaside resorts of Jesolo, Riccione, and Cattolica, near Venice. He murmured.

"Empty paganism, a cult of bodies, they are complimented on everything, all mystery and possibility of transcendence is voided. They talk so much about love, but it is love in the end that is extinguished."

After a few thoughtful moments, the cardinal showed himself in the peasant priest.

"One must be willing to recognize that the sacred fled Venice centuries ago. Perhaps these magnificent churches are an expression of guilt more than of faith, and an aesthetic opportunity to have Carpaccio, Tiziano, Bellini, Tintoretto, and the best carved chalices of all Europe. Perhaps is God not also there? Is art not the highest and most worthy possibility of our tiny human condition?"

Cardinal Patriarch Luciani accompanied me to the door of his office where his *familiar*, that is, his assistant, was waiting for me. He told me that he had great affection for Argentina and that some of his relatives had emigrated at the beginning of the century. "I always have Argentina in my prayers." I bowed to kiss his hand, as the ritual demands before the most reverend excellencies, and I came out into the sun of San Marco. I looked toward the pagan chariot, atop the basilica. Its bronze horses galloping in full sun, as if fleeing to their native Byzantium, where they'd been kidnapped by the Crusaders. The patriarch had suggested that among all the symbols it represented, Venice had been the pagan and sensual resistance to medieval Christianity. A guilt-ridden Christianity, cruel in its demands and orthodoxies. Curious that he would say it to me with such naturalness.

5

I PAY A formal visit to the consulate offices located on the main floor of the *palazzo*. My desk is separated from the offices by a grand vestibule that is presided over by a *Descent from the Cross* attributed to the workshop of Tiziano. During the war, the Italian government had placed it in the tenancy of foreign representatives. Before greeting the consulate's ragtag skeleton staff, Rega shows me with pride the sumptuous spaces and marble floors that had been refashioned into terrazzo according to a secret formula.

"They remain at the same temperature; in winter they don't feel like marble but rather like hardwood ...," says Rega. He takes pride in having done his job for more than thirty years, in a historic building, whose details he has been able to explain to each of the consuls who've successively passed through Venice.

The old desks are varnished, but since 1946! Rega introduces me to *Signora* Adela, who will retire soon. She's standing at her desk before her wide-carriage Olivetti typewriter, with its infinite roll of the Daily Ledger, where all the operations are recorded by date, time, reason, and fee. The petitioners leave the document to be certified (consular invoices, authorizations, records, etc.), then stop by the

Banco Ambrosiano, just a few steps away, and return with the receipt of payment. The consul must sign all the originals. I prepared a special pen, with black ink, for this purpose.

The *Signora* Adela has a hard smile. She's sporting a fresh gardenia on her chest, with dewdrops, bought for the occasion. She explains her work to me. Rega officially introduces me to Idilio Milossi, whose responsibilities are split between running errands, cleaning desks, and maintaining the hall. He's a sullen, efficient, and silent type. Of vague and long-suffering Balkan origin. Neither he nor the *Signora* Adela ever evoked their private lives torn apart by deaths, migrations, broken dreams. They have the dry courage that Europeans had before the current recovery and welfare.

"All I'd like to say is that I wish the best for each of you who are already part of the consulate. We'll upgrade by adding a much-needed counter for assisting the public. Please give me your suggestions on how we can work best together," I said.

Milossi invited me to follow him through an adjoining dark corridor to visit his empire of broomsticks; shelves of cleaning supplies; a basin of beat-up marble, from the time of the "new building," as Rega calls the construction of 1751; and a small table covered by an oilcloth with a gas heater and a dented aluminum pan where very black, bitter, but essential, coffee grounds are always kept warm, but dilutable with tap water.

"In case *il Signor Console* so wishes or for a guest. We have four French porcelain cups...," and he pointed to them. Then, in a very low voice, he ventured an explanation: "Those two have hated each other for thirty years. If they speak to each other, they insult each other immediately; that's why they work like mutes, using gestures."

I don't answer. I get the impression that my skeleton staff seems to work well together, but it hides a bureaucratic cold war.

To end the morning of introductions, Rega pulls me aside to my office and points to the file cabinets in the room through whose window enters the happy murmur of the Grand Canal and the hustle and bustle of the market on the opposite shore, with all its stands of various edible treats—maritime, terrestrial, and aerial.

With the solemnity of a secret, Rega shows me a small card written in ballpoint pen with the combination to a 1920 Italian safe, painted brown. Rega takes out the code book and ceremoniously hands me the sealed envelope signed by Zubiaurre, the outgoing consul. The code system, in that consulate with so few secrets, was transmitted using a manual punch machine, letter by letter, according to the key code. I would only have to use it once.

Rega wanted to show me the interior gallery on the same floor of the hall that led to the area that the owner, Count Cini, kept reserved but unused. They say that this gallery had a magnificent library. They also say that the astute English Consul Smith protected the brilliant Canaletto and even had him paint in this space overlooking the courtyard of Villa Lisetta, at the entrance. He was a great collector and Canaletto, a modest artist.[3] Many of his paintings can be seen today. In London, of course.

---

3   The sobriquet of Giovanni Antonio Canal, an eighteenth-century Venetian painter. His paintings were widely collected by English gentlemen on their Grand Tour through Europe, of which Italy, and Venice in particular, were principal destinations.

He opened doors leading to darksome spaces with the locked-away air of an abandoned house.

"Allow me to show you a relic…" He opened a final door to an incredible accumulation of furniture buried in poorly rolled curtains, clothing, and bedspreads.

"The Count believes that this could be a valuable piece that the French refused to recognize and pay for… It's the bed where Josephine Bonaparte slept, when the brazen Bonaparte seized Venice in 1797 and defied the Grand Council, demanding unconditional surrender, delivered by an insolent French sergeant, written ignominiously on a drum skin."

"How did they respond? I mean, the Venetians."

"They surrendered. They were all merchants. There was no longer any military pride. Simple cowards. That night, for fear of a backlash, Napoleon stayed aboard his captain's ship and Josephine, who was seasick, slept here in the palace."

I recounted the story of Josephine's relic at dinner. As a consequence, the next morning, at my request, Milossi opened the lock of the side gallery and from my desk I was able to see Sabine, Delia, Iván and even the cat Ada pass one after the other in single file toward the bed of the empress who became seasick from the sway of the ship. All they saw was an amassment of old rags, but they returned in awe. And Iván looked up "N" for Napoleon in the Espasa encyclopedia and showed us the uninspiring portrait of *Joséphine de Beauharnais*.

6

M ORE THAN ENTERING Venice, I was entering an idiosyncratic life, even if only as a temporary citizen. Learning the rhythm of the house. Learning about the flowerpots that the caretaker Lisetta, kind and helpful, waters in the afternoons. Chinese jasmine, spring herbs, rue, linden for sleep, basil for pesto. Her husband, Renato, who is quite old, grumbles in *vèneto*[4] as he places his rickety old chair between the entrance to the gallery and the court-yard and plays his mandolin. They have two Persian cats, slight and mean, who don't set foot on the street. When they smelled and saw Ada, brought by Delia and Iván to live with us, they pricked up their ears, distrustful of a ter-ritorial invader.

Ada comes to my desk to say hello. The two of us would isolate ourselves in the back of the palace, where there were pieces of junk, well-traveled and weather-beaten valises, a carpentry bench with rusty tools. I restored a small room

---

4   The Venetian language, which many refer to as a dialect. This categorization, however, is wrong. Rather than a dialect of so-called Standard Italian, Venetian is a linguistically distinct language, spoken by some 5 million people, both in Italy and in the diaspora, including immigrants to Argentina.

that had a window with rusty bars that overlooks the *canaletto* of Santi Apostoli.

From the first days, Ada had surprised us by not showing the feral signs that could be expected from a cat that, although young, had lived in freedom on the streets and alleys of her city. She didn't scratch furniture, jump on tables, and she had soon become accustomed to the litter box. In reality, there was no reason to be surprised; Venice is one single palace, a residence for all, with her watery walls that have protected her since the barbarian invasions in the fifth century. Ada had always been a citizen of a house with long corridors that turn into a labyrinth. The Venetians say that only cats can return to Venice by the same path by which they left.

We subjected her to the barbarity of a bath. She became anxious. She put out her claws just enough to let me know that she was there in case she reached her limit of tolerance. Iván laughed seeing her close her eyes as the warm water trickled down her muzzle. The worst part was the electric hair dryer. But finally, she stopped lashing her tail and relaxed her ears as she felt the unexpected pleasure of the warm air backwards against her coat, held by friendly hands. Belonging to those barbarian friends: humans—capable of believing that cats should be bathed!

Repairs, purchases related to settling in. The house begins to move, it ignites. The noise of pots and pans arriving from other azimuths. Some broken pottery. Paintings protected for the journey with pressed cardboard as if masterpieces ... because you never know.

Sunday in the *palazzo*, without people or service. Touring the bowels of the building. I'll dive into its hidden nooks and crannies. In the main hall I touch with my palm the withered silk of the stuccoes that adorn its walls. High above I discover traces of gold paint on the acanthus leaves on the ceiling. I pilfer through the chests of drawers used to file the old consular documents from the thirties and before. Wooden pens, quills for cursive writing used to write in the Daily Ledger, buttons, a single cufflink, metal clips eroded by decades of sea air. In a deep, ramshackle armoire in the side corridor that no longer leads anywhere, decades-old and decommissioned typewriters are piled up. Reams of forms tied up with cord, moth-eaten overcoats, dead and forgotten clothes, broken umbrellas that once belonged to forgetful consulate clients. Letters and packages that no one will ever pick up.

The wistfulness of a Sunday afternoon.

7

LANDING WITH ALL your belongings, and for a long time, in a new city, brings the feeling of renewal and even the illusion of rebirth. I slip off into the street and drink a coffee, standing at the snack bar next door. I am *il nuovo console*. That might last five or six months, then I'll become the consul.

It's a new life inside our old life. A space of possibility that we'll inhabit with new answers. As I sipped my *ristretto* I felt that this Venetian experience would serve to enrich my writing voice beyond that of the novel and style that I'd captured in my first two published books. During the voyage, I'd felt the impulse of a different expressive form rising to the surface, more linked to my own particularity, my character, my central ideas, my rejections, obsessions, affections, hatreds, mistakes. Closer to that enigmatic totality that we feel as "what we are." I sensed that the most efficient and intense form of the literary is produced in that dark zone of being, when what we've been in the process of being, and the thinking and feeling, and instinct and reason, alternate successively on different paths of writing. By assembling—or disassembling—that totality of oppositions, one can arrive at one's own voice.

I believed then that I should free myself from my first two books, even if they'd been discreetly noticed in the anonymous and depersonalized sea of bookstores. They were works born of what Gide called the writer's will to enter into dialogue with the possibilities of living in his time.

After coffee I walked through the alleys leading to the *Fondamente Nove*. I was convinced that my first two novels were born of this ideological and narrative Frenchness of the *porteño* writers, that is, the writers of Buenos Aires. The *porteño* I, the lost conversations in the café at Parque Lezica with Bazán, Requeni, Ballester, Teme, and sometimes with the anointed: Nalé Roxlo, Castelnuovo, Rafael Alberto Arrieta. The free university of the *porteño* café. While walking along the *fondamenta*, I asked myself: after Borges, Lezama Lima, Rulfo, or Arguedas, could one continue to be a narrator only of the socio-cultural and political themes of his time? Except for Borges, Cortázar, Enrique Molina, and the poets, we Argentine writers were on the margins of the great experiment of the Latin American novel. Borges made fun of the realism of Balzac, "those writers who enter a room and feel the need to describe all the furniture and even the mood of the doorman who showed them in."

One begins to write without giving much thought to the direction and meaning, or the effect, that this curious decision or passion may have. I preferred to move forward in that search which resulted in what was most useful and necessary: the will to write according to a new thematic path and form, without the desire to repeat myself. I wanted to *crack-up*,[5] to break the apparent or intellectual self.

---

5 This is probably a reference to Fitzgerald's posthumous collection of essays *The Crack-up*, which the author quotes twice in the book.

I returned home and began to arrange the papers and notes from my novels, to line up my pens and prepare the 1917 typewriter, the Continental, which guaranteed typographic slowness and noise, the 1930 Underwood, which must have been used to take down the statements of gangsters in the Brooklyn of Lucky Luciano or Marlowe, that independent moralist.

8

I HAD JUST arrived in Venice when Sabato called unexpectedly from Rome. It was the first bit of proof that Venice is indeed a universal drawing room,[6] a sanctuary for pilgrims and pilgrimages. In this case a refuge. He disclosed that there were threats against his life and that he was doing interviews in Rome with the press. He was looking for a kind of PR deterrent effect. He'd made statements on the radio against terrorism.

Rega went to pick him up at the train station; he was arriving from Rome. He greeted us with the seriousness of a furrowed brow, as if he were fleeing an attempt on his life. He took the opportunity for a literary quote, from Thomas Mann, how arriving in Venice by train is like entering a palace through the back door.

"But what can I do! López Rega's goons threatened my life… The clock started ticking on my life back in Argentina."

"How so?"

"With calls to my home in the middle of the night. I'm sorry, I don't want to get you involved, but this is

---

6   This is a reference to Napoleon's alleged description of the Piazza San Marco as "le plus elegant salon d'Europe" [the most elegant drawing room of Europe].

not a pleasure trip," and he gave a smile with a wince of bitterness.

"I read your interview in Rome, in the *Repubblica* newspaper."

"Yes, I thought the best thing to do was to come to Italy and denounce what is happening to me. The only thing that can stop them is the press or an international outcry. It's the Triple A.[7] The people in Rome were indignant; they even offered to let me stay until the danger passes."

I show him to the guest room. It's still in need of furniture, only two single beds separated by one of those bedside lockers with a little door to store the chamber pot. The nineteenth-century remains of the *palazzo*. The guest bathroom has a bathtub from the same period as the bedside locker, with lion's paw feet, and extraordinarily deep, so deep that someone could drown if they fall asleep. I say to Ernesto:

"By the way, your friend Nilda called me and told me that she'd traveled to Italy to do an article for the *Clarín* newspaper and that she'd likely pass through Venice. I told her to make sure to call me when she arrived."

Sabato looked at me and smiled at my discretion. Nilda was his young female friend. We used to run into each other when she was with him at the Café Dandy on Libertador. Nilda was ironic, sexy, charming, and anxious to the point of biting her nails, writing and becoming depressed, to the point of wishing to die. She had a good novel, *The Sect*.

"She made a reservation at the Hotel La Fenice," Sabato told me quietly as if to reassure me.

---

7   The *Alianza Anticomunista Argentina* [Argentine Anticommunist Alliance] was a Peronist death squad operated by a branch of the Federal Police and the Argentine Armed Forces.

In 1966, we had created, along with the musicologist Ernesto Epstein, Tomás Maldonado, and Sabato, the magazine *Crisis*, thanks to the generosity of Federico Vogelius. Tomás Maldonado had arrived from Italy; he was Inge Feltrinelli's partner and a communist senator. The European *gauche divine*. He'd been director of the revolutionary Bauhaus, which was the experimental center of European plastic arts. Although Maldonado had more fame than work, the Bauhaus, as an aging avant-garde, gave him prestige.

Crisis was originally conceived to be a preeminent cultural and pluralist magazine. Its objective was to lift us out of provincialism, with an aesthetic directed at the profound and permanent, following the extraordinary literary boom in Argentina and Latin America. Faced with the reality of my transfer abroad, I disassociated myself from the magazine in December. I felt that Argentine politics was taking a dark turn. Months later, Vogelius dedicated *Crisis* to the politics of the revolutionary left without calculating the consequences. But it became a magazine of the time and an inescapable reference. Sabato also distanced himself.

It was then that I began to understand that my diplomatic career helped me to free myself from stranding and snags, whether existential, personal, or historical. Crises of love, sex, money. By then I already felt like an able sailor: destined to set sail. Always pulling anchor and setting sail. There is destiny, which is a mystery, and there is a will, perhaps naïve, to improve one's destiny, even though we know it is inexorably written. Believing in destiny relieves us from accepting fortune and misfortune as surprises.

We were having an aperitif with Sabato on the balcony of the consulate before the radiant spectacle of midday.

Ernesto recounted the episodes of Argentine politics and especially his own, with invariably dramatic tones. I tried to distract him toward our splendid reality by showing him the bustle of the *Pescheria* market. I pointed to the *traghetto* that the Venetians use to move people along the Grand Canal, a few seated, and six or seven standing, balanced by experienced sailors.

"You deposit a hundred lira coin and cross," I said. The *Pescheria* is the oldest market: a thousand years in the same place.

"Charon," said Ernesto somberly.

But nothing really caught his attention. Not even when Iván appeared, who'd returned from school, followed by the cat.

"Say hello to the most famous writer in Argentina," I said to my son. Ernesto seldom paid attention; he was always distracted by his ideologies, judgments, protests. Reality was never visible in his words; it was merely heard in an eternal attempt to transform it or to remember it, or to revile it with irony and enthusiasm.

From the consulate balcony, the view stretching from the *Pescheria* toward the sun-soaked palaces of the opposite bank and the porcelain-blue sky formed a gigantic smile. I understood that it was a futile effort by Venice to break the stubborn Argentinianness of Ernesto Sabato, who continued talking to me about the crisis of the *Crisis* magazine as if he were accompanying me from the door of his house to Santos Lugares train station. I stretched out my hand toward the flock of pigeons that were gliding over the Canal and the party of seagulls cleaning the crates of seafood being discarded at what was now the market's closing time. Sabato continued, engrossed in his complaint.

"Vogelius was dumbstruck when I told him to no longer count on me for *Crisis*. He tried to change my mind. I was already a communist back in the thirties—when it cost a life or martyrdom! What is coming in Argentina is regrettable childishness. For God's sake! A Guevarized Peronism. Who would even think of such a thing! As you must know, Eduardo Galeano is now in charge of the magazine."

"Jorge Vázquez, the Montonero-diplomat[8]—you'll forgive the extreme oxymoron—told me that Perón, when he met with them, had told them: 'Boys, you're going to start with communism when communism is leaving history without anyone pushing it out...'" Sabato burst out laughing and praised his much-hated Perón.

"What a tremendous son of a bitch!" he said with warm approval.

---

8   The *Montoneros* were a left-wing Peronist guerilla organization in operation in the 1960s and 70s, which took their name from the nineteenth-century cavalry militias called *Montoneras*.

9

I HAD READ in *Il Gazzetino*, the local newspaper, that on that evening they were to award the *Premio Campiello* for best Italian novel at an event in the Palazzo Ducale. It occurred to me to ask Ernesto if he would like to go, so I called Professor Vittore Branca, director of the Cini Foundation, suggesting the possibility. I sensed that Branca was quite keen on the idea. Sabato was a well-known figure at the time. Branca's perceptible enthusiasm opened the possibility for me to add Argentines from journalistic and cultural spheres who were in town: Mario Trejo and Alberto Cousté, director of the Círculo de Lectores de España, and his wife Mónica Feimberg, head of publicity at the Plaza y Janés publishing house.

We met at nine o'clock to have a few drinks as the sun slowly set, then we walked along Calle Merceria toward the Piazza San Marco, dodging museum-weary tourists, forever lost in the circular labyrinth that is Venice. Burning feet, bottles of mineral water. Flabby bodies, spent by walking and queuing to enter museums and vaporetti. By obligation or ritual. Intoxicated by the struggle of trying to understand what would turn out to be almost impossible for them: art. During those years, the seventies, tourism was a cretinizing disease. Today it's a pandemic.

In the Doge's Palace everything was duly solemn. Two cuirassiers in their shiny helmets and dress uniform saluted the entrance of the prefect and the mayor. Branca welcomed us with affection and showed us to a row for invited guests. There, where the protagonists of greatness, successes, miseries, and defeats had passed, Venice displayed all her grandeur, her aesthetic of ritual and power. It was incredible to watch as the officials in their tailored suits, dark gray or administrative blue, were arranged next to the prefect. They should have been encouraged to wear velvet cloaks, feathered hats, or bejeweled pointed miters like those worn by the doges on ceremonial days. That republican and municipal uniform reduces power to an anonymity that can only foretell anarchy or boredom. Venice was floating with indifference above the little men of postmodernity.

The event consisted of reading the vote of a multitudinous jury from all over the Veneto to award the annual Campiello Prize. A friendly announcer read the votes aloud. At a certain point, the name Sgorlon, Sgorlon, Sgorlon, Sgorlon began to be repeated and at the end finished with a resounding lead. There was a round of applause for the winner. Sgorlon took the podium and expressed his thanks with caution and modesty, as if he suspected a favorable injustice. He seemed inhibited and insecure like a belated graduate. I thought it would be difficult for him to write a self-portrait as efficient and true as the one Borges made in 1928: "I am a more or less mournful man who travels by streetcar, but I think it is good that there are coaches and automobiles and a Florida Street with dazzling shop windows."

Sabato looked at me and made an ironic gesture in relation to the ceremony and Sgorlon's conceptual paucity.

We were already standing, applauding him, when on the dais I saw a resplendent couple whom Sgorlón greeted with more deference than the mayor himself. As I'd just been dropped into Venice, I dared to ask Professor Branca who those elegant figures were who seemed like the true envoys of the Doge of Venice to represent him at the award ceremony. Branca told me that they were a married couple, he, an important engineer, named Balder. She was his wife, Andreina Venier, a descendant of the Doge and of the admiral who, together with Andrea Doria, commanded the decisive battle of Lepanto. A professor of Slavic languages.

Sabato was approached by a reporter from *Il Gazzettino*, as I stood watching that extraordinary couple in the box seat against the backdrop of the entrance hall of the Doge's Palace. And beyond, high above, the disproportionate ninety-eight-meter-tall Campanile, "not counting the angel," which, golden and resplendent by day, now floated in the blue night. Venice was outdoing herself.

Andreina tossed her hair back, laughing in the box seat next to the timid and happy Sgorlon, and her hair blended into the tower of the Campanile and the moon-dressed angel.

We laughed at the same thing with Professor Branca.

"Consul, I assure you that it is rather difficult to add to Venice another splendid woman!"

Trejo, too, could not take his eyes off Andreina Venier, who was leaving the dais and walking away.

"I don't know who, but someone said that elegance is a matter of the bones," he commented.

We waited for Sabato who was finishing his interview and decided to go to the Caffè Florian with tables on the edge of the colossal square, where we stayed for a couple of hours around a very happy Sabato. The improvised gathering seemed like a tribute in his honor. He repeated jokes already very familiar to his friends: about Perón, who "when he went into a brothel, he came out married," about Borges and his "erotic pinching," about Isabelita Martínez... Until he thought it was getting late and chivalrously decided to accompany Nilda, tired from the trip, to the Hotel La Fenice.

10

WE ARGENTINES HAVE the tendency to identify with that "more or less bereaved man who travels by tram."[9] We transit that nothingness, that no man's land, the quotidian, until we end up at the exaltation of happiness or pain. Venice caused me to feel this that Saturday in August, when I awoke with a rare and stimulating feeling of happiness. Sometimes the gods smile on us. I'd heard the bells of Santi Apostoli toll eight or nine o' clock, not sure which, because I became distracted counting them. A radiant morning that foretold a hot day. The beams of light passed through the slits in the shutters like floodlights that crossed the penumbra of the bedroom and created golden circles on the wall and ceiling. As the vaporetto passed by with its invariable rumbling I heard Iván's cautious little feet on the mosaic of the corridor. I pretended to sleep, and he waited for a moment, then I barely moved my hand, and he ran to dive into bed and hug me. It was the ritual of summer days. Sabine would roll over for another stroll through the dream lands. I liked to stroke Iván's back like a feline cub. Then I would hold him in the air above my chest

---

9   *The Cultural Life of the Automobile: Roads to Modernity.* Guillermo
    Giucci. Trans. Anne Mayagoitia and Debra Nagao. UT Press.

and he would kick about and flap his arms like wings. He called the game "playing little bird." His golden hair that he inherited from his mother. His muted laughter, cosmic harmony.

When I opened the shutters, I beheld the spectacle of the Grand Canal. The cargo boats, the cry of *uée! uée!* announcing their entrance into the Rio dei Santi Apostoli, which framed the side of Palazzo Valmarana.

I stood there and for the first time in a long time I felt liberated from the inner mourner, that misguided gentleman who nevertheless takes the appointed tram and sometimes arrives where he didn't expect to arrive. "Happy as a bare foot on a beach," wrote Ricardo Molinari. I sensed that in the valley of tears happiness sounds like insolence; it was more appropriate to complain.

My colleague Medus—who had read very few books, had formed a practical philosophy of life, without any salvationist, ethical, or militant aspirations—said: "You can't go round and round with that word happiness. Happiness is a good salary for your professional level, security in the short and medium term, family, children, a dignified death, nothing else."

Nothing else? And what about sleep? Without sleep you die; that's common knowledge, it's a cliché.

Iván was already having breakfast with Delia. I remained facing the morning that was unfolding along the canal. I felt an innocent existential enthusiasm. I'd bought a white desk that I placed in that very bedroom next to the window. There I began to write during the caliginous naps of that summer. Like in our northern provinces, I avoided the sun's glare by adjusting the opening of the shutters and creating air currents that reached the distant depths of the palace, Ada's territory, a warehouse of useless junk, and a backroom transformed into a study, where I erected the shelves of my wandering library.

I thought I'd truly fallen into my voice, the voice needed for the novels I'd set out to write. I was becoming estranged from my two published books. I wrote several pages by entering a freer, riskier, and more natural terrain, and I sought to find the story from my more integrating and just aesthetics insofar as the famous questions of substance and form and of concept and language are concerned. That will to break with what had already been done meant the end of a literary stage. I wanted to distance the lecturer from the artist-writer, to break from the nineteenth-century French tyranny as a general aesthetic.

I had my pens with their different hierarchies and paper that held the pen and ink well. They were hundreds of expired forms in the consulate's Daily Ledger. The sheets were wider than normal paper, which left me a sizable margin for additions and corrections. What would become my novel *Daimón* was born there, with all the violent fits of an eternal Lope de Aguirre and the anarchic madness of Spain; his declaring war on King Felipe II and pretending to organize an army of Amazonian monkeys to destroy the Empire. A serial criminal, a determined and self-confessed supporter of the devil. And his Marañones, his troop of assassins, failed saints, visionaries, conspirators.

I shift to the America I saw in Peru, in Brazil, in the *altiplano*. Immense mosquitoes, leeches sucking the pale ankles of the Iberian hordes, birds of regal plumage, schools of piranha, announcing themselves as the frightful boiling of the waters, capable of devouring a wild ox in half an hour and a Spanish knight in three minutes. A theocidal crusade of slavery, of all the natives herded and guarded by mastiffs that the chronicler Oviedo praised for their ability to recognize and destroy "effeminate, insubordinate, and deserter Indians." He even wrote the apologetic biography of Becerrillo, the champion mastiff of the Christian Americas, trained to kill indigenous fugitives from slavery, or homosexuals. (How would he recognize them?)

The ramshackle palace was beginning to feel like home. The *piano nobile* with its eighteenth-century stuccoed hall and its attributed Guardi, and the *Descent from the Cross* from Tiziano's workshop, was set aside for administrative use. Below our floor, the *mezzanino* was developing a familial warmth. Delia was already beginning to get along in Italian. We enrolled Iván in the Istituto San Giuseppe, the traditional Venetian primary school. We took our son, dressed in coat and tie, to the school, fifteen minutes from the consulate. Mother Lucrezia, the Superior, was waiting for us. We had all the necessary documents with us. Iván was very nervous because his Italian was at a beginner level, logically incorrect and still short on vocabulary. He remained silent when Mother Lucrezia asked him if he liked Venice. The nun ruffled his hair resolutely.

"In three weeks with your new companions, you will understand Italian and even Vèneto!" Iván smiled in relief.

We walked down the corridor along which ran the classrooms. We could sense the smell of erasers, the pencils shavings, longing for their original forest and curling around the pencil sharpener, the pencil box, the ruler, and the protractor like a derisory brass rising sun. The silence and the clean, neutral, and perhaps neutralizing smell of every religious school in the world. The chapel, the foyer with the latest "honor roll" and the outburst of a huge and unseemly Murano glass chandelier, surely a gift from a powerful family.

We went out into the crowded street and walked hand in hand, Iván, Sabine, and I, dodging more tourists than Venetians. Mother Lucrezia had given us a list of school supplies and uniforms, with the addresses of some of the stores. We decided to go immediately. Iván was skipping, his fears left behind, and he accepted and wanted to dive into the first steps of knowledge. One knows well that there, on that first day, the end of childhood begins. The inevitable attack on innocence. What to say, what to comment as a parent? Iván would take the first steps of his gentle taming in the serene Istituto San Giuseppe. He was to begin his second entry into the world.

Must we hand our son over to the world as it is or set him apart and keep him in the world we would like? Those who are set apart suffer. There is no solution to this question. We cannot make a child do what we didn't do. I felt sad, and I couldn't and shouldn't express anything. I suggested that we have a soda at a little bar on the *salizada* of San Zulian and the three of us went on to the stores to buy the uniform and the supplies and the books.

11

PROTOCOL REQUIRED THAT I meet the accredited consuls. Giavi, the Honorary Consul of Mexico, organized meetings twice a month on the breathtaking terrace of the Gritti Hotel on the Grand Canal, near San Marco. A floating *pontile*, swaying from the passing of the vaporetti, was outfitted with a handful of tables with large orange umbrellas. It was there that those pleasant meetings of the "Club of 13" were held. I was welcomed by the dean of the consular corps, the Swiss consul, Richard Hurny. He introduced me with a few brief words and a sense of humor: "We knew that you were bringing in young blood, as they say, into our group of more or less sixty-somethings. We'll soon get to know each other and you, Consul, will tell us what crime you must have committed to be sent to this prison." Everyone laughed and applauded. I expressed thanks, including to my predecessor in our consulate, and added new laughter by saying that "my punishment is surely much greater than yours, as I hope to turn sixty-five in this prison, just as you said."

The dean introduced me to the two groups: the career diplomats, all threatened by their fateful retirement day, and the group of honorary consuls, very talkative and welcoming. I was coming from an Argentina threatened by political violence and entering a cycle of death and lawlessness. Some made a cautious allusion. In reality, the Europeans' refinement prevented them from making a diplomat uncomfortable. I was already familiar with that delicate evasiveness, similar to talking to someone who has an idiot child or an abusive father in the family.

Gritti's *pontile* could not have been more comfortable for that meeting on a sunny midday at the end of spring. I was the newcomer and the two waiters who served us welcomed me by offering me Negronis, the famous Bellinis, or sparkling prosecco. Lake, the British consul, was a gaunt man, of few words and lithe gaze. Baron Giunti was a delegate from the European Union, a cordial Florentine. They felt me out about golf, bridge, and tennis. The Swiss Hurny talked about Italian politics, which was starting to heat up, the result of attacks orchestrated by the Red Brigades and a sea of uncertainty and conspiracies. The Communist Party led by Berlinguer was closer than ever to seizing power, and the Christian Democrats and the right wing were beginning to react in a process that would end with the death of Aldo Moro.[10]

Baron Giunti, as an Italian, complained about the corruption of many Venetians in connection with the Mosè Project.[11] Which, as its title indicated, consisted of "saving Venice from the water" by building a gigantic, flexible, and

---

10 Prime Minister Aldo Moro was kidnapped by the far-left Red Brigades and, two months later, following a "people's trial," assassinated.

11 The MOSE (an acronym for *Modulo Sperimentale Elettromeccanico* [Experimental Electromechanical Module]) is a project designed to protect Venice from flooding. Whether by design or coincidence, the acronym evokes the Italian name (*Mosè*) for Moses.

retractable rubber dam that would be assembled when the onslaught of the sea reached the heights of the historic 1966 flood that was thought would sweep away *la Serenissima*. That delayed project is considered to be the cause of all of Venice's corruption. The generous foreign aid, compelled by aesthetic reasons, was controlled by a political bureaucracy. Moses wasn't able to enter Canaan, nor the *Serenissima*. This was one of the topics of the consular corps.

I surrendered to the armchair, with my eyes on the *Ponte dell'Accademia*, full of indefatigable visitors to the museum. The noise of the water taxis, the roar of the vaporetti, the water lapping gently on the *pontile,* making it sway. Atop the elegant mast nailed to the bottom next to the mooring, an idle seagull with bulging eyes enjoys the Canal's movements.

"Really, it's a glorious day," Lake murmured in English.

I resisted a third Bellini. The consular snack consisted of prawns, fried *calamaretti*, Venetian-style sardines, assorted cheeses, and a small risotto served with care.

Consular problems: passport theft, eviction of hippies, prefectural bureaucracy, exemptions denied by the Finance Office. And the threatening situation of the smiling communism of Berlinguer and Napolitano.

"A laundered Stalin," murmured the Neapolitan Dalogia, Honorary Consul of Malta. The careerists almost never ventured an opinion on politics. It was not worth risking the last months or years of that pre-retirement spring.

12

SABATO HAD THE idea to visit Stravinsky's tomb in the San Michele cemetery. The Coustés, Mario Trejo, and Nora Jaureguiberry, a visiting colleague and friend, tagged along. The painter González del Real and his female companion as well. We'd walked to the *Fondamente Nove* where the vaporetti leave for the cemetery. We sat with Ernesto in the seats at the bow, the best place to enjoy Venice. With his characteristic scowl he predicted a time of horror for Argentina.

"My only protection is that I am internationally known, otherwise I would have to go into exile ... at this stage of my life!"

"Are you going back to Rome?" I asked.

"No. Nilda and I will go to Paris for a few days; she's never been. I have an interview with the people at Gallimard."

"But hasn't your novel had success at the Seuil publishing house? Sarduy is your biggest cheerleader; he never misses an opportunity to praise the sales of *Alejandra*, the title they chose for your *On Heroes and Tombs*."

"Yes, but I want to change. Gallimard is Gallimard ... "
I thought that Ernesto already thought of himself as among the Pléiade. He lived with his vanity like Faulkner with his

alcoholism or Borges with his blindness. The difference is that visible vanity discredits and arouses neither pity nor understanding. On the contrary, it summons ridicule and slander. A crushing Argentina raged against him until he was cornered with an ignoble and choral belittling that would accompany him until his death. Borges himself added a certain ironic phrase against anyone who considered himself his literary peer.

He wanted to be the Sartre of Argentina, but his great intellectual resemblance was with Camus, who inspired his first essays *One and the Universe*, *Men and Gears*. Camus, or the useless, intellectual passion to reconcile social justice and power, social revolution and justice with democracy and law.

In Italy, Sabato was praised for his attempt to give the novel a transcendence that was lost in the prevailing decadence. This flattered him. Enzo Bettiza and Claudio Magris singled him out as a response against "telquelism" and aestheticizing mania. (Sabato's self-esteem was always threatened: he believed more in the word of others than in his own foundations as a writer).

The walls of the Arsenale and the coast of Murano and a forest of cypresses and pines were now in sight, which signaled the floating cemetery of San Michele. We felt the salty breeze. Sabato had brought me as a gift some pages from his *The Angel of Darkness*, which he was convinced I would welcome as an heirloom.

When he asked me about my work I chose not to go into details about my search for the "other voice." He had been so generous as to take my first novel, banned by Spanish censors, to the Sudamericana publishing house, to López Llausas. And for my second one he'd written a few paragraphs of praise, for which I will always be thankful.

The vaporetto grumbled abruptly with its propellers in reverse and we got off at the island of the dead. While I was asking how to find Stravinsky, Sabato went over to the flower kiosk and lingered until he found a splendid rose. We walked slowly among the famous and anonymous dead.

It seemed as if the birds, which abounded, were following us to greet us as liberators from so much silence and stillness. Mario Trejo turned off on a side path. We called out to him, thinking he was distracted, but he gave us a nod and we continued on without him.

We stayed for a while in front of the tomb, with that undefined will to express respect or a feeling of gratitude before someone of such greatness. Sabato stepped forward decisively and bent down to lay the rose on the gravestone. He was not theatrical, but he had the reputation of being so, and sometimes he lacked the good judgment not to look like a politician. No one came up with anything to say. And the silence grew heavy. González del Real's wife, an innocent Black woman, smiling, profoundly oblivious to everything thanatotic, stepped forward toward Sabato and said to him with quasi admiration:

"I can see, maestro, that you deeply appreciated Stravinsky, did you not?"

Trejo was waiting for us on the pathway out. We thought he'd found the toilet, but in fact he managed to locate Ezra Pound's grave site on the map at the entrance. He was a fervent admirer of the American poet who lived in Paris during the years of Gertrude Stein, Toklas, Joyce, and Fitzgerald. Pound during the war had been an intellectual collaborator, via radio, via his pro-fascist lectures. He was living in Rapallo and saw in fascism an anticapitalist and antidecadentist revolution, which led him to confront his own country in arms. Neither Cousté, nor Sabato, nor Mónica Feimberg, who was Jewish, accepted Trejo's defense of Pound. Actually, I think only I and Trejo had read *The Pisan Cantos*. In fact, they weren't fond of Trejo with his ironies, in his gaze or words. A controversy arose that lasted the entire return trip. Sabato, as was to be expected, demanded "an ethical imperative" in every creator and preferably in thinkers and poets. Trejo told him that Pound had wanted to found an ethics by denouncing usury as the essence of capitalism and, above all, by establishing as his objective not capitalism but a community devoted to artistic and creative values.

And so it went on. The unending accusations and refutations clouded the contemplation of the Doge's Palace, which the vaporetto reached at sunset.

13

A RECEPTION WAS planned for the 25th of May, which we postponed until the 9th of July in order to have the house better prepared. Protocol required inviting Argentines residing in Venice, authorities, and prominent figures. In reality a consulate needs a very close relationship with the police, the *Guardia di Finanza*,[12] the judiciary, port authorities, and academics. There are a lot of moving parts to managing all of this. Visiting institutions as well as public and commercial figures requires agility. With banks it is essential. Emigration from "the three Venices" to Argentina was perhaps the most extensive. The juridical and documentation problems required continuous negotiations with state offices. The industrial port of Venice, in Marghera, was the passage point for exports to Argentina, not only from that part of Italy but also countries of Eastern Europe, of all the materials for the Aluar aluminum plant.

But a strange restriction arose prior to our inaugural cocktail party. The *cancelliere* Rega and Milossi burst into my office with the guest list in hand. There were too many. They explained to me that the floors of the *piano nobile*

---

12 An Italian police force under the authority of the Ministry of Economy and Finance responsible for financial crimes.

could not support the weight of three hundred people. They took me to the main hall. The floor was made of ancient "reconstituted marble," a traditional preparation for Venetian palaces that guaranteed a more comfortable temperature than that of cold mosaics. The material is flexible, supported by wooden slats. Milossi, nimbler than Rega, jumped and I heard the tinkling of the crystals on the central chandelier. Since the construction of the Palazzo Mangilli Valmarana, supposedly in 1758, those floors have been a staple that imposes a notion of exclusivity within a mass society. Palaces are limited to the aristocracy, obviously.

"Six or seven years ago a floor collapsed due to overcrowding on the San Marcuola side," said Rega.

I imagined with horror my guests falling from the *piano nobile* to the living room, in the *mezzanino,* where we live. I had a horrifying flash of Professor Branca, of the colonel from the Alpini A. Franzetti,[13] of the patriarch's representative, all falling to the lower floor, some with a canapé or glass of prosecco in their hands.

"Don't laugh, *Signor Console*," Rega said, "it's an important matter; in fact, you can call the mayor's office, and they know how to estimate the weight that a similar floor can support. It's a common thing in Venice."

"All right, Rega. Two hundred would be fine?"

"Yes, *Signor Console*. Besides, not everyone comes, or even at the same time, which is usual."

---

13 The *Alpini* is the name given to the Italian Army's alpine infantry, the first being the Gruppo Bogno di Bosozzo, founded in 1930, and renamed in 1947 for the *alpino* (infantryman) Alfredo Franzetti, who died fighting in the former Yugoslavia during WWII.

For a week, Sabine, Delia, the caretaker Lisetta, and Amedeo, the one-eyed waiter from the yacht club, a specialist in Venetian risotto, had worked to organize properly our first cocktail party. On the evening of the 8th, the eve of the banquet, while watching the news, I heard angry shouting from Delia, a race to the back of the house, and thunderous laughter from Iván. The empanadas that had entailed so much work for two days, stored in an antique cupboard, supposedly the coolest and most guarded space in the palazzo, had been nibbled on. Several dozen were ruined. Ada was thought to have slipped through a crack between the two lopsided century-old wooden doors held up by a hook. When I went to the back, I realized that Ada had managed to outwit Delia's attempt to catch her. She was running toward the living room and the huge Amedeo, who'd come to arrange the tables, was trying unsuccessfully to block her way. As she ran past, she looked me in the eye for an instant then continued on her way, probably to take refuge under the bed or in some emergency hiding place that no one had discovered yet. Delia came running from the back, furious, carrying the trays of the surviving empanadas. There was nothing that anyone could say to her. The cat had bitten into them, not wanting to eat them. She must have bitten into them for pleasure, thinking that those white objects lined up in rows, waiting to be fried and that no one had ever seen in civilized Venice, were a regiment of appetizing sleeping mice. Could a Venetian cat imagine the existence of empanadas from Tucumán?

The cocktail party was well received. It was a good idea to use the ground floor, with its large doors that open to the balconies that overlooked the Canal. There we served the final glass of champagne to those who'd stayed to enjoy the long July sunset with its cooling breeze that provided a relief from the heat.

There we had the first long conversation with Andreina Venier. We spoke about Russia, where I'd been stationed during the final Stalinism, Brezhnev's.

We didn't talk about politics. We spoke of the Russian people, obstinately Dostoyevskian, extremist, cruel, unpredictable, as is often said, and of their great literature. During her travels, she often visited the creators of the final Sovietism and some of the first dissidents, consolidated during those years, praised by the Western press, by Brodsky, Voznesenski, Tarkovsky. Andreina spoke a fin-de-siècle Russian from before the post-revolutionary period, which she inherited from, and was influenced by, a Russian grandmother from Tsarist times, who'd been decisive in her education, as she put it. Andreina was about thirty-two years old, an age when some women of her kind become aware that they have the possibility of avoiding repetition, tedium, and comfort without risk. Women who have become aware of bourgeois morality and decide to challenge conventional power. It's the best contribution they can make and make for themselves. She was one of those women who had to jump over every hurdle. She was already a mother of two boys.

"How long were you in Russia?" she asked.

"Three years. From sixty-seven to seventy. Before that, in 1963, I went on a short trip for students organized by the Intourist agency."

"Where did you study? What did you see?"

"I was doing a doctorate in Political Science at the Sorbonne. I saw what everyone is seeing, with the exception of European or South American intellectuals. I saw boredom.

They lived through a bloody and even heroic fight, at least against Nazism. And they ended up as I saw them: waiting for the West ... Godot. The new Godot. Reduced to idiocy by a pair of jeans. And now allow me to ask you the same question but changing the verb tense: what do you see in Russia?" Andreina laughs, throwing her hair back gracefully.

"As I talk to the survivors of that horror, on every visit I notice the same thing: nothingness. Nowhere is nothingness the same as in the steppes and the tundra. There, mirages and demons appear. At any rate, it's less boring than Venice. No, I don't see anything. The Russia of today is nothingness after something ... That's the disease of our time: waiting without much hope."

"And your communism?"

"I still go to meetings with Carlo Maria Santoro, who's a professor. We go so we can laugh. People speak who believe that Russia, communism, is still a channel for their personal resentment. Napolitano, the deputy, is the best.[14] However, the Italian Party under Berlinguer is on the rise. They will achieve an electoral success, albeit a bourgeois one, leaving the Revolution hanging on the rack. It's well known today: if you remove the hatred, the revolution ends in nothing, no? Do you know what Mussolini said after Stalingrad? Ciano noted it in his diary. The two of them were alone in the Duce's office, which looked out onto the Piazza Venezia and muttered: "Only I could imagine an imperial destiny for a country full of vulgarians and barbers."[15] And she

---

14 The speaker may be referring to Giorgio Napolitano, one-time member of the Italian Communist Party, who went on to be Italy's longest-serving president (2006-2015).

15 Although the author attributes this quote to Ciano's diaries, I

laughed, as if not wanting to forget, smiling with a certain mockery in the sparkle of her eyes. The Venetians of today were included in this. "To many intelligent communists, shall we say, all over the world, something very unique happens, and I think you will understand me. After so much—ideologies, violence, hot and cold world war—after Togliatti, Thorez, and so many of Stalin's lackeys, we're left with the final, ineffable conviction that always returns to us: the stupid capitalist society has no possibility of organizing the world. It can be said, when it's all said and done, that we believe in an inexorable future of elimination of capitalist concentration, of transnational blocs. The present decadence of Europe is proof of this future reality. Men like Berlinguer or Napolitano believe in that future, and in the meantime, they are lukewarm Social Democrats, resigned Mensheviks. Like me. We're enduring, shall we say, the end of the infantile disease of progressive leftism."

When all the guests had gone, around ten o'clock at night, the colors of the sky in slow sunset, a pink-reddish-blue twilight, faded with the slowness of a cosmic oil lamp. It was as if Canaletto had decided to go to sleep, putting away all his colors in the museum of the *Accademia.*

Only those of us from the house and Rega and Milossi remained. Delia and Amedeo brought us a glass of champagne and a platter of empanadas. No doubt Ada saw me and Sabine finishing the party with her last sleeping mice.

---

was unable to locate it in either the original Italian or the English translation.

14

*T*HE BLUE HOUR, the blue hour! I said to myself, recalling the whiskey I drank alone, watching the gondolas full of tourists with their overdose of romanticism. Sabine
was overseeing the renovation; the consulate was transitioning
from the public day to family privacy. I managed to remember
verses about the blue hour from Lugones's poem.[16] It's when
day approaches night and everything turns blue. I'd heard that
phrase spoken by my uncle or one of my cousins on a car trip
to I don't know where; I would have been six or seven years
old. The serene hour, "It's short-lived," said my cousin or uncle.
"Then, night." Could the horses and cows near the barbed-wire
fences along the road have been tinged with blue? I couldn't remember. The blades of the windmills, the eucalyptus, the ombú
trees, and the houses were dissolving.

Venice, after so many centuries of sunsets, was sinking
majestically into another blue hour, a color that must have
been considered by the meticulous Ruskin. I stretched out in the
two-seater and drank my whiskey with a feeling of harmony
rare for me. Venice, the family, the forward march of my work,

---

16   The author is referring to "La hora azul" [The blue hour], a poem by
     prominent Argentine poet Leopoldo Lugones, who, coincidentally,
     committed suicide by drinking cyanide with whiskey.

placed me in a moment of quiet, without my recurring anxiety of not wanting to be and of running from the past to the future and from there to nostalgia. Without respite. Like an unhappy apprentice of existence.

Just as there is a blue hour it occurred to me that there will be a Blue Age. An age in which the essential was lived and, by then, there's a right to the final selfishness and freedom in the face of death. A quiet liberation from that terrorist.

I felt that Venice, with her nine hundred years of history, remained in the serenity of her triumph without expecting anything from so-called History. She had lost. She had created an Empire, had defended it at Lepanto and lost in a final humiliation in 1797 to an Attila from the West, five feet, six inches in height, who sent the cowards of the Great Council of the Republic an intimidating message written on a drum skin, with the revolutionary cockade of 1789. The petit caporal. *It was May 16, 1797, Venice fell into her new life. She reincarnated herself and is now in her Blue Age. Both of us, until she's swallowed by the sea, her most luxurious tomb.*

Venice lost her Empire but grew as a symbol of the adventure of illuminating life from her long-foretold existence-for-catastrophe. Now she symbolizes the entire West in its death throes. She awaits a single blow from the sea, scarcely stronger than that of 1966. The West, as a culture, in its final stage, is Venice. To be in Venice is to be aware of a long end, which one senses as inescapable, the end of an exhausted civilization. A blow from the sea or the annihilating blow from technolatric and consumerist capitalism.[17]

---

17   In his collection of essays, *Apologías y rechazos* (Apologies and rejections) Argentine novelist Ernesto Sábato wrote critiques of the West's "technolatry" (the worship of technology or material progress).

From my Blue Age I see the sphere of Venice as a unit without a before or after where six years mix facts and protagonists in a single high instant, capable of arousing nostalgia. A six-year day. The chronological mania ceases: all the hours of those six years are simultaneous. There is no before or after. The hours and years revolve in a unified sphere of time and space, beyond human measurements. We are all in all her times.

Blue Age: the possibility of freedom, without ethics, ambitions, or nostalgia. An unexpected valley without tears or laughter, after the so-called life and before a death no-longer feared. Blue Age: to leave public life, with others and from others and to return to the deep self, which has been awaiting us since we betrayed childhood. Blue Age, new freedom. Grateful nostalgia that today brings me back to Venice and all those faces and so much forgetfulness.

"The blue hour and suddenly it's night..." said my cousin, as we were returning from Mar del Plata in my uncle's car. "Suddenly night."

15

AFTER SEVERAL WEEKS of pleasing sunshine, we had ten days of heavy rain, with storm clouds blown in by winds that came down from the Alps and roughed up the waters of the Grand Canal and navigation in the Adriatic. We were still novices at the winter handling of the palace. At night a shutter would become unlatched and begin flapping in the unbearable storm. I'd have to get up with a flashlight to close the boisterous window—when I still didn't know where the light switches were in many rooms! Electricity arrived two centuries after the palace was built by Consul Smith.

It was at that particular time that Delia suffered a bout of depression. She was irritable at work, which she occasionally expressed by banging pots and slamming doors. During the long boat trip to Genoa and before, the month she'd been with us, she'd forged a very close relationship with Iván. They'd laugh late into the night in the *Augustus* cabin, next to ours, at the mistakes in Italian they were learning together. I had to settle them down by banging on the bulkhead.

Delia's childhood had been stolen from her. She was raised in Misiones, and her birth wasn't even properly registered, just a hurried scrawl in the baptismal book of a parish in Eldorado. Raised by a Ukrainian stepmother. "When I was Iván's age it was my job to sweep the henhouse with a broom made with a stick and dry willow branches held together with wire," she told Sabine during the initial interview in Buenos Aires. "I had to sweep barefoot so as not to get my shoes dirty... That lasted until noon, and I'd never complain: when I finished I'd run to the farmhands' spring and sit with my feet in it, waiting without a peep until my stepmother, who yelled a lot, came, and I'd receive, as if in secret, the best possible prize: she'd pump a huge jet of cold water so she could clean the shit off the chickens, and then came the best part, the moment when she'd rub my feet with her hard, cold hands, spreading my toes wide. I felt happiness and rest; I'd close my eyes, and I could have slept for an eternity. When people say the word caress, that's what I remember. Just that."

Delia went to school briefly, the first two grades, but she didn't learn to read or to add and subtract. She had learned the alphabet and then to read, when she was left alone for a while. She was self-taught by neglect.

The person who was to travel as our nanny and helper in our home became ill a month before we embarked. Diego E. recommended Delia: "She's a strange woman, very intelligent." She worked at the home of one of his relatives. So we enlisted her in the Venetian adventure, with all the risks of improvisation. Delia, I believe, wanted to be six thousand miles away from her native Eldorado and from that Buenos Aires where she'd been brought as a maid. She accepted with enthusiasm. We obtained all the necessary documents through the Foreign Office, even her passport as "diplomatic service personnel."

Her life, before working in Buenos Aires, since the age of seventeen years, consisted of not asking too many questions. The new identity documents and passport would be her rebirth certificate. Iván, according to Sabine, would be the reflection of what she'd lost and what should have been. So the bad weather wasn't the only reason for her depression.

Taking advantage of Iván's absence at lunch on Saturday, we confronted the reality of her change:

"What's going on, Delia? Something's going on."

"I don't even know what it is."

"We'd decided ahead of time that if you weren't able to adapt, you could decide to do whatever you wanted. It was always clear to us that this leap for you could … Would you like to go back?"

"I don't know. I really don't know. Sometimes I get lost and overwhelmed with no answers."

I was afraid Delia would tear up. I resolved to tell her, somehow, the essence of Sabine's theory.

"Iván is starting school. Why don't you go on the journey with him?"

"What's the point? What good would it do me now?"

"One can make of oneself what one wants. It's never too late. You have to have the courage to say to yourself, "Am I going to move forward? Then I will do … ."

"As if I could choose."

"You can. What would you choose?" And Delia with irony:

"I once saw myself in a white coat, as a doctor. Doctor Delia. Pure silliness."

(What happens in the end, when what seemed unattainable is achieved? Is that happiness? Yes? But luckily Delia doesn't ask herself or us any questions.)

"Do it. Have the courage to start now. We'll arrange for you to study the remedial education program for adults, which is very common here in Europe because of the many wars, and all the refugees... Sabine and I have been watching you; you learned more Italian than Iván during the three-week boat trip. Are you up for it? Or are you going to be a shirker? The disgrace of the missionaries' zeal."

"Alright, maybe I'm up for it." And she smiled. "Dr. Delia Balbastro! Ha!" And it seemed as though she'd looked out the window and hidden a glint of unexpected joy.

The rawboned Delia, with her Brazilian customs and mannerisms, her frizzy hair straightened with a hairdryer, her brown skin, the autumn rain falling relentlessly in the background, embarked on an educational odyssey: She finished elementary school in two years. The European baccalaureate in three more years followed by her incredible admission to the demanding medical school at Sant'Antonio di Padova. That "strange intelligence" that Diego E. had mentioned when recommending her to me began to unfold during that conversation when she came to retrieve the coffee cups. It was there that Delia's famous adventure in Venice began. The strange building of a destiny. And its consequences.

16

THE SAME MONTH I received, during that delightful summer lounging in the sun on Tigre Island, the newspaper in which the Chancellery had published the decree confirming my transfer to Venice, a young poet was expelled from the USSR amid threats, pushing and shoving, and a thrashing to remind him of the beatings in Lefortovo Prison. His name was Joseph Brodsky. He was thirty-two years old. He was rebellious, Jewish, and anticommunist, refusing to be used as an "official dissident" like Evtushenko or Voznesensky. At the age of twenty-three he had surprised the Soviet catacombs of true literature with a poem dedicated to the English metaphysical poet John Donne. It was a hymn of exhalation, an apologia. However, Brodsky, without intending to, managed to convey a poetic feeling by identifying poetry as the extreme and purest form of freedom, the verses listed all the objects of the world that would fall asleep, accompanying the final sleep of the extraordinary John Donne.

To fall asleep, to die, was also to extinguish the world and the universe. Had he been self-critical, Brodsky would have applied to his style the words: "illicit fervour," "length."

The misfortune or persecution or exclusion of a writer can become his public fame, especially within the context of a worldwide tension so extreme that Anglo-Saxon Western capitalism could be presented as the protector of freedoms and creation. Years later, in 1987, the unknown Brodsky would receive the news of his Nobel Prize in the United States, where he lived as a beloved refugee. Brodsky wrote, recalling his Gulag: "I have braved, for want of wild beasts, steel cages, / carved my term and nickname on bunks and rafters. [...] Munched the bread of exile: it's stale and warty."[18] Indeed, Brodsky threw himself into the life and wild freedom of the wolf expelled from the Soviet zoo. As chance would have it, the Aeroflot flight left him in Venice, after a brief stop in Vienna, and it was Andreina Venier with her otter coat and mink collar who was responsible for retrieving him and placing him in the *Accademia* hostel.

God becomes distracted, and sometimes lives are manipulated by a minor, playful demon. No one can explain why Brodsky, recently expelled, traveled as part of a group of official writers. First to Vienna and then to Venice, to continue after a few days as a refugee to the United States, a politically pious homeland to the exiled poets of the other empire.

Brodsky recounts how he arrived in the middle of the festive group of poetasters and intellectuals at the Santa Lucia train station. In reality, they'd put the former prisoner on the charter of the regime's sycophants in order to save money. It was the end of a freezing winter afternoon. For the Soviets, it was a burst of spring. The pro-government intellectuals were chattering and laughing, elated with the reward of being able to visit the perverted West after

---

18 This is the author's own translation of his Russian poem, which appeared on May 29, 1987, in *The Times Literary Supplement*.

years of danger and the steppe. Brodsky didn't understand anything. They were told that they would be guests of the Italo-Soviet Cultural Institute.

That was when the woman in charge of collecting them at the station like a lost herd appeared. It was Andreina. Brodsky notes in his books about Venice: "Then came the 'Veneziana.' I began to feel that this city somehow was barging into focus, tottering on the verge of the three-dimensional. It was black-and-white as befitting something emerging from literature, or winter; aristocratic, darkish, cold, dimly lit, with twangs of Vivaldi and Cherubini, in the background, with Bellini/Tintoretto/Tiziano female bodies for clouds."[19] The *mujik* didn't hesitate to place all the names of the Venetian pictorial canon at the service of Andreina Venier. She, from her distance and luxuries, treated everyone as *tavarishchi*, comrades, even the man they'd kicked out. Brodsky added in his account, "If I can, the first thing I will do is to return to Venice."[20] And indeed he did return several times, until the day, they say, when Andreina threw him down the stairs of the apartment in San Samuele, where Brodsky, drunk and shouting, had managed to slip in, despite no one answering him on the intercom.

---

19 Here and elsewhere, the quotes that the author attributes to Brodsky differ in varying degrees to Brodsky's own words in *Watermark: An Essay on Venice*. Rather than back-translating from Spanish to English, I have chosen to quote Brodsky's own English text. In some cases, where the quotation is significantly different, I will provide a footnote to explain the difference.

20 The text closest to this quote in Brodsky's Venetian memoir is "And I vowed to myself that should I ever get out of my empire, should this eel ever escape the Baltic, the first thing I would do would be to come to Venice."

A strange story, that had interested me personally ever since I lived in Moscow, had begun. I knew what its prisons meant, the ongoing risk of death, the hell that are the others, prisoners and guards, et cetera. Brodsky was sent to a work farm, which was the way to drive a political opponent mad and destroy him, as had happened in 1967 to my friend Yulia Kirilina. In short, Brodsky had emerged from the horrors of the concentration camp and when he arrived in Venice, he was received warmly by Andreina Venier on behalf of the Italian Communist Party. The bait was irresistible. It seemed like a trick staged by the demonic KGB. Perhaps he said to himself, "Now they're really going to kill me." Brodsky could not yet know that Venice was Byzantium and that Italy, the Empire, was surviving behind modernity. He understood nothing in those first hours on planet West. He felt that he was being led amid smiles to the gallows. This was confirmed when, looking at Andreina, it seemed he'd known her for a few months in Moscow, only superficially, during a dialogue between poets and Slavicists, but hidden by felt boots, a fur cap with earflaps and coarse one-piece gloves. But her lips, her profile, and her height were probably those of that Slavicist, scarcely memorable, a Mayakovsky scholar. There was no doubt in his mind that the *Veneziana* was a KGB agent, extraordinarily disguised as an aristocrat, descendant of one of the admirals of Lepanto. The supposed intellectuals, two Armenians, a Georgian, a Chechen, all metics, were simply hired assassins and subjects of the Venetian ICP. For Brodsky, the apparent expulsion was the final stage of a cynical execution.

The Soviet group descended the steps of the *Ferrovia* and, dragging bundles and suitcases, reached the vaporetto stop with an excess of tourists. Amid the crush of people, he remained glued to Andreina's otter coat, unsure whether she was his paradise or his hell. Then, in Russian, he was only able to venture, according to his own account, to propose a single lofty and refined literary topic:

"What do you think of Eugenio Montale's recently published motets?"

This man had been thrown out of Russia with a gray T-shirt, a frayed serge jacket, several duffel bags and a portable Olivetti with a Cyrillic alphabet hanging on his back, all hopelessly Soviet. The question was endearing and contained the utmost willingness to show his poetic devotion. Brodsky narrates that the *Veneziana's* only answer was a thunderous laugh and then silence, despite his bewilderment. The official writers got off at Rialto. Someone met them at the pier. Andreina Venier, in a conspiratorial tone, told Brodsky that she'd reserved a separate hostel for him, because of his refugee status. He followed her through some alleys dragging his belongings and his Olivetti. His ambiguous guide was now on his side, contradicting all CP orthodoxy. She spoke to him almost in a whisper, and Brodsky inhaled again the Shalimar perfume that was so delicious to his steppe and prison pituitary. She gave him a motherly farewell kiss on the cheek, as one treats a mujik rescued from an avalanche, and left him in the hostel reserved and paid for by Berlinguer's CP. Italy...

Brodsky writes of Andreina: "So we gave short shrift to her membership in the Italian CP and her attendant sentiment toward our avant-garde simpletons of the thirties, attributing both to Western frivolity. [...] The measure of her visual properties. Five foot ten, (Brodsky notes as if he had measured her in her sleep), fine-boned, long-legged, narrow-faced, with chestnut hair, hazel, almond-shaped eyes, with passable Russian on those wonderfully shaped lips with a sly gaze and a blinding smile on the same." Anyone would sign these words by Brodsky. The exile would find Andreina's legs again in the films of Cyd Charisse's or in *The Blue Angel*. Her angular, sensual face, almost an anatomical oxymoron, her mouth and her restless and ever-moving hair, like the sea. Her double would be Raquel Welch, the sixties sex-symbol.

Brodsky: long legs and bony body, his emaciation the result of prison deprivation. A thick mane, almost red, which he lost amid daily protests in front of the mirror. A large forehead, intense, wounded gaze, with a glint of someone who mocks himself. "Certainly, I'm losing my hair. And my mind!"[21] Literary lucidness and poems of maturity that no longer had the intensity of those that had impressed Anna Akhmatova. A mouth like a gash that was loosening and opened to hurl terrible guffaws of joyful Russian alcoholism.

He seemed to be trying hard not to look like a Soviet "dissident" fallen for Cold War propaganda. He was one, and he would be awarded the Nobel Prize in 1987. But he was a character and a true writer, with more of a critical sense of a reader than the felicities of a great poet. When he recited his poems in Russian, his voice took on an extraordinary timbre, harmonious and strong.

Perhaps this was the main point of attraction for Andreina. When he recited in English, choosing Auden, Eliot, or Lovell, he was rather boring. But in Russian he was thrilling with his voice and the themes of his humiliations

---

21   Interview with Sven Birkerts, *The Paris Review*. 1982.

and prisons. With the last dramatic verse, he'd cut himself off and laugh at himself and look at his friends and say:

"It's no use; I'm a Mayakovsky. 'But with me / anatomy has gone mad: / nothing but heart / roaring everywhere.'"[22] And he'd explode in bursts of laughter.

---

22 From the poem "Adults" by Vladimir Mayakovsky, trans. Harry Maxwell Hayward.

17

TO LIVE IN Venice is to enter into the codes, keys, and secrets of this exotic place where we will spend years of our lives. The thick, humid summer sends the Venetians to the shores of the Lido. Along with them we entered the world of the Excelsior Hotel and its rows of cabanas facing the sea, in the radiant light of our first summer, where Iván whiled away the day in his orange rubber dinghy anchored in the breakwater. Roque, the bathing attendant, passes out buckets of fresh water to each cabana to wash off the salt and sand before a frugal lunch and a siesta. Between two and four, the children aren't allowed to run or scream. Cured ham, sardines, salads, yogurt. Everything prepared by Delia. Between five and six, the short walk to the pier of the Palazzo del Cinema and then, on the bow of the boat, the much-anticipated appearance of the arches of the Doge's Palace, the mechanical *Giganti dell'Orologio* chipping away with their hammers at the human hours, and the *Campanile* disproportionately tall, in hopeless defiance, and then the walk to the consulate through labyrinthine alleys that allowed us to progress toward our neighborhood avoiding the exhausted herd of tourists. A stupid, delicious beach routine that I always detested, with its gossip and bellies smeared with suntan oils.

Before the intense heat we were overcome by the already identified disquiets that foreigners new to Venice suffer: illness, insecurity, anxiety at the loss of the century in which we were born, streets of water and a floating city that must annually renew her contract of existence before the sea. I believe the origin of these fears during initiation is undefinable. When Iván caught a cold, his mother heard a wheezing sound in his breathing. Our reaction was not one we would have had in Buenos Aires or Peru. We worriedly asked Rega for a list of doctors and urgently called Dr. Graziani. He told us when he arrived with his traditional leather bag, used in the West until the beginning of the twentieth century: "Don't worry, everything seems serious to people arriving from Italy to Venice." He examined Iván and declared: "It's the beginning of asthma." The news troubles us. Asthma in Spanish is a disease that defines and even ruins a person for life. Asthmatic children are raised on the margins, affected by a precocious culturalism. They are children of warm interiors, with a hovering mother and aunts, like the *tante* Léonie, who makes them witty but pansies like Proust; or arrogant, heroic, but ultimately tragic like Guevara, the Che. But asthma in Italian is a benign word, temporary, which refers to bronchial stubbornness. He gave us his prescription and within two days the disturbing wheezing had disappeared and Iván returned to the Istituto San Giuseppe.

However, our fear returned with another scare just ten days later. My head "felt heavy," I told Sabine. She called Dr. Graziani again, and he received us in his modest office on the Strada Nova. He took my blood pressure and told me that the top number was a little high: 180.

"That'd never happened to me," I told him, "in my life."

My voice must have conveyed distress. Graziani told me that it wasn't high enough for hospitalization rather merited close attention. He wrote a prescription and said, "Buy these tablets and call me if the symptoms persist." One hundred and eighty seemed like borderline syncope or stroke to me. We bought the tablets at the first pharmacy. At the next drugstore I had my blood pressure taken, which had already dropped to 160. Delighted, we passed by the consulate but continued on to a third pharmacy two hundred meters farther on, in San Vio. There my pressure read 140, and I was relieved of the idea of an impending heart attack.

When I got home, I called Dr. Graziani to let him know that my blood pressure spike had disappeared:

"My device may not be working correctly. Sometimes it happens, but it always errs toward the serious; it would be bad if it were the opposite, wouldn't it? In any case, heed the warning. Go on a white diet: chicken, fish, noodles, white bread, milk, and a single glass of white wine per meal," he told me calmly and without professional guilt.

The fear of dying is a Venetian trauma, said the Consul of Mexico, the refined and skeptical Giavi. Venice herself spreads fear of death. She'll die from a catastrophe, we, only from disease.

We were living in another century, in the hands of a sublime, moribund Venice. I came to know this; she was a prison without bars. Everyone wanted to flee from her, from her charm, from her attractive fragility. She was Buñuel's *Exterminating Angel*: no one could save themselves and ultimately pass through the threshold of the salon.

18

OCCASIONAL TUESDAY EVENINGS, conversations with Andreina in her little "Slavicist" office at the Università Ca' Foscari or sometimes at the Italo-Soviet Institute of Culture. We'd talk about Russia, exchanging hilarious anecdotes about the Russian people, brutal in their gestures but hypersensitive in the deepest fibers of their being. Brodsky wrote that there were two moments in Andreina's gaze, mustard and honey. Two shades linked to her mood. Mustard dominated because she felt better in a game of ironies and criticisms. Her intelligence prevented her from lingering too long on kindness and affection. It was curious to see this splendid woman, elegantly dressed, discordant with her environment, speaking in a loud voice, bursting into laughter, "the familiar flash of her pearls, thirty-two strong," as Brodsky wrote, that when she abandoned emotion, she became extremely mathematical, another Russian passion. Andreina spoke loudly, laughed, seemed like a provocation in that Institute that was more Soviet than Italian, with its white Formica tables and chairs, illuminated by implacable neon tubes attached to the ceiling. The cheaply framed picture of Lenin with his bald head and penetrating gaze. The poster of last year's *Festa dell'Unità*. Four or five gray entities worked at the Institute who moved about and communicated in mumbles. There was a large photo, smiling and in color, of Enrico Berlinguer, and farther in the back, the portrait of Gramsci with his expression of terminal prisoner, consumed in Mussolini's prison, the price of his ideology of taking power by means of cultural action. I understood that between Berlinguer's humanism and Debray-Guevara's "revolution in the revolution,"[23] the hard, imperial, Stalinist communism would soon be over.

Standing in front of me, under that light, as if for interrogations, was Andreina, swathed in a perfume that Brodsky called or believed was called Shalimar, one of those perfumes that Soviet hierarchs buy for their secretary on some official trip to the West. Andreina is hard on Italian literature:

"Here poets matter. Language, the height of expression, lives in them, Leopardi, Ungaretti, Montale, Pavese, Dino Campana, Zanzotto. Prose is weak in Italy...Here everything comes from the Roman Empire, from Virgil."

"Do you write?"

"I'm rather shy. I'm a bit like Pasolini, more personality than inner world. I always make my notes and lectures on Russian authors. Because of my Russian grandmother, I've been bilingual since birth, shall we say. The shadow of Russian literature is too strong to take the Italian literature of today seriously. I often go to Moscow; I gather information about the murder of the Romanov family. It's all so horrifying that there's no way to add fiction to the

---

23 The author is referring to French philosopher Régis Debray's text *Révolution dans la révolution*, published in 1967 in Cuba, where Debray befriended Che Guevara, later becoming a brother-in-arms in Bolivia.

facts that I discover. Since they consider me a "comrade," they let me talk to the silenced witnesses. It's an historical investigation, shall we say. Women have a hard time with literary immodesty. They're able to undress in public, but unable to describe it if they masturbate or murder... In short, nothing stands out in Italian literature. In Italy there's no Faulkner, no Kafka, no Joyce, no Proust.

Someone passed by the door, and she made an authoritative gesture, worthy of the Institute's director.

"Would you like some tea?" she asked. I said yes, and she continued talking about her strange relationship with politics: "I've known the Russian horror, for many years. But I also hate this decadent, final, plebeian capitalism. Fortunately for the world, the Russians are hopelessly, genetically, pre-technological. When they sent the dog Layka into space, what interested the Russian people was the dog, not the military technology. In their homes there are as many pictures of the dog as of the cosmonaut Gagarin. They're underdeveloped in their souls; they're mujiks, and the West led them to technology and consumption for reasons of State, or rather, of military superpower. They screwed up. They picked the wrong battlefield. Russian strength lies elsewhere. The Russians are denaturalized... I married a communist when I was very young. It was a matter of luck: he stayed with the USSR, and I stayed with the deep Russia of my grandmother and the poets. Not bad, no?"

Someone brought two teas in silver cup holders and two tiny blue rectangular packages with three lumps, which I knew well from my years in Moscow. I smiled.

"I recognize this sugar that doesn't dissolve, as if it were made of marble."

Andreina laughed, and said:

"When my comrades come, I offer it to them and watch them use the spoon to stir and stir to try to sweeten something. They never dissolve completely. It helps me to not get fat. I submit them to the torture of the empire they want to spread around the world. An empire where the sugar doesn't dissolve and the pens spit splotches of ink."

Next, I told her about my presence at the celebration of the fiftieth anniversary of the October Revolution in 1967. Red Square, the pigeons frightened by the roar of the tanks, flying desperately over the domes of St. Basil. The Politburo led by Brezhnev, Podgorny, and Kosygin, atop Lenin's mausoleum. As if carrying the weight of his mummy's revolutionary emanation. The diplomatic corps on the side platforms. And the moment when we felt a tingling in our feet: Red Square was vibrating like crystalware in an earthquake. The missile launching platforms carrying intercontinental missiles advanced, like a provocation of triumphant extermination. A gray granite dust rose from the square, ground by the steel caterpillars.

"Yes," says Andreina, "and people form opinions based on space or nuclear achievements ... Intellectuals like Suslov, the most intelligent member of the Politburo, still don't know that empires fall because of bad coffee makers and those Hungarian razors that make a noise like a lawnmower."

"The dream of the USSR was surely present at that celebration in 1967," I continue. "I'll never forget the festivities, with Marshal Rodion Malinovsky and the Politburo, all covered in medals, the hammer and sickle in rubies and diamonds. The Kremlin illuminated, the celebration of the first snowfall of the year and vodka and Armanianski for marshals and politburocrats."[24]

"It was the historic burial of cruel heroism. The logic of mediocrity was taking off," said Andreina. "The disaster was Khrushchev when he thought he could be a Stalin of consumerism and light industry. It was like pretending that an elephant could dance the rumba. A bourgeoisie with a car of their own was created. But it was the Moskvitch, which sometimes caught fire in the street, until Agnelli began manufacturing them in Togliattigrad. The middle class is a degeneration of capitalism; it tolerates anything, including the Gulag, but not a newly purchased car stalling in the street or a razor making that noise."

All this happened at the Italo-Soviet Institute as we drank Russian-style tea barely sweetened with indissoluble cubes. Before leaving, I looked at her in silence for a moment longer.

"But your communism . . . ," I said.

"Yes, of course. I see where you're going. I don't think I could ever be bourgeois. I think I hated, unfairly, the petite bourgeoisie. Perhaps . . . I think I was unable to accept the reality of a Venice without heroism or greatness, inhabited by heirs who are nothing more than bored guardians of a spectacular museum with rusty swords and *carpaccio* . . . These little men who have the nerve to bear the surnames of doges and admirals. Is that what I'm telling you? My grandmother, brought up in the best of Tsar

---

24 According to the author, *Armanianski* is a Russified pronunciation of *Armagnac*, a strong brandy produced in the Armagnac region of Gascony, which, according to the author, the Russian military and diplomats drank in staggering amounts.

Nicholas's Russia, preferred the world of opera. Its men, their exile to the United States ... I don't know. I don't have the slightest sense of reality, I know."

"But the matter of militant communism was no joke."

"Of course not. Perhaps I have a rebelliousness, a flirtation with provocation. I've already lived through the ruins of despicable Sovietism, a Judeo-Christian farce, but I surely can't imagine that this capitalism of merchants and business executives can continue to be supported by Western culture. Of this I have no doubt: there will be an acceptable society and a return to natural time and space. I sincerely believe this. Thank you for prompting me to remember who I am! Because I really don't believe anymore ... "

19

THE PAINTER BALDOVINO arrives with his wife. He checks into a room in a hostel in the poorest part of the city, in the Castello *sestiere*. He wants to paint Venice. Oils and tempera. He has the necessary confidence. He tells me that as a boy he helped his father in his greengrocer's shop. A teacher at school praised him in drawing class. "She saved me a life of doing odd jobs," he tells me. The long journey of the artist.

Days of intense heat. Summer begins to die, yet has its law, its scorching sun. Having finished his tasks at the consulate, around two o'clock in the afternoon Idilio Milossi, who assists me in various matters, leaves with a bag of old newspapers and a large bottle of water. He sets off on a long trip, of more than an hour, to Malamocco or Punta Sabbioni.[25] He walks along the stone *murazzi* that protect Venice from the sea on the Lido coast. He endures the scorching sun against his head. He places old newspapers on the rough, hot stones; he undresses and in absolute solitude dozes or looks at the sky next to the sea. Milossi is a lone wolf: he prefers to be wild and solitary.

---

25 Although not geographically contiguous, both sites are popular beach destinations.

The humblest come together: Milossi invited Baldovino to eat tagliatelle with tomato sauce that he prepares on the gas stove used for the official coffee, which is served to the consul at eleven o'clock, when the customs bills are brought to him for his signature, or is offered to certain visitors in the French porcelain cups that the *cancelliere* Rega keeps under lock and key. (Once, after hours, I went in search of water and discovered that Idilio ties together six or seven bunches of spaghetti with sewing thread, so as not to overdo it or end up short, and puts the bundles, his rations, back in the Buitoni box).

Baldovino told me he was delighted with the excursion to the *murazzi*. They lay near the lighthouse and Baldovino would climb down among the rocks to go diving. He told me that he plans to come back, because it was the first time "he really saw the sea." From there he became an admirer of Guidi, the Venetian painter of the still sea and its horizons of warm mist. Baldovino scrapes up the lire to go to the few theaters, the exhibitions, and even to *La Fenice* to see Carla Fracci dance.

I would lock myself away with the blinds drawn and the drafts, which is the most reliable cooling system for summer naps. I was making progress with my *stil nuovo*, taking advantage of the house's silence, while Sabine and Iván were at the Lido. Almost at dusk, when the temperature was more bearable and the sun wasn't beating down on the tables of the bar in Campo dei Santi Apostoli, I had a cup of coffee and corrected the large sheets of paper I'd recently written. Glossy sheets of obsolete consular forms. The novel was progressing; I was carried away by the joy of an unconventional style. I felt that rare enthusiasm or exaltation that comes from believing that the right path has been taken, amidst that uncertain jungle of blank pages. Baldovino, Carla Fracci, and I, all lost in the labyrinth of so-called art. Picasso, it seems to me, never doubted; neither did Borges. I feel the joy of believing I can get it right. Style is character and character is man. But man is an undefined haze and part of the mystery of everything. And above all, error, illusion. And character itself can be an occasional frame of mind, pure will.

I find a phrase by Sartre, interesting given the exclusiveness of his ideas and mental labyrinths: "One believes he is in Venice, and immediately, he feels that Venice is elsewhere. It is a general feeling. There is something that cannot be defined. Venice is a symbol, a protest, a detour, an urban heterodoxy."[26]

---

26 I have been unable to locate this quote; the translation, therefore, is from the Spanish, not the original French.

20

BEFORE CONSULATE CLOSING time, Rega brings me the news from the Foreign Ministry by teletype. Death has come in Argentina. Barracks are being attacked, guards shot. Organizations at the margins, shadowy gangs, face off in a dirty, nighttime war. A cycle of death picks up speed, and death will be the only winner. Perón returns to government and consolidates power, Cámpora is excluded because of his concessions to those who sought to use the centrist bastion of Peronism, which is evolutionist, reformist, not revolutionary like a Guevarist revolution, something that might have made sense two decades earlier.

Here in Italy the *Brigate Rosse* shot Indro Montanelli, the great liberal of Italian journalism, in the legs, kneecapped, *gambizzato*, as some newspaper editorials cynically call it. Everyone is under threat, journalists first and foremost. The security service recommends that those threatened take refuge in another location. So Moravia showed up in Venice. Alberto Moravia, the antifascist militant and intellectual resistance fighter, author of *The Indifferent One, The Woman of Rome, The Two of Us*, and *Boredom*. A man of Italian-style Marxism, he went into exile in Venice like a Giordano Bruno persecuted by the red inquisition that supported the ideology of revolutionary violence. He'd raised crows that were now posing a threat to him.[27] Lauro Bergamo, the editor of *Il Gazzettino* of Venice, organized a small get-together and the Albrizzis received us in their stupendous *palazzo* in San Polo.

Moravia arrived under discreet guard in a water taxi. His victimhood was less pathetic and more real than Sabato's. They were writers of the same stripe, with more politics and sociology than art. Both had extensive commercial success, and both were growing old with the notion that they weren't valued as writers. They'd believed in permanent fame, and in an admiration that was based on book sales and newspaper interviews. The writers who achieve this kind of literary populism are not usually the ones who remain deeply valued. Joyce, Proust, Kafka, Borges, Nabokov, Broch, had to pay themselves or have help becoming published. They didn't win the Nobel Prize.

The Albrizzis, extremely refined young people, greeted Moravia, whom they certainly didn't know well, like a friend in trouble. Lauro Bergamo introduced us to the refugee. Renato Mieli and his wife Bianca were there, with Tem, their detestable little Chihuahua, Ripa di Meana, president of the Venice Biennale, and her friend Marina Lante della Rovere, two deputies from the Veneto, the socialist De Michelis, and the professor and essayist Carlo Maria Santoro.

They had prepared a cold buffet, with an ample selection of wines. Moravia explained the threat and the Roman police's fear of not being able to protect him.

---

27 The author is alluding here to a Spanish proverb, *Cría cuervos y te sacarán los ojos* (Raise crows and they'll gouge out your eyes), which is an admonition against rearing thankless children.

"Venice protects me with her sea curtain, this marble castle with moats, cut off from the rest of Italy. If you want to flee, go to an island, or to an archipelago with palaces like this one. I'll try to save myself from the Huns, like the original founders of Venice in the fifth century."

Moravia was far from pleasant. He moved about like an author who was not only consecrated but also undisputed. Champion of outmoded Italian realism. Many of the writers of socialist realism, following Togliatti's death, were already in favor of a modernist aesthetic and of forgoing the "social commitment" imposed by Stalinism. In those years of Western capitalist renaissance, they had become respectable people. Moravia, with his melancholy prostitutes and his facile psychologism, had remained behind; he was closer to the cordial Edmondo de Amicis than to his adored Tolstoy and Dostoyevsky.

We were able to talk for a short while, seated on one of the palace's open terraces. He was interested in Perón's recent return to Argentina. Perón, in Italy and in Europe, had been the target of a campaign of discredit in the press. He'd been accused more or less of being a fascist, both by the communists and by those who'd colluded with fascism, some of whom were present at that meeting. Moravia asked me if Perón supported the urban guerrillas who claimed to be Peronists.

"Perón had periods of exile. He never lost political power. He tacitly supported the Guevarist-Castro line until they, a minority with small arms, had the bright idea of taking over Peronism. Peronism is a centrist social Christianism but with the subversive language that was in vogue," I said.

A tall, elegant man overheard me; he was a liberal senator from the Veneto, and he interrupted boorishly:

"There was a clear idea about Perón here. When Eva Perón came, in Rome they threw rotten eggs at the door of the embassy, in the Piazza dell'Esquilino."

"Well, it was twenty people. The Communist Party wanted nothing to do with Peronism. Because Evita was going to be received by the pope, by that pope, they mobilized. Pacelli had a different idea about Argentina and the political forces in Latin America, which was beginning to be a reliable bastion for the waning Christianity in Europe. The true favorite daughter of the Church in times of Marxism and liberal decadence was Ibero-America. He received Eva Perón with the utmost graciousness, but not with the honors she sought."

"No one could imagine Pacelli as a *homme à femmes*," said the mistress of the house, Countess Albrizzi, with an amused and smiling grimace. Everyone laughed. I attempted to move beyond the subject. Moravia was growing impatient. Some people brought chairs closer to listen to his final words on the matter. It was an extraordinary night, like being on one of those *altane* they build on the Venetian rooftops, among friends. Starry night. Absent the *foschia*, that damp haze that softens Van Goghian nights.

"The Church has a more universal idea and knows that there is a bastion of culture, style and blood, Italian-Argentine, shall we say. Perón himself was of Italian origin. His grandfather emigrated from the Kingdom of Sardinia. He was here for a while, in the *Alpini* regiment. At a difficult time, during the immediate post-war period in Italy, when people were starving, as president he ordered ships with grain and meat diverted to Italy. It was neither a publicity nor a demagogic gesture; he did the same in relation to

Spain. Both countries run in the blood of the Argentines through immigration."

"Yes, but then the Argentines charged us an international price," said the liberal senator.

"At that tragic moment neither Perón nor the Italians thought about the price. It was not done for the price," I told him firmly.

Miranda Bergamo took the floor decisively, annoyed perhaps by the senator's misplaced aggression:

"I have sympathy for Eva Perón. She was strong. The pope was right to receive her with high honors. He decorated her, didn't he?"

"A medal and a decorative rosary. She left the Vatican in a rage," I explained.

"What did she expect?"

"Everyone receives a medal, just like in Catholic school, as we all know. But Eva wanted to be named a Pontifical Marquise."

"Pontifical Marquise?"

"Yes. She had no official responsibilities. She thought that all her society problems would be covered up, erased, with such a noble title, Marquise," I said.

"*Guarda un po'!*" exclaimed the senator. "I don't think she had much of a history as a Catholic."

"I don't think Eva Perón cared about being a practicing Catholic. But I am sure, from what I was told about the incident on her trip to Rome, that Eva felt as Christian or more so than the pope himself. I have no doubt ... "

They laughed. They thought it was a joke, but I had no doubt that Evita felt more Christian than the pope. I sensed, like many other times in my diplomatic life, a certain critical reticence toward Argentine issues. As if we were under observation, as if we were unreliable.

After the Argentine digression, which was amusing to those present, Moravia focused on questions and comments about his work. He lingered on the real person who inspired *The Woman of Rome.*

Moravia spoke sparingly and with a total lack of charm. He even spoke impersonally about the personal, such as when he alluded to his ex-wife, Elsa Morante, who was a more profound novelist than he. His droning insistence on the working class since the time of France's Popular Front and the war made him look like a retired metallurgical worker: he was a robust man who bordered on square or cube-like, with an uncultivated face that fell short of being refined by success and the consequent worldliness. Whatever traces of a distant Jewishness that might have conferred a more refined expression were abolished, it seemed, by so many decades of Stalinist internationalism.

Moravia said, energetically, that the Red Brigades movement was politically insignificant:

"It is the last instance of the infantile leftist disease. They'll plant bombs, shoot off the legs of journalists and officials, but they'll never have the people. In reality, all of this is nothing more than their own historical funeral. Europe, its peoples, the public, want nothing to do with Trotskyist nostalgia. The Communist Party distances itself from all that. Neither Russia nor China support these uprisings of intellectuals and students. Cuba itself is frozen, without a truly revolutionary destiny. It's merely a satellite, an infertile moon that revolves around the USSR."

The owner of the house entered, preceded by the waiter from the yacht club, Amedeo, with a large dish of risotto, her specialty. The house cook brought a bowl of tagliatelle and an assistant with bowls of various pasta sauces. Wine flowed. Moravia was served first and chose the tagliatelle, with a gesture not to be misinterpreted as contempt for the local specialty.

It was past eleven o'clock and from that high terrace, discretely illuminated, one could see Venice's rooftops and the Campanile with its sleepless angel.

Moravia ate with the decision and clarity of a laborer at his midday meal. He handled his fork with extraordinary dexterity: he twirled a few tagliatelle around it until they formed an even ball without it falling apart—as often happens to the rest of us—as he brought it to his mouth. He swallowed it with the determination of a Roman soldier, indifferent to the conversation, his eyes lost in the pleasure of taste.

Because I'd been stationed in Russia, he asked me about the situation and about Brezhnev's will to hold on to imperial power that was being increasingly overtaken by "the allies forever." He was interested in the break with the Chinese and the seriousness of the confrontation on the Sino-Siberian border. He asked me if the Russians supported terrorism in South America, in Chile, Brazil, Uruguay, and Argentina.

"They don't want anything to do with it," I answered. After the missile standoff in Cuba, they don't want anyone to determine their course in the perilous global politics. I was in Russia when Guevara died in Bolivia; there was barely a mention in *Izvestia*. They even attempt to discredit Debray. They say that he was Guevara's informer, and that the Bolivian army spared his life due to De Gaulle's intervention."

"I know that version," Moravia tells me, "and I know it's false. I noticed on my last visit to Moscow that they broadcasted that message because they believe there is a germ of a new ideology, an anti-Soviet schism. But Debray had nothing to do with Guevara's surrender. What happened was that the CIA was aware of Tania's every move since she, a KGB agent, settled in Cuba at Guevara's invitation, whether sentimental or sexual. It was enough to follow her. And that's how it went down. They followed her from La Paz and captured him."

He invited me to go with him to the other end of the terrace to see the lights of the *Canalazzo*. He wanted to tell me something:

"Actually, Consul, I want to tell you that I am very worried about my situation. I'm glad I found you. I fear for my family. The threats, death threats, are very real. The services believe that they want to eliminate a political figure, like Craxi or Moro or Fanfani,[28] or someone with a high international cultural profile. That being the case, I'd like to know if I could call on your embassy if the need arises."

Obviously, I reassured him and told him that having him in Argentina would be a source of honor for our country. But nothing happened. Two weeks later I saw that he was giving a lecture on culture and politics in Milan. Already by then I had certain diplomatic experience that I'd learned in Moscow: Those who feel persecuted usually manufacture ways out, alternatives, to be able to be at ease where they are.

---

28 Bettino Craxi, Aldo Moro, and Amintore Fanfani all held the post of prime minister during a very volatile period of Italian politics, which included the kidnapping and assassination of Moro.

21

TO LIVE IN Venice was to steer the home ship. Its tedium and its joy, child-rearing, professional life, marital arguments, the tenderness, the shouting, the smell of the old kitchen of the decaying *palazzo* that necessitates putting horribly pink weather-stripping under the hundred-year-old doors. Personal freedoms nullified, barely subsumed, in a network of higher conventional values. After hitting forty-one one no longer believes enough in oneself to break with anything; the home—companionship, the breath of fresh air that comes with a child, along with his enchanted environment—triumphs. With his army of figurines and castle drawbridge that we made from a packing crate. The childhood of a little prince Siddhartha. Until, perhaps due to our carelessness, at some point, he saw the horsemen of the Apocalypse galloping through the streets: disease, misery, death. In the meantime, Iván kicks around a ball on the Campo dei Santi Apostoli. I am sitting at the tables outside the café. He's playing with Luca Bressin against two boys from San Lio.

Shouts from goals. Protests. Happiness for the goals abounds: 10 to 6, 11 to 8.

The pleasures of family life: one leaves, slamming the door, furious. Since it's raining, he yanks the umbrella and almost knocks over a coat rack. He rushes toward the Strada Nova, barely greeting the doorman Renato with his mandolin. He opens the umbrella violently and runs into a narrow *vicolo*. The ribs of the umbrella scratch the walls. I walk toward the Campiello Widmann. Even the steps are violent because flattening a spouse's nose or vice versa was not an option. One sinks into Venice through her lost labyrinth, *palazzine* in ruins, which belonged to families emigrated from the *Serenissima*, or from the world. The rattle of water drops on the umbrella's taut nylon. Venice welcomes me, in her empty streets, and absorbs the rage and sorrows. Until I find the *cafecito* that I'll lose again in the labyrinth and run into the poet Federico Gorbea, also lost. He's looking for the Arcobaleno Cinema or the Arena, or the Ritz or the Coliseo. They all have similar names in all of Italy's cities. Federico Gorbea is looking for the cinema "that's around here," but he can't find it and invites me to join him to see the then pornographic film *Emmanuelle*. A distant bite of the subconscious libido, the crumbled raincoat left on the coatrack of an abandoned train station.

Afterwards we went for a pizza and recalled the Argentine poet Ricardo Molinari, whom we both admired, visiting him in the Congressional Library, where Federico held the post of librarian. Gorbea recalled passages from the "Oda al mes de noviembre junto al Río de la Plata."[29] And that verse that neither of us knew to which of Molinari's poems it belonged: "*Feliz, como un pie desnudo en una playa.*"[30]

Three days after the tantrum at home, when values and resignation in flip-flops had restored the routine, I went

---

29 "Ode to the Month of November by the Rio de la Plata"
30 "Happy, like a bare foot on a beach."

out into the radiant sun of the cool morning to the San Lio branch of the Banca del Lavoro. I stopped at the bookstore next to the Rialto Bridge and discovered Abbagnano's *Dictionary of Philosophy*.[31] The price discouraged me. On the table of new releases, there was a book filled with the opinions of illustrious visitors, and I came across a short poem by Nietzsche about the city that was "the only place on earth which I love,"[32] as he confessed:

> *O happiness! O happiness!*
> *O happiness! O happiness!*[33]

Two very unusual verses for an Antichrist, a man deeply in mourning who travels from solitude to solitude. The seeker of the origin of tragedy. Only Venice could animate, give a vital breath, to the genius who would animate the philosophy of two condemned centuries, shortly before embracing and kissing in a *piazza* in Turin the lips of a horse whipped by a drunken coachman. Only Venice could have made him cry out in such a way, "Happiness!" Sartre could never allow himself to use that word to refer to his life, not even during orgasm with his most beautiful pupil while Simone de Beauvoir spied on him behind the library. Perhaps Nietzsche sensed the possibility of supermen in a civilization that was dedicated to pleasure and had the luxury of courage, which left us as a keepsake its majestic

---

31 The author here refers to a *Breviario di Filosofia*, but I could not find that title in Abbagnano's bibliography.
32 Letter to Franz Overbeck, March 24, 1887. Trans. Christopher Middleton.
33 Chapter LXX, Noontide, *Thus Spake Zarathustra*. Trans. Thomas Common.

mantle of palaces, casinos, *boudoirs*, violins, libraries, and harlots, famously revealed in classical poetry.

I was happy that morning on the *Salizada* San Lio.

I returned from the bank with almost three thousand dollars to cover my expenses that had been delayed and the improvements to the consulate's customer service area. A new counter, calculating machines. Rega still used one with a crank and gears that she oiled monthly. Lamps and three new desks. Our modest consulate was also a wheel in the world's machinery. Its receipts were constant and even important. In my memory, those meters of my life were engraved on the *Ponte* San Lio, under a splendid light. That moment, a few steps of revelation in which I felt happy to exist: a good salary, a nice city, a family and the rest … as my colleague Alberto Medes used to say.

Sabine and I celebrated with a champagne dinner. The *satori* of happiness justified it. I fell asleep with the blinds open to the night and with the sublime murmur of the water of the Canal on the steps of the palace. It must have been two o'clock in the morning when we were awakened by the phone; I answered it in the living room. It was a call from the Foreign Ministry. Ambassador De la Plaza's chief of staff told me that Perón had appointed his superior as the new ambassador to Uruguay. This was a new Perón, who believed in multiparty national unity, because De la Plaza had been an exiled anti-Peronist during the First Peronism, precisely in Uruguay.

"De la Plaza asked to take you along as his political advisor." As Bianculli communicated my vaunted appointment to the new post, I felt as if life's deviltry were communicating that appointment to me when I had the dry and joyful taste of champagne in my mouth, in celebration for having felt happy. I broke out in a cold sweat.

"It's an offer, I suppose," I asked.

"No, consider it a decision, the decree has already been drafted. In fact, you'll be the political advisor, *el Negro* chose you specifically."[34]

"I want to talk to him. I've settled into my post and organized my family's life here. I'd prefer they allow me to talk about making the transfer toward the end of the year."

"I don't think that's possible," Bianculli told me. "Perón's inauguration is speeding everything up."

I sunk into the armchair in the living room and remained there. It struck me that I was in a paradise disguised as a minor, one-person post. I wouldn't be able to forestall alone the decision that would send me back to the idiotic and dreaded hell of what would degenerate into an orgy of violence. I decided to leave that very morning for Rome, to communicate to Ambassador Adolfo Savino, who'd just arrived, and from Perón's most intimate circle, my desire to stay in Venice, in the post I'd been asked to choose that distant afternoon in November. I told Sabine that the call was to inform me that the ambassador could receive me for the protocol visit I'd requested. I chose not to worry her.

I saw the Po countryside still covered in morning mist, then radiant with spring when I crossed the vineyards and the delicious hills of Tuscany. I drove without even stopping for coffee. If the draft decree of my transfer was signed, it would be useless to complain after the fact.

---

34 The sobriquet *el Negro* [the black man] used here is a reference to Guillermo de la Plaza. Often employed as a term of endearment, the term often referred to skin tone rather than race.

The ambassador received me in the afternoon and fortunately he was upset for not having been duly consulted. He called Buenos Aires and later told me that everything was resolved, and I'd continue in my post in Venice. I would not be withdrawn from the center of the world.

I'd run a great risk: I was progressing in my new style, writing *Daimón* and passages of *The Dogs of Paradise*;[35] Iván was beginning the school year, which he would complete without the ruptures that affect the children of diplomats. Home had been reborn this time in a *palazzina*, run-down but charged with prestige and antiquity. I took the Fiat along a secondary road near San Sepolcro, in the heart of Tuscany, where I stopped at a tempting country inn to eat a magnificent plate of tagliatelle with a glass of fresh barrel wine from Orvieto.

The flames of hell were licking at my door. The deathless idiocies of the same old Argentina had transformed into times of enthusiastic assassins. A dark and monstrous cruelty. Adolfo Savino, one of the men who carried the most weight with Perón, tried to help me and did me a favor, a *gauchada*.[36] Years later, when he fell into disgrace, expatriated and persecuted by the military government, he stopped by the consulate to ask me for a favor, which for a Consul would constitute a crime. I didn't do it. And the episode was seared into my deepest self forever. I betrayed

---

35 Each of these novels have been translated into English, *The Dogs of Paradise* (1989), by the late Margaret Sayers Peden, and *Daimon* (1992), by Sarah Arvio.

36 The word *gauchada* is any action typical of a *gaucho* as a result of skill, boldness, or bravery. By extension, it has come to mean a favor or good turn. In some circumstances, however, it can connote a dirty trick.

gaucho amorality. And that made me—still makes me—feel terrible. I'm Argentine. I feel terrible for not having acquiesced to the misdeed and returned the *gauchada*, as Martín Fierro would have done, without hesitation, for the *gaucho* Cruz, who went out as a police officer in search of Fierro and ended up defending him with a sword so that justice would not be merciless against an innocent man for the "minor crime" of having killed someone, drunk, at a dance ... [37]

---

37 Here the author is referencing the nineteenth-century Argentine epic poem *Martín Fierro*, composed by José Hernández.

22

URING THAT CIRCULAR six-year day, Borges and María Kodama arrived in Venice.

They traveled frequently and all over the world. Borges was in the midst of his most intense years of worldwide fame. He had been denied the Nobel Prize for having accepted Chile's highest national decoration, but from the hands of Pinochet. We know that European hypocrisy makes noise from the left but lays its eggs on the right, like the *tero* bird.[38] They didn't give him the Nobel Prize, which in the end is an annual award, handed out more frequently than creative literary talent. Instead, destiny corrected the oversight with the unavoidable diligence of María Kodama. One must consider what would be to his greater interest. Kodama accompanied the absentminded Borges with discretion and kept his presence alive in the world, moving about with astuteness and efficiency, carrying his name *urbi et orbi*. In those days I thought that she had rather rejuvenated Borges himself, in certain literary lacunae in relation to post-World War II literature. He eased, as best he could, his tenacious

---

38 This metaphor is a reference to the South American *tero*, which is said to lay its eggs in one spot then emit loud noises in another to draw predators away from the eggs.

and sincere views on politics. I believe, I think, that because of Kodama he stopped praising South American dictators and became aware of the tortured and disappeared.

He arrived very Borgesianly. They took rooms at first in a hotel with a name worthy of Southeast Asia or Mandalay, located impractically and a hundred dollars away by *motoscafo* from the historic center and the consulate.

The Italian editor of the Biblioteca Borges, Franco Maria Ricci, helped María find accommodations in the historic center. Borges didn't want a five-star lodging other than the one he used in Paris, which provided peace and quiet, not to mention the prestige of having been the abode of his admired Oscar Wilde.

They found one a few steps from the Doge's Palace and moved in the next day. Borges believed he'd caught a glimpse of the hotel's letters and logo. "What does it say?" he asked. "Albergo Londra," María replied. He told Ricci and María that it seemed like a coincidence, but it wasn't a coincidence. "It's the same hotel where we stayed with my parents sixty years ago."

"Am I perchance fifteen this morning? Is time circular and we're where we were and will be again? Will my parents be waiting for me downstairs in the lobby for our first walk in Venice, just like before?"

When I was seventeen or eighteen years old, I'd met Borges at some festivities of the Society of Writers, in the old house donated by Victoria Ocampo on Calle México. Then Borges was indeed "a more or less bereaved man who travels by tram." But when I saw him arrive at the consulate sitting in the back of the water taxi, and as he got out at the pier holding Kodama's hand, I noticed his elegant gabardine suit and silk tie of matching colors that Borges would never have imagined as he ambled through the Florida neighborhood after drinking his glass of milk at La Cosechera on Avenida de Mayo. I walked by him more than once as I was leaving the Nacional Buenos Aires, when he wasn't blind and not as admired worldwide. Around 1950, Angel Battistessa, a renowned professor of Spanish and Literature, invited our class to the Alliance Française, where Borges was giving one of those lectures that allowed him to survive, because he was on Peronism's blacklist. The Alliance was a small theater, with a dais and comfortable seats. I was on the far side of the second row and was able to see, between the side wings, Borges's head leaning toward a hand holding a tortoiseshell comb. He was a boy whose mother demanded that his hair be combed. And I speculated much later, as he would say, that it was his mother, Leonor Acevedo. His sweet but inescapable guardian angel.

Borges could only see certain shapes in intense daylight. He entered the *Palazzo* Mangilli Valmarana without hesitation in his step, rather as if his blindness possessed an unbelievable quality or were a negligible minor difficulty. He was at the height of his fame in England, where he was translated by Norman di Giovanni, and in France by Roger Caillois. He'd spoken at the great world forums, from the United Nations to UNESCO, Honoris Causa at Yale. Yet he had a natural Taoist shyness, born of a certain skepticism or visceral precaution toward worldly convention. No situation, no matter how exotic, ever removed him from his distance, his aesthetic self.

23

TWO NIGHTS AFTER his arrival, the enthusiasm to meet him—without ever having read him—led Venice's intellectual group to invite him to eat at the home of Renato Mieli, a member of the communist resistance since 1938, when he had to flee Italy. Founder of ANSA, the Italian news agency, former Marxist idealogue, and editor of *l'Unità* until he rebelled against communism in 1956.[39] During the war he was a British agent and participated in Montgomery's advance in Sicily and Clark's from Anzio. A Jew from Alexandria, he was a discreet gray-haired gentleman with the appearance of a mild-mannered corporate lawyer. Alexandria had bequeathed to him an ineffable gnosticism, and at the same time the agnostic and spiritual refinement of the deep Mediterranean. In Venice he was married to a former comrade from his Party days, Bianca la Rossa, as the Venetians called her. They received us along with María, Franco Maria Ricci, his fiancée, and other friends interested in meeting that exotic and cosmopolitan product of literature. Borges, who greeted everyone with his head held high, meeting the hands that reached out to

---

39 Literally "The Unity," an Italian newspaper founded in 1924 as the official newspaper of the Italian Communist Party.

him with the experience of a "non-seer." His eyes open, as if looking at anything in general, or everything, but in some way at the passerby who was greeting him. They were not the eyes of a statue. It invited the assumption that blindness was something avoidable, in any case unseemly to call attention to.

Andreina Venier and her husband, Ripa di Meana and Marina Lante della Rovere, Bianca la Rossa, Miranda and Lauro Bergamo, editor of *Il Gazzettino*, Vittorio Gregotti and others.

It was as if they were greeting Valéry, but without having read "The Graveyard by the Sea" or *Monsieur Teste*. I understood that Borges was the Valéry that Europe had failed to replace. Borges was also a last moment of a great Western literature on the verge of its swan song, in a decadence whose inexorable arrival was already in sight.

"Literary fame..."

"The literary fame that I was previously denied, now precedes me and even makes my literature imaginable. Few read it. Everything is abnormal in this regard. It's inexplicable. A favorable imposture."

The table livened up with the Riesling, Tokai, and Amarones from Friuli that Mieli himself was serving. Borges occupied the place of guest of honor, Kodama to his right, by now an expert in cutting into small pieces whatever was served to him. Bianca explained to him that she and Mieli had broken with communism in 1956, with the Soviet repression in Hungary.

"My husband wrote a period book denouncing Togliatti's collusion with Russian policy in the Spanish Civil War and with executions ordered from Moscow. I'll give you a copy of the book on Togliatti in French."

Borges listened with his head raised.

"Ah, Togliatti..." was the only thing heard from Borges's deep voice.

And Bianca:

"Renato also denounced the Trotskyist essence of the apparently non-violent tactics of Gramsci. At the end of the day the strategic result is a bloodless seizure of power, of cultural penetration, but necessary to apply an inexorable dictatorship of the proletariat, another Stalin of benign appearance, shall we say."

"Ah, Stalin..." Borges muttered.

Borges sometimes didn't fully understand certain words in Italian and asked me for clarifications in a whisper. Communist politics was certainly not his subject.

The table livened up with a discussion between Vittorio Gregotti, the architect-aesthete who worked with Ripa di Meana as head of the new *Venice Biennale*, and Lauro and Miranda Bergamo, who mocked the transformation of the visual arts into a biennial spectacle.

"An Israeli, allegedly an artist, demanded that they pay his first-class ticket from Tel Aviv as well as the transport of a dozen sheep, probably plucked from the peaceful hills of Tiberias." Everyone laughed, even Ripa and Gregotti, who'd had to approve the project to exhibit the flock of sheep that the artist had dyed blue.

"Is it true that the sheep had to have a veterinarian on duty because the artist dyed them with blue and orange aniline dye?" asked Miranda sarcastically. Gregotti had no choice but to nod his head as he ate his prosciutto di Parma.

Franco Maria Ricci recalled that, some time ago, an Argentine painter had dyed the waters of the Grand Canal. He was referring to Nicolás García Uriburu, who'd hired several boatmen and overseen the process of dying the canal. He'd studied the lagoon's currents and the timing of the high and low tides. The next morning, the waiters at the Gritti Palace, while serving breakfast, found the wharf stained blood red, which they took as a message from the Red Brigades. By contrast, on the magnificent steps of the Basilica della Salute, a yellow coating climbed the steps as if to make the sacristan who swept the entrance believe in a miraculous greeting of faith in the color of the Vatican, translucent on the marble of the basilica's *fondamenta*.

"The Argentine was prosecuted, and I think expelled," said Miranda Bergamo. Since they were looking toward our area of the table, I felt obliged to say:

"Only an Argentine could think of improving Venice!" They laughed. Borges raised his head. He fumbled with his fork and then poked at the morsels as best he could. He did everything with ease, as if it were natural. No doubt he'd received from his English grandmother a certain Protestant stoicism. Suddenly, as the topic of the *Biennale* still dominated the conversation, Borges leaned over to me and asked:

"Have you read Delmira Agustini at length? I was thinking of a poem of hers; I'll tell you about it ... "

The table was inclined to speak in French, as a courtesy to the guest. And Borges answered a question from Andreina:

"Yes, I always read the Italians, starting with the fundamentals—Dante and Virgil. Croce seemed honest to me. He didn't separate ethics from aesthetics and politics. Boccaccio, of course ... Years ago I was also interested in Papini, who lived in Buenos Aires. I found Momigliano's analyses admirable. But truth be told, I read very few of my contemporaries. I'm under the impression that poetry in Italy, and almost everywhere, is more important than prose, is it not? Everyone listened in silence without daring to mention Pasolini, Bassani, Guido Piovene, Elio Vittorini, nor Manzoni himself, or Italo Calvino, whom the journalists were by then describing as Borgesian. Borges seemed to sense in the table's eager silence a certain disappointment. It was as if he'd spoken to them about Edmondo de Amicis, from another century. He continued:

"Dino Buzzati caught my interest with those Tartars who never come. The Tartar who does come for the protagonist, the lieutenant, is that of his own death, as occurs for everyone. Quite original, no? Everyone's Tartar ... and Buzzati's lieutenant would have wanted a hero's death, a warrior's! All the great marshals of Germany died in their eighties and nineties, in bed. Hindenburg, Moltke."

At one end of the table there were reminiscences of the illustrious writers who visited Venice or left anecdotes behind:

"Sartre comes often, without showing his face."

Miranda Bergamo spoke of Nabokov, who that year hadn't yet ventured down to the Gritti, from his hotel in Montreux.

"The other day, on the vaporetto, sitting in the front seat, enjoying the palaces, I saw Ernst Junger," said Bianca Mieli.

"Venice didn't used to pay much attention to writers; we're very provincial. We always contrived anecdotes to avoid reading them. We ridiculed Byron; he was a much too haughty lord, arrogant."

And Vittorio Gregotti added:

"He lived like a hero. He fell in love with a baker's daughter in Brenta. A true love, with all the limitations of constancy that a libertine can possess. Venice hated him. He rented the Palazzo Mocenigo, where Codognato lives today, and he'd dive into the water from the vestibule above the *Canalazzo*. Sometimes he'd swim to San Lazzaro degli Armeni, the island belonging to the Mekhitarists, the Armenian Christians. He studied the Armenian language. There they say he finished writing the third canto of the *Childe Harold's Pilgrimage*.

Borges, as if someone had called out to him, raised his head as if looking above everyone's heads, and with his deep voice, devoid of solemnity, whispered:

All heaven and earth are still—though not in sleep,
But breathless, as we grow when feeling most.

We all joined in an admiring silence, perhaps without understanding, Borges's poetic eucharist. Gregotti continued:

"The Venetians couldn't stand him. They said he swam so as not to show the deformed foot he was born with. When he died in Missolonghi with the insurgents, "to free Greece from Turkish domination," the Venetians said that he'd actually wanted to kill his deformed foot that humiliated him. Cruel Venetians!"

"He took it too far. He knew how to create a hero's death, and for a lost cause," said Andreina de Venier.

"Rilke would have envied him for having attained 'a death of his own.' No one wants death, neither their own nor that inflicted by our kind brothers."

Miranda Bergamo took advantage of the good spirit at the table buoyed by Renato Mieli, who was replenishing the glasses with wine. She recounted:

"Someone else who didn't fare too well in Venice was Hemingway at the end of the war. He put on airs of a liberator. He wore a military uniform with unique insignia, fake, although he possessed correspondent credentials. Arrigo Cipriani, Sr., the true founder of Harry's Bar, told me a very funny anecdote. Hemingway was in the habit of going out at dawn with a boatman who'd pick him up and he'd hunt ducks on the tiny islands around Murano. He'd get off at Harry's as early as eleven o'clock in the morning and drink martinis nonstop. The not-so famous and inexpensive martinis from when Harry's was an unassuming bar for gondoliers and drunken Englishmen."

Miranda's tale was interrupted by a sudden invasion of barking, jumping, and running from Tem, Bianca's Chihuahua.

"*Scusate! Scusate!*" she implored, trying to catch him as he attempted to climb up on the table. He was no more than eight inches tall, and his perfect little head displayed a gleam of joy in his eyes and menace in his teeth. Renato called out to him, "*Tem, caro Tem, per carità!*" Bianca wrapped her hands around him, kissed his little head, and took him back to the pen from where he'd made his escape.

"One loves these little dogs so much because they are so hysterical, nervous, anxious, like poets. Worse than poets!"

Tem made himself heard though no longer with hysterical, rabid barking but with long demagogic whimpers that eventually grew silent out of boredom.

"Do you have dogs, Señor Borges?" asked the engineer Balder, Andreina Venier's husband.

"The cat is the calmest animal but the most ferocious in the face of aggression. It has the utmost dignity: it doesn't hesitate in the face of death. A cat is respected, a dog is loved like a child; they're too human. A dog can be enlisted by armies, police, or torturers. A dog can be a guardian of property. A cat never. His nobility prevents him from identifying so much with humans and their terrible feelings. I have an old white cat; his name is Beppo. He's very convenient for me, because Beppo has that British timidity and aloofness that is so useful for coexistence." Several people laughed while others looked on with a certain puzzlement.

Miranda continued with her tale about Hemingway at Harry's, perhaps believing that Borges might be interested in this famous man:

"As I was saying, Hemingway moved about with the authority of a liberator. Already in Paris he'd thrown in with the American army that followed Leclerc's retaking of Paris. To hear him tell it, Paris was reborn by his military action. Already by then he was being teased and people were joking that the only thing liberated by Hemingway was the bar at the Ritz, and that many bottles of Bordeaux and of the Veuve Clicquot champagne were missing. At Harry's, Hemingway, dressed in his military or duck hunter's coat, sat at the end of the *comptoir* and chin-wagged with the old man Cipriani who was experimenting with new formulas for Martinis and Negronis for him. Before noon someone would arrive whom many of those present know, and whom I shall call the Countess G." Several guests made knowing gestures and Miranda demanded: "No, let's not say names; it's not necessary. At that time the countess was as inscrutable as she is now. Spectacular and distant, and she dressed with the convenience of post-war discretion. We all depended on the ration book; we were all treated more or less like fascists. I remember: One was forced to slither along the walls. We lived threatened by fascists disguised as pro-Allied *partigiani* liberators!" Everyone laughed. "The truth is, Hemingway had his eye on the countess. He began to greet her with his most Colgate smile when she entered, and G. responded with an imperceptible gesture of distant propriety. Arrigo would then take her a *tartina* and a glass of champagne. And this is what Hemingway contrived to seduce her. He obtained from the Soviet military delegation a couple of those blue half-kilo tins of Malossol caviar. Does anyone remember? The seam of the tin was covered with a wide elastic band, a Soviet invention for vacuum sealing. It was the finest bait, even if it was given as a gift, that Hemingway, the famous tropical fisherman, had ever used. Cipriani told the countess that the American gentleman had left the gift for her. Since the liberator of Italy hadn't arrived yet, Cipriani took off the pink band, which he rolled up like an elastic band, and opened the circular tin filled with the precious sturgeon eggs. They shone like perfect steel-gray ammunition in their moist Caspian Sea magma. Then the Countess said to Cipriani in Vèneto: 'How much is a kilo of caviar?' Cipriani told her the exorbitant amount in dollars. And she replied: '*Caro* Cipriani, you keep it and add the amount to my account. Please thank the American gentleman for the gesture, which I appreciate, but please tell him that beyond fifty grams caviar loses all meaning and distinction.'"

Miranda's tale was greatly celebrated. It synthesized what they felt and knew about the figure of Hemingway. I noticed that between Ripa di Meana and his friend Marina della Rovere a game of aggression had begun. Marina gave in to the champagne at Renato's insistence. In order to conceal the tension, Ripa addressed the guest of honor:

"Is this the first time you've been to Venice, Señor Borges?"

"No," Borges said, "I came with my parents in 1916. I saw it then and admired it, an inescapable fact for any sensible person. It is difficult to remember it now, without the light from that time. I try to recall buildings, places, some sounds. But everything is far away, perhaps only a confusion of marble palaces, swaying in the silt of the lagoon, floating, enduring. I believe, however, that I remember that already then, more than half a century ago, people feared for the fate of Venice. In short: my memories, my Venice is sepia-colored, like those old photos, from 1916; it was 1916, shall we say?"

I watched him as he spoke and thought that that light was helping him to reconstruct the vision of reality that he could no longer see. Something similar to that light of stars extinguished millennia ago and that still reaches us traveling through space to compose that starry night that we admire from our garden. Light that arrives from the death of its origin. Light, the surviving traveler.

But Marina returned to the charge against Ripa. It seemed to me that he said something antagonistic to her when she was about to light a cigarette she'd taken from a silver cigarette case. The table began to abandon the overlapping conversations to pay attention to the quarrel. Ripa was annoyed but maintained his calm demeanor. He signaled firmly to her not to light the cigarette. Prevented from doing so, she closed the cigarette case and instead stood up to thrust it into the St. Basil's Cathedral-style ice-cream dessert that Bianca Mieli had placed in the center of the table. Then Marina sat down, cool and disdainful, and looked at Ripa di Meana, who made a gesture of apology to Bianca. He then reached down and removed the cigarette case, wiped it with his napkin, and put it in his pocket. From this brief dramatic eruption, the mood shifted to laughter. Ricci and his stunning wife were unable to contain themselves, and everyone laughed uncontrollably. Bianca had regained her humor after her brief matronly indignation. She took the dessert platter and passed it to the waiter with instructions to rebuild the architectural disaster as much as possible and then serve the dessert with the help of an assistant. Marina della Rovere took her glass of champagne and leaned back in her chair, happy to have waged another slight battle against convention and to have enjoyed a good deal of attention.

Borges hadn't perceived the events or the reasons for the commotion. No doubt he attributed it to a story or jokes he hadn't understood. As the comments and laughter continued, he leaned over to me and said:

"I asked you a while ago to remind me of Delmira Agustini because she wrote a poem about non-physical blindness, because she wasn't blind, but rather spiritual blindness, shall we say. I just synthesized from memory those verses that have to do with that light that the blind man remembers and uses from memory, shall we say. The topic we've been talking about."

Then in a low voice, taking advantage of the comments and exclamations due to the antics of the descendant of Pope Julius II, he recited verses by Delmira Agustini:

I fall into a strange luminous blindness
A strange blindness that erases my world,

Give me your light and just snuff out my world forever.[40]

"Don't take it literally; I added my own touches. I was so bold. Without the 'just' that I added, this eulogy of shadow wasn't as effective ... What do you think?"

"It changes the verse, and suggests that behind the injustice of blindness there is a more or less indifferent god. Sounds like elegant contempt: 'Just snuff out my world.'"

"Forever, forever!" said Borges. "Forever; don't insist on life again!" And he laughed, throwing back his head.

---

40 Besides adding *nomás* (just/only), Borges altered the poem slightly, replacing the verb *velar* (to veil) with *apagar* (turn off/snuff out).

24

"THEN CAME THE Veneziana. I began to feel that the city was barging into focus."[41] This is what the poet Brodsky wrote after his first brief stay in Venice, having been expelled from the Soviet Union. This happened before our arrival. "Tottering on the verge of the three-dimensional," Brodsky noted. Many months have passed since then, and when the former Soviet poet earned his first salary as a lecturer at a university in the spiritually deserted center of the United States, he bought a round-trip ticket from Detroit to Venice. He wanted to regain the vision, and perhaps even more, with which the deceptive West had welcomed him just after being shoved onto an Aeroflot flight. During that brief stay he believes that Andreina Venier was something absolutely abnormal, but he couldn't decide whether she was a misguided divinity or a sophisticated KGB assassin sent to kill him. With her perfume, her otter coat, her hair of a galloping filly, her gaze ever alternating between mustard and honey. No one can know the content of that brief and presumably unforget-

---

41 The author's translation here reads: "Apareció la veneciana y poco a poco la ciudad se prendió fuego" (The Veneziana appeared and little by little the city caught fire).

table relationship. What is certain is that the battered mujik is shaken to his most intimate core and seizes biblical majesty to give pathos without resorting to secular parlance: "And the Spirit of God moved upon the face of the waters. Then there was that next morning. It was Sunday, and all the bells were chiming." He wrote this in *Acqua alta*: "Spirit of God that next morning, presumably bells of alleluia."[42]

It can be presumed that they dined and drank together, during the birth of an intense friendship. What is certain is that Brodsky commits the carelessness of crossing the hunter's path for the second time. Or Diana, the Huntress's. Brodsky quotes Francis Bacon: "Hope is a good breakfast, but it is a bad supper." Actually, he described, in rather delirious language, the feeling he had, trying to escape from the second empire that used him as a writer of genius expelled by the USSR and welcomed by opportunist Western freedom. Brodsky promised himself, and wrote it down, that if he weren't able to return to Venice: "I would [...] buy myself a little Browning and blow my brains out on the spot, unable to die in Venice of natural causes." At least die in Venice. But he wasn't able to do it, because he would die prematurely in New York. However, he was buried in the cemetery of San Michele Island, near Pound and Stravinsky, whose tomb we'd visited with Sabato during his sincere spectacle of placing a rose on Stravinsky.

What's certain is that Brodsky returns in search of a lost dream, that of his first passage through the *Serenissima*.

42　As the author references the title as *Acqua alta*, I presume that he is referencing the French edition, which bears this title, the title of the Spanish edition being *Marca de agua*. In any event, this quotation does not exist in the English edition.

He takes a grueling trip from Detroit with multiple connections and hours of waiting in airports. He finally arrives in the city of miracles. Surely there was a phone call from the United States, and she's waiting for him in a caffè where no sane Venetian would go in winter, in the Giardini dell'Arsenale, the Caffè Paradiso. Striking in a taffeta dress, she was waiting for him with two small volumes of poetry: Propertius in Latin and Pushkin in Russian. Brodsky notices the ridiculousness of his zippered canvas bags, his forehead covered in beads of sweat from the anxious race to the Arsenal, crossing twelve bridges, as he writes, feeling anxious about the reunion and guilty for being late. To top it off, he's wearing a cloth cap and a thick Soviet serge jacket. As he deposits his Soviet-Yankee traveler's cargo on the table, she scrutinizes him with her mustard and honey gaze and says to him:

"What a belly! Neither Mandelstam nor Akhmatova were able to put on weight in the West, you, on the other hand, were lucky."

Putting on weight after several Soviet prisons is the first thing one notices about an exile flung into the West, except for the mystical Solzhenitsyn. Brodsky jotted down the words "flop" and "winter light." Andreina had likely been waiting for more than half an hour, reading Propertius in the light of the melancholy Arsenal, which had already been converted into a summer venue for the dreadful *Biennali*.

25

IT WAS THE painter Baldovino who was going from the Rialto Bridge in the direction of the Basilica della Salute. It was a Sunday morning at seven o'clock, and Sabine and I had gone for a walk before tourist Venice awoke. It was our friend Baldovino who was carrying a small wooden easel and a box slung over his shoulder, probably with tubes filled with colors, palette knives, and brushes. Behind him, carrying a bag, was Mirtha, his wife, with a canvas folding chair and a plastic bag. She walked behind him, almost with ancestral Eastern obligingness. We decided to follow them from afar in that deliciously cool late summer air. Venice was waking up, gondolas and boats swayed, tied gently to the colored *paline*. Pigeons flapping, shutters opening to the light, someone stretching in a nightshirt.

The Baldovinos, apparently, have a creative program. We follow them from afar but aren't afraid of losing sight of them because they're following the Canal along empty *fondamente*. The only sound is the dragging noise of tables and chairs in bars and the gush of the hoses that clean the walkways. A clear sky, a centuries-old peace. A persistence of incredible beauty which the painter is hunting. We follow them cautiously, but at times we lose them in the labyrinth until the jungle returns them to the clearing of

Campo San Polo, or to the inescapable street of Ca' Foscari or San Barnaba. They move along in a rigorous and quiet line of twos, at a comfortable pace, in the direction of the *Accademia*. We're overconfident and we lose them; we go exploring along the Campo San Vio. Nothing. Half an hour was lost and finally we decided to go back to the Canal to return to the consulate by vaporetto. But Sabine insists, she has a hunch, and we head for San Trovaso. In front of the famous *Squero*, the old gondola shipyard, the painter was there with his easel set up; and his wife, on the small stone staircase that leads down to the San Trovaso River, was preparing *mates* with an aluminum kettle and alcohol heater. It was as if they were hidden on that small stone stairway, and nothing disturbed them. Baldovino made charcoal outlines prior to applying oils. He was a painter at the purest moment in the life of every nascent artist. He wanted to add to his palette the colors of Canaletto, whom he admired. Shades of sky, more or less luminous, difficult and unexpected reflections of shifting waters, from sea to lagoon and those that escape from the lagoon to become purified in the sea.

Months later Baldovino would achieve tempera and oil paintings with an admirable and humble interpretation of Venice. (Some of his paintings, on wood, will be successful.) But that morning he existed in the happiness of pure, improbable art.

He was certainly living the initial exaltation of the successful strokes of the broken gondola supported by piles in the workshop in the *Squero*. Baldovino interrupts himself and doesn't take his eyes off the canvas. He sips the *mate* and eats a biscuit that Mirtha offers him. The enthusiasm, *la enthusía*, on that cool morning. Feeling touched by magic, or the muses, before the blank canvas and the overwhelmingly remarkable reality. Perchance that painter could not have had a moment of greater faith in art and with the happiness of his wife, the *mate*, the colors, and the solitude of the *canaletto* of San Trovaso.

26

WE'D GONE TO lunch with Borges and Kodama at the Trattoria di Raffaele in San Marco and agreed to book a gondola ride for the next day. Later we went to the *piazza*. He reiterated his admiration for Lugones as our *miglior fabbro*,[43] even though, at a very young age, he'd once yielded to those who violently criticized him. He tells us:

"There was a rather mysterious element for my life. Lugones killed himself on February 18, 1938. The national shock of his supreme protest coincided with my most serious and personal shock, the death of my father, during those days of February 1938. Now, over time, the two events are one. They will forever overlap."

We came out in front of the colossal square under the scorching two P.M. sun. Borges told Sabine, María, and me that Italy's brightness wanted to push aside the penumbra of his blindness.

"How do you see me?" I asked him.

---

43 "Best smith or craftsman"; a reference to the Provençal troubadour Arnault Daniel in Canto XXVI of Dante's *Purgatorio;* T.S. Eliot borrows this epithet to refer to Ezra Pound, to whom he dedicates *The Wasteland.*

"To see is saying a lot…"

"Am I wearing a tie?" Borges lowered his face to my chest and said:

"I see something vertical … Something dark, it seems."

"Indeed, my tie is dark blue." María said to him:

"Borges, from here the Campanile is visible." This time Borges raised his head.

"I think so. I think it's something enormous to support bells and an angel. I think I see; it's something like his tie but going up." We laughed and he added: "An immense vertical shadow, but I don't know if it's from now or what remains of the Venice of my first trip, more than half a century ago … I can't be sure. But it would be the same."

27

THE FOLLOWING DAY and at my request, Rega hired a gondolier from the neighboring Ca' d'Oro station. The question we asked ourselves was: how would Borges get from the steps along the side of the canal into the gondola half a meter below, as unstable as these historic contraptions are? But for situations such as this the Venetians have answers from centuries-old experience. Fortunately, the strapping Amedeo hadn't retired. While the seasoned gondolier held the boat still against the steps, Amedeo, in his white jacket, lifted Borges (in suit, tie, and his silver watch fob pinned to his buttonhole), and, to our anguish, deposited him, with all the nautical expertise of his Venetian genes, right in the center of that narrow floating violin. Borges forced a smile, which I thought evoked sensations of the distant trip with his parents, when the gondola was still the usual vehicle, before it became denatured by tourism and luxury. It was an afternoon of heavy air, cloudy, with listless birds. We moved along the Grand Canal. We were seated in plush chairs facing each other, in admiring silence, certainly evocative for Borges. We heard the gondolier's movement, leaning on his oar, his body tilting forward, without much effort. His only rudder was the strength of momentum, along with the secret of unbalancing the strange center line of that asymmetrical invention with the weight of his body and dominating the course with admirable precision.

We continued along the Grand Canal, and we then entered the narrow Cannaregio *rios*. The urge one feels when passing under those stone balconies and between brick or marble walls, eaten away by centuries of salt, is to stretch one's legs and lean back for the abandoned contemplation of one who dozes off listening to Chopin. Silence and receiving that strange burden of centuries-old existence.

Kodama whispered to Borges what she was seeing. I commented to them about a curious interpretation by Élie Faure concerning the palaces, the luxury, Venice's aquatic madness. "Why so many palaces?" Borges asked me. I told him that Faure suggested that they were not houses to live in. A normal house, even a luxurious one, engenders and shelters a family. The Venetians discovered that every *palazzo* creates or obliges a lineage, which is much more. The descendants of the founder must be military heroes, great merchants, jurists, inventors, poets. It is the residence, the habitat that guarantees the pride and even the republican ethics of the *Serenissima* at her peak. It was possible to decorate the salons with gold, without Christian guilt. It was known that the gold would be a school of imperial power. As it has always been. There was always empire. Borges protested:

"'Another empire, another tomfoolery.' I think it was Nietzsche who said that."

I continued:

"They condemned the Doge Venier to death. The Venetians knew how to control their leaders, like the English, who also beheaded their king to secure parliamentary rights."

Borges felt comforted. He was genuinely a republican. I had told him my story of how a young Jesuit recruited into the first squalid convent of the Order in Venice, newly founded by the disciples of Loyola, escapes one night through the window and walking toward San Marco finds a fallen white plaster mask. He puts it on, as the Venetians used to do to free themselves from being the "other" and of having to be an individual in the public sphere and not one of many, as we are. The young Jesuit feels that he is leaving behind a prison and at the same time the vertigo, the whirlwind of freedom, starting with sex. His imposed correction, his aspiration for sainthood, to continue his journey with the other, the deep self, the liberated transgressor. Venice knew the freedom and fullness of being on the side of sexuality, luxury, war. For the British, Puritanism and the Bible as a power of subjugation and domination.

We headed back toward the Grand Canal. The sky was thick with clouds and rumblings that announced an abrupt summer storm. Without a word, the gondolier's rowing grew quicker. We grew nervous. The storm unleashed lightning and torrential rain. The gondolier managed to shelter us under a stone bridge. We had barely gotten wet. He steadied the gondola with his feet and, to still the gondola in the slight current, placing his palms on the arch of the bridge. A downpour of heavy drops to say goodbye to the summer. Water over water, as in the *I Ching*. Lightning and terrifying thunder as if to shatter the palaces' crystalware. And then, when the din ceased, the muffled, extremely intimate, intense voice of Borges, without the facile emphasis of recitation, with the verses of the *Rain Psalm* by his teacher Lugones, about whom we'd spoken the day before:

The sky was a somber cave of water;

thunder, in the distance, rolled down a hill... [44]

He reveled in every word. We were all worried, except him. Within ten minutes the rain began to ease off. It was like a rain fleeing the rocky ground of the Río Seco, Lugones's homeland. To that end, in cosmic harmony, Borges delivered us:

And a distance breeze in crooked flight
Smelled of acid, a subtle lemon chill.
[...]
The blue hill smelled of rosemary,
and in the deep valley fields a partridge whistled.

"The partridge, that's the only thing that's missing today in Venice!" he said.

The cloudburst had passed, and we rowed toward the consulate. We saw the trouble from faraway. Delia, Milossi, Lisetta, Iván, Amedeo in his white jacket and even Ada in Delia's arms. They'd been thinking about the disaster of a soaked Borges who seemed like an invalid, helpless, but who in fact had surprising strength.

(A conversation that B. had with his mother:
"Good morning, Mother, shall I draw the curtains?"
"Georgie, am I alive? How awful! Another day! What an imposition! I thought I died last night..."
"No, Mother, no. I've had the water put on for tea."
Recounted to Sabine by Kodama with an ironic gleam in her usually impassive Oriental eyes.)

---

44 Translated by Julie Schumacher.

28

PHILEMON AND BAUCIS, the mythical Greek couple, was what Sabine, an expert in mythology, called our acquaintances Captain Sievers and his wife Amalia. He'd retired from the Merchant Navy after the wreck of the *Andrea Doria*. They lived in a small apartment near the tony Campo San Samuele. A house full of memories. Everything was going quite splendidly, in the reserved manner of the Northern Italians. But at some point, there was a feeling or an impression that the Sieverses were experiencing the anguish of growing old and the dilemma of dying and suffering alone the death of what in seventy years had merged into a single being.

I liked to think of the Blue Age. Those final years that the Sieverses were already exhausting. When love's wings are clipped and it transforms into the tenderness and companionship of a long coexistence.

We ate the very delicate Austrian dessert that the Sieverses, *un po' triestini*, considered a trademark of their home. But above their candelabra-lit table flew that silent hornet of death. We walked back to the consulate and Sabine said to me:

"I heard from *Signora* Giavi that the Sieverses had a son who died at sixteen.[45] Didn't you see the photo on the piano? They poured their love out onto each other." And Sabine told me the story that Goethe includes in the spectacular ending of the second *Faust*. It's not merely a topic of erudite or inaccurate mythology.

"Does it have to do with death? I barely remember the myth."

"Yes. Philemon and Baucis, old and extremely poor, offer cheese, honey, and wine to two ragged travelers whom the rest of the village rejected. The astute Philemon understands that they're all-powerful, divine beings. They are none other than the omnipotent Zeus and Hermes, moved by the old couple who exhibit an innocence rare among humans. The story is long: Zeus decides to reward them by transforming their hut into a marble temple that the old couple will tend for the rest of their lives. They accept with joy."

"Could they be the Sieverses? In their apartment in San Samuele?"

"And instead of cheese and honey, Norwegian pink salmon and beef stroganoff," says Sabine. And she continues: "But then comes the essence of the myth. Baucis encourages Philemon to tell Zeus what they most desire but always conceal out of modesty: they ask Zeus to allow them to die together. That they not suffer the anguish of one seeing the

---

45   Little could the author and his wife know at this time that in 1983 the same fate would befall their son Iván, about whom the author writes so lovingly in this memoir, while the family was living in Paris. Twenty-seven years later, he would write about this tragic event in a memoir titled *Cuando muere el hijo* [When your child dies].

other die and continue to live. No, they didn't want to say farewell or to hasten it."

"And Zeus?"

"He understands everything. He grants their wish. They will no longer fear arthrosis, autumn phlegm. Alzheimer's ridiculous discussions between the forgetful old man and the deaf old woman: 'Did I tell you?' 'No. You didn't tell me!'"

"You didn't tell me! But I just told you! What was our son's name? ... The mental decline, the worst punishment."

"And love?"

"No. They can't be bothered any longer by that abnormality. With Zeus's promise they go forward free, without desires, without fears."

"They're in the Blue Age."

"Yes. And Zeus agreed to remove the last concern, the farewell, and the weeping for the one who departs first."

"Of course, that's the supreme spiritual comfort. Now they'll no longer fear death or cling to the desire to repeat life."

"It wouldn't even occur to them. They forget everything. The sanctity of oblivion."

"Well, to hell with the Sieverses!"

"To hell with them." And I say to Sabine, as we arrive at the vaporetto pier: "And will those of us in the Blue Age remember the Sieverses and Venice?"

"Venice? Which Venice? There's a pizzeria called Venice in Belgrano.[46] Belgrano, what Belgrano?" And we laughed as we boarded the vaporetto.

---

46 An upper-class neighborhood of Buenos Aires.

"Finish the myth. What happened to Philemon and Baucis?"

"Zeus kept his word, perhaps happy to have found a couple of human beings noble in their humility. He allowed them to die together and in some forest of some planet she's a linden tree and he an oak, with the branches intertwined, naturally. Thus concludes the myth."

"There're the Sieverses and also our friends, Dr. Solomon and his wife Emma, and others, perhaps the Giavis. And in the future us too, no?"

"All of them, all of us. All plays in the theater of life end badly. Even comedies."

29

VENETIAN MISCELLANEA. Iván asked to be allowed to walk home from school on his own, to not be walked by Delia. The boys are making fun of him. We reluctantly agree to cancel the escort. On my way back from an appointment at the Prefecture, I decide to take a detour through the Campo de la Guerra, where the school is located, and like a spy I wait for Iván's class to let out. Once outside the entrance, the shouting, the laughter, the pushing and shoving starts. They swing their satchels filled with notebooks and supplies. They run while kicking a beer can. They lean on the canal bridge to watch the delivery boats go by. I follow Iván who races the Da Tos brothers; they hit the brakes and bump into passersby. The Da Tos brothers turn in the direction of their house and Iván continues on his way, swinging his bag. There, under the radiant light of midday, it's pure freedom. When he arrives at Piazza San Bartolomeo he stops in front of the statue of Goldoni, with a permanent smile, watching the pigeon perched on the poet's tricorn, until the pigeon shits on the poet and Iván bursts out laughing.

That's what Iván wanted, using the excuse that his classmates were making fun of him. He desired vulnerability, those fifteen minutes of autonomy, to feel the street and the city against his skin. And when he crosses the consulate gate, I understand that he is absolutely right to want his freedom: children's games, races, shoving, laughing at an irreverent pigeon, that nothingness that is everything, freedom as an instinct. A just-because, a just-for-the-heck-of-it.

30

THE LAST LONG, peaceful siestas, with half-closed blinds controlling subtle breezes. Expired forms are there, yellowed, flipped, where I write as if scribbling on the back of bureaucracy. I add, correct, what I think I like: Columbus discovers Paradise in the peninsula of Aparia, at the mouth of the Orinoco, and respectfully communicates it, like a modest heir in the direct line of the prophet Isaiah, to the Reina Isabel and Pope Alexander VI. In 1492 he'd discovered the unknown part of the world, during the voyage of 1498, Paradise. I laugh as I note the prophecies of the promise of the return to the land without evil. Enoch, the Abbé d'Ailly. I copy verbatim the letter that Columbus sent to the Queen: "It is as if the world, round like a ball, were a woman's breast, and the nipple the highest and closest to Heaven." It's the Omphalos! Columbus is both proud and humbled by the tremendous responsibility of having landed in Openness since the expulsion of the hapless Adam, the sinful Eve, and her murderous, hard-working, half-naked, God-doubting progeny, prone to low-hanging fruit.

The Spaniards believed that the Orinoco was the Euphrates and the Tigris as they opened into a delta that reminded them of the Venetian archipelago. That's why they called that region Venezuela. The communiqué to

Pope Alexander is concise and absolute: "On 4 August 1498, I reached the lands of the Earthly Paradise."

One need simply read the story to discover the lost fantasy, the surreal driving the sacred History. Lunacies that one can consult in the Archive of Seville.

I entertain myself by jotting down on a separate sheet of paper the effects of the return to Paradise. Columbus would dictate the "Ordinance of Nudity" for the entire population. Modesty, a consequence of sin, would no longer make sense, nor would the Catalan textile industry and the resulting tailoring industry. On the other hand, having reached Openness,[47] Jehovah's condemnation of work makes no sense. Columbus orders hammers and axes to be laid down. Those who have a vocation for farming, for commerce, for aggrandizement, despair. Columbus, unflappable, dictates the "Ordinances of Mere Being," forbidding all will to do, to have, and even to exist.

I like it—it works. It's in my mood and my voice. When the sun goes down, I'll take the written pages and rewrite them in the café at the Campo dei Santi Apostoli, at that hour when Iván, Luca Bressin, and their gang play soccer against the wall of the church.

---

47 "Openness" is a reference to Rilke's concept of *das Offene*, which he treats in the eighth of the Duino Elegies, which begins, "With all their eyes, animals behold the Open." Trans. Edward Snow.

31

AN EXISTENTIAL CRISIS for Ada the cat. Major disturbance in the house. Since there was a costume party at the Istituto San Giuseppe, Iván wanted to dress up as Batman. Sabine found him a rubber cape and a black mask at the Standa department store. Since Iván was still at school, she thought she'd surprise him and lay out the costume on an armchair in the foyer: the feline mask, cape, and boots. It was a hollow Batman, as if waiting for Iván's body. It is common knowledge that cats furtively sniff out anything new that comes into the house. It appears that Ada came from the back of the house and found this creature of her own zoological family sitting in the entryway. What's certain is, when Iván arrived he found Ada transformed into a monster with a glowing stare, showing her fangs. Her body resembled a hedgehog, her hackles raised, her tail lashing as in a language of imminent attack. She wouldn't allow anyone to approach her. We didn't know how to subdue her; she was giving off a strong odor. She exuded the decision to confront to the death that immobile creature that was watching her from the chair, usurping her territory. Moreover, I began to deduce that Ada was feeling disappointed by all of us, her family. She'd given up her freedom and her position on the gondola mooring to become part of our home. And we'd allowed this crypto-feline creature of Hollywood's commercial imagery to move in. Its black mask with vacant eyes and pricked ears aroused criminal aggression. Ada was right.

Delia, ever astute, ran to the chair, grabbed the rubber creature and opened the door and tossed it into the outer hallway. Ada was appeased, but it took no less than ten days for her to enter our bedroom. Cats are very reflective, even critical. And their resentment is long.

32

WE CROSSED THE Rialto bridge with Borges and filed through the labyrinth in the direction of Santa Margherita so as not to have to dodge so many tourists. It's clear that he was interested in my account of the adventure of the Jesuit Sorge.

"If one puts on a veil, a mask, one is no longer oneself," Borges said, recalling my idea of the young seminarian who finds the plaster mask in the street and puts it on. And everything begins to change.

The weariness of not wanting to continue to be oneself is quite explainable: one usually feels limited and even crushed by others. What's more, the mask can help us to free ourselves from ourselves and free some of those others we carry inside. Freedom, which is what Sorge, the Tyrolean who was recruited by the earliest Jesuits, discovers.

"In fact, Venice did away with its Middle Ages three centuries before the rest of Europe. When one lives here, one understands that the use of the mask continued to spread until transforming into a culture. Living in Venice without a mask would be like living in an unbearable tenement. Here sex was the key to entering reality from the Judeo-Christian metaphysical catacomb. From there it would become a part of occultism, heterodoxy, philosophy. *La*

Serenìsima Repùblica, the Most Serene Republic. A curious republicanism that did not equate the bumpkin with a lord, or the wise man with a donkey. And as I told you before, they even cut off the heads of the doges who believed they could steal, or allow to be stolen, public goods. Historians estimate that in the fifteenth century there were about three thousand patrician women, two thousand women who belonged to the bourgeoisie, two and a half thousand nuns, and twelve thousand harlots."

"Twelve thousand, eh? Don't you think that's a bit much?" says Borges.

33

CHATEAUBRIAND, WHO ALWAYS tried to be original in his observations, declared, in fact, that membership in the guild grew substantially when, beginning in the eighteenth century, patrician and bourgeois women relegated prostitutes to the gray area of mere professionals. Rather than besting them in the streets they did so in bed. A Venetian husband, from the century of her heyday until that of her decline, felt honored if it became public knowledge, such that he took it upon himself to spread it about, that his wife had been dishonored, and at the same time honored, by some illustrious visitor from the nobility, the great aristocracy, or high culture. Over time, erotic memories are among the most vivid left by visitors such as Henri IV, François I, Rousseau, Byron (and La Fornarina), the unsuspecting Montaigne, Musset and his quarrels with George Sand, d'Annunzio and Duse, the ambiguous Thomas Mann, and so many others.

"Ambiguous Thomas Mann?" Borges asks me. "He never interested me much as a writer. But ambiguous?"

"Well, the whole thing with *Death in Venice*..." Borges hadn't read it. He told me:

"His best book is *The Holy Sinner*, which no one chooses to read or even knows about. Everyone talks about *The Magic Mountain*, with all its pretentiousness," he said.

Once at Campo Santa Margherita we sat down for coffee and I went to the tourist bookstore and bought an edition of the pamphlet *Tariffa delle puttane di Venezia*,[48] from 1535.

I read him a few sentences:

Rate:
Cornelia Griffa: A veritable gift, delight. She's haughty; she'll ask you for 40 escudos and even more.
Lucietta: Frenchified and unhealthy, 2 escudos, mostly out of pity.
Cecilia: the great Francis, king of France, took all her charms. But still…
Diana: beware, she swindles and cheats.
Lucia Alberti: madwoman, take care not to approach her.
Lucrezia Squarcia: she pretends to be a student of letters. She always has a Petrarch, Virgil, and even Homer on hand.
Perina Lavandiera: the most vile. 2 escudos is a lot.
Paula, her sister, half an escudo.
Laura: uses the name Petrarca. Half an escudo.

And several pages of advice and prices follow.

There was a note about Veronica Franco, the most famous prostitute from that time, the intermittent lover,

---

48   The rates of whores of Venice.

during his visit to Venice, of Henri III of France. She was worthy of the memory of Montaigne, to whom she dedicated poems that the independent skeptic praised.

Rousseau, the eminent educator and moralist, narrated in his *Confessions* his astonishment at the courtesan Zulietta, who receives him in specially designed lingerie, with pink bobbles, and begs him "not to try to make love in the French style," as if it were something backward for Venice.

The use of lingerie was centuries ahead of the medieval woolen unisex pantaloons of civilized, Nordic, preferably Protestant and even Calvinist, Europe. Burano today is visited by embroiderers of the centuries-old tradition. These hard-working women make napkins, handkerchiefs, tablecloths, table covers, and doilies for world tourism. They don't even know that they are heirs of the erotic lingerie suppliers for those twelve thousand courtesans who helped to alleviate the male condition throughout Europe and even the Near East.

"Twelve thousand, *che*? That's an outrageous number," says Borges.

"According to the archives … "

"There are so many, it's almost too commonplace, it might as well be none at all. That would be discouraging, don't you think? The ease, that is."

"But that heyday was short-lived," I tell him.

"I imagine the Inquisition would have intervened."

"No. Something happened worthy only of Venice. Here the Inquisition was hindered because it was at the discretion of the patriarch, who was usually a man of the local gentry. Something happened that will surprise you: ladies became courtesans and even self-declared prostitutes, with a license.

The others, pitiable professionals, were left for the seamen and the proletariat of the Arsenal ... "

"More or less like now, no?" murmured Borges. Of all those minor palaces that we saw, worn, transformed into humble dwellings, there nevertheless remained an insolent joy of living, or rather, of having lived. A light drizzle lingered, forcing us to return to the vaporetto.

34

LIKE ALMOST EVERYONE, but in his peculiar style, he was mortified by his sexuality since adolescence.

Stemming from that defenselessness, an extraordinary guardian angel had kept him safe in his metaphysical and aesthetic bastion. No woman could harm him there or rob him of times of passion. He had abductors who were certainly sent by his guardian angel: his mother, Doña Leonor, with an oedipism of *mother-patroness*. At the end of the thirties, he became friends with Bioy Casares, snob, tennis player, fluffhead, with his cumulative gymnastic Don Juanism, his absolute opposite, who didn't interfere in Borges's creative solitude but kept him isolated within a club of four or five people. And, ultimately, until his death, María Kodama, who protected him in life and assured his glory much more than the Nobel Prizes he was denied. These three "abductions" allowed Borges to not so much as stick his nose out of the aesthetic palace. To devote himself fully to his most private cult.

Estela Canto narrated with certain callousness some aspects of her love with Borges, between 1936 and 1952. She suggests that their love failed to progress because Borges did not know how to stop the incursions of maternal oedipism in their relationship. Canto was a Communist without class complexes. She knew the upper-class codes, so as to mock Bioy Casares's bourgeois exclusions and values. Estela had been born into an aristocratic yet impoverished family in Uruguay. She was polemical, insolent, cultured. She regarded Borges as a man deeply and perhaps definitively wounded in his sexuality, but she admired and respected him. She recounts a weekend trip with Borges to the countryside with the Casareses. At that time Borges was rather unkempt and Bioy asked him to shave because his parents would be attending the luncheon. As he was afraid of cutting himself with the razor, Estela shaved him and wrote down in her memoir: "That was the closest our bodies ever got." The mother could not give her son's hand to a woman who believed in communism and who was not shy about narrating the anecdotes of her occasional jobs as a barmaid and dancer in the cabarets of El Bajo and Avenida Paseo Colón. "I pay for my freedom by faking my slavery," she'd say, laughing, scandalizing the supposedly unprejudiced members of the Sur group.

I met her, a translator of Proust, and a great reader, the year she'd distanced herself from Borges. I was in the first year of university during that era of cafés and great conversations of literary initiation. She and Patricio, her brother, talked to me in the Bar Florida about Jean Genet, still relatively unknown in Argentina. They sent me in haste to the Galatea bookstore, around the corner from where we were, because there was only one copy left of *Querelle de Brest*, and *Pompes funèbres*.

Perhaps it was out of secret resentment that Bioy Casares wrote, in that vile book of their conversations at home,[49] that Borges ended up proposing marriage and that she replied, "I'd gladly do it, Georgie, but don't forget that I consider myself a disciple of Bernard Shaw: we can't get married if we don't go to bed first." Bioy adds that Borges replied: "Can I hug you?" and then called a cab to take them to a horrible restaurant in the Plaza Constitución, El Tren Mixto, telling her in English, "We must celebrate." A curious accuracy, written and published by Bioy to disparage his lifelong friend.

It was in 1935 at a dinner at his home where he met Estela and the love began, perhaps the most complicated for Borges, a man besotted but with abstractions.[50] Bioy was a serial and inconsequential seducer. I always suspected that, before Borges, it was Bioy's omnipotent Don Juanism that had been defeated by that extraordinary Estela Canto, whom he later introduced to Borges. Estela Canto would mock Bioy's membership in Buenos Aires's Lawn Tennis Club, his white sweaters with blue collars, his intrinsic superficiality. She'd take the floor at the group's dinners and enthusiastically explain "the permanent revolution of Trotskyism" and the necessary violence in "the solution of contradictions." Nal Roxlo believed that the unfailing Don Juan, Bioy Casares, had been defeated by someone he believed sexually irrelevant, a mere witness to his stories. Estela Canto had preferred the brilliant, the defenseless, the reserved. A curious mimesis of Borges as the apparent little

---

49   The author is referring to the biography *Borges*, written by Bioy Casares and published in 2006 by Ediciones Destino.

50   Canto states in her biography of Borges that they met in August 1944 at the home of Bioy Casares and his wife Silvia Ocampo, "a few days before the liberation of Paris."

man on pink corner who with his little dagger kills the bully, Francisco Real, the Yardmaster, and saves everyone from cowardice, without telling anyone, out of sheer humble courage, without boasting to everyone.[51] Estela wrote in her (almost banned) book *Borges a contraluz*:[52]

"I liked what I was to him and what he saw in me. Sexually I was indifferent... His clumsy, abrupt kisses, always at the wrong time... I never pretended to feel what I didn't feel."

According to Nal Roxlo, this long affair was a bone that Bioy could never swallow: the unprejudiced and seemingly invincible adulterer had this time played the role of the cuckold!

What is certain is that perhaps Borges's most important story, "The Aleph," was dedicated to Estela Canto, who typed it. Sometime later, to help her out, Borges gave her that original as a gift. She sold it at Sotheby's for thirty-thousand dollars at the time. It was bought by the Biblioteca Nacional de España.

What is more certain is that Borges suffered discretely and with courage these intimate conflicts, which he perhaps only knew how to overcome at the end of his life. He experienced the nonfictional temptation of suicide. María Eugenia Estenssoro alerted me to a passage from the black notebook belonging to Jorge Luis Borges, found in the Hotel Las Delicias in Adrogué in 1940, according to the refined

---

51 The author is referring here to the short story, "Hombre de la esquina rosada," first published in 1935, and translated as "Man on Pink Corner" by Andrew Hurley.

52 This biography, published in 1989 in Spain by Espasa-Calpe, has not been translated into English. The title translates roughly to "Borges against a backlight."

collector Nicolás Helft, who published it in part. It reflects Borges's depressive state in those years perhaps coinciding with the ambiguous relationship with Estela Canto. In the annotation the supposed suicide victim writes: "The other J.L.B. (the other and real Borges, the one who justifies me in a sufficient but secret way) carried out that afternoon (perhaps for the first time) his duties as second assistant (two hundred and ten pesos a month; with deductions, one hundred and ninety-nine) at the small library in Boedo.[53] He purchased a revolver in one of the gun shops on Calle Entre Ríos, and curiously, a secondhand copy of a novel (*Ellery Queen: The Egyptian Cross Mystery*); in Plaza Constitución he bought a one-way ticket to Adrogué-Mármol-Turdera, went to the Hotel Las Delicias, consumed and left two or three strong beers unpaid and discharged a definitive bullet in one of the upper rooms ... "

Helft explains that "Borges did not succeed in committing suicide in the hotel in Adrogué," but he felt very hopeless. He was forty years old and was only recognized in a small circle, and his books sold few copies. His money was barely enough to buy a few books and sometimes go to the movies. He lived with his mother in an apartment at Pueyrredón and Las Heras. He worked in the neighborhood library mentioned in the note."

He felt that this mediocre life was false or unreal, and that what was real were the stories he wrote, usually in that dilapidated hotel room where he'd spent his childhood vacations. The black notebook with gridded pages also contained a fantastical tale. The first drafts of "Tlön, Uqbar, Orbis Tertius." "So, at the moment of his

---

53 Slightly less than $50.00 USD.

greatest crisis," Helft points out, "as his life seems to be falling apart, Borges concludes his most powerful and enduring work on the annihilation of reality by power of imagination."

Palazzo Mangili Valmarana

Detail of the ceiling, Palazzo Mangili Valmarana

The hall of the Palazzo Mangili Valmarana

Abel Posse. Snow on the Piazza San Marco

Sabine Parentini Posse and Delia Barboza on the Piazza San Marco

Delia and Ivan on the Piazza San Marco

Abel Posse and Ernesto Sabato

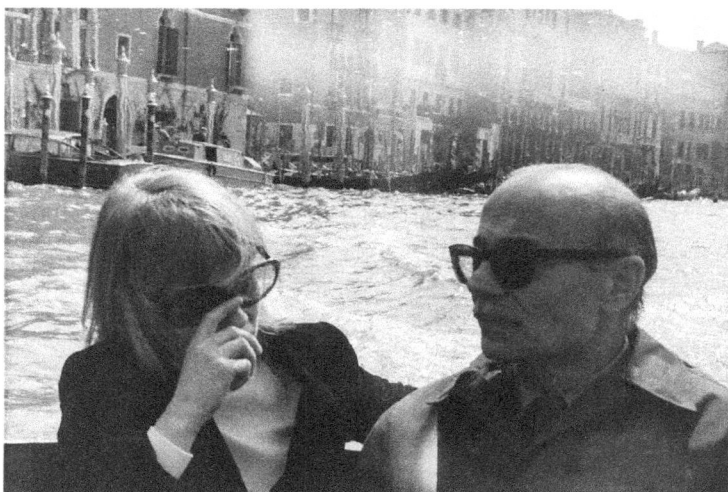

Sabine Parentini Posse and Ernesto Sabato

Abel Posse and Jorge Luis Borges in the Consulate

Borges and Maria Kodama in the Caffè Florian

Joseph Brodsky

Alberto Moravia

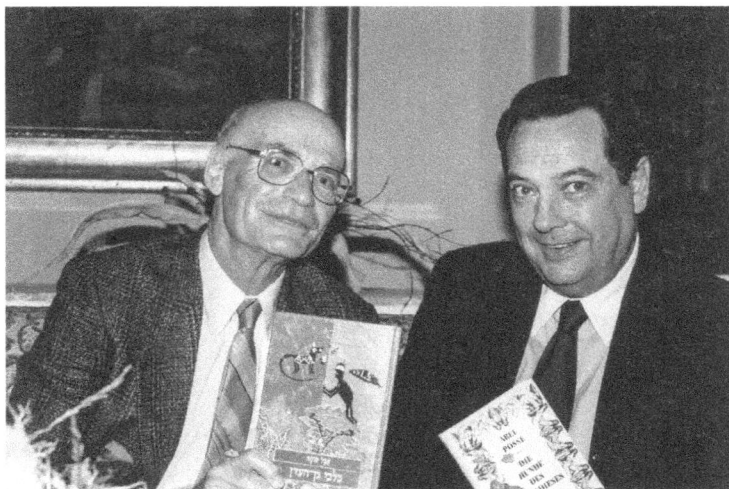

Abel Posse and Seymour Menton

Juan Rulfo

Poet Federico Gorbea in the Consulate

Manucho Mujica Lainez in the Palazzo Mangili Valmarana

Abelardo Arias

Alejo Carpentier

Delia in the patio of the Consulate

Ivan on the Lido beach

At the Igor Stravinsky's grave in the San Michele Cemetery

Diana Vreeland, Andy Warhol and Fred Hugues on the Piazza San Marco

35

BARELY WESTERNIZED BY his position as "poet-in-residence" at the University of Michigan, Brodsky returned to Venice transformed by his fame. He was the ideal dissident child prodigy for the Nobel Prize, which would eventually be awarded him in 1987. Andreina's rejection and coldness at the meeting in the gardens of the Arsenale were fuel on the fire. The Venetians saw him reappear—he was invited to London by the British Council—and they understood that everything about Brodsky in Venice happened, or was presumed to happen, because of Andreina. Shrewd, she occasionally showed herself in public, at the Institute of Slavic Studies of the University, or in Germany's cultural center. But the mujik began to assail her incessantly. As with all Russian men, for Brodsky the submerged part of the iceberg was not only the largest, it was infinite and ultimately sinister. (Dostoyevsky's characters, according to Andreina, are the prototype of that people). Brodsky possessed the talent of a poet-literary critic, according to her, who did not value him as the poet Akhmatova believed she'd discovered.

The unsuspected complexity of the seemingly messy red-haired man began to reveal itself. And I think that from that moment on the problems began for Andreina.

She had taken him for a mediocre poet, an unruly young man, expelled for claiming freedoms in a genetically tsarist empire. No one knows where they rendezvoused. It was no longer at the university, least of all, of course, at the Italo-Soviet Institute. But everyone began to know that they did and even ventured preciseness. As is often the case, the subject had become obvious beyond all proof.

After the extraordinary incident with the engineer's dogs and long before Brodsky's definitive physical defenestration (actually, a non-metaphorical plunge down the stairs), I learned in my weekly conversations with Andreina of the impact that Brodsky achieved, beyond the rejection of the Arsenal Gardens, on his next trip. Brodsky was foolish enough to believe that the stunning Andreina was the direct incarnation of Venice, but even more serious: to have compared the *Veneziana* with the greatest Russian poet of the twentieth century, Anna Akhmatova, who was also a dazzling aristocrat, considered at the time of the 1917 Revolution as the most magnificent woman in St. Petersburg and Moscow, until she was finally subjected to the suffering and misery of Stalinist resentment. Brodsky felt that Andreina was the reincarnation of Akhmatova. From this combination of delirium and reality he could not be saved—he made seventeen trips or passes through the *Serenissima* in his brief life.

He would die in New York in 1986, but he would ask his son Andrei to bury him in Venice's island of the dead, the cemetery of San Michele. A request heeded by his Russian son, a child of love and danger, and by the grandchildren who lived off capitalist abundance with him in New York.

Andreina was to learn of Brodsky's amazing existential record: a poet praised at the age of twenty-four by the already globally mythical Anna Akhmatova when Brodsky was launched with a "Great Elegy to John Donne"; in reality, Andreina understood that this great poetic attempt had not reached its height; there was more poetry of extension than of intensity, but Akhmatova, already very old and condemned to live in the kitchen of an apartment shared by three families in Leningrad, had understood the precocious talent of her friend, the red-haired man, as she called him. Soviet brutality awarded this poem, dedicated to an English metaphysical poet, with trial and imprisonment. ("Who has enrolled you in the ranks of poets?" asks the judge. And Brodsky, "Nobody. Who enrolled me in the ranks of mankind?")

Until the miracle of the prison sentence that will make him spend "the best years of my life": eighteen months in the extreme Arctic, after the KGB had put him in an insane asylum for a year and considered him unbearable, even for the insane. He's sent to the village of Norenskaia. He takes all the books on philosophy, theology, and poetry he wants. The KGB believes that in such solitude the cultural plague won't contaminate anyone. He's alone, possessionless, facing the harshest weather of the God of his atheism.

Andreina tells me while we drink tea in the café of our get-togethers at the Academia bar:

"When he was twenty-two years old, Akhmatova introduced him to the painter Marina Basmanova from a family of well-to-do artists. Brodsky's best friend was Bobyshev, who also fell in love with Basmanova. Today we know that this so-called friend encouraged a note in a Leningrad newspaper accusing Brodsky of being a 'pornographer and anti-Soviet.' He couldn't beat the wrap.

That's also the Russian soul. A country of baseness, calumny, and mystical grandeur. An unbearable mixture, no?"

"And Basmanova?"

"She had Andrei, Brodsky's son. Later the relationship ended because she was threatened. After being expelled in June 1972 via Aeroflot to Vienna and then via Venice to the university post in Michigan, he didn't return to Russia and never saw Basmanova again. He didn't even return when Gorbachev handed Russia over to capitalism."

"No. I never considered him a great poet. But his knowledge of world literature was extraordinary. I, who'd believed him to be an insolent Hebrew pursuing a career planned by the CIA to obtain another victim of 'Soviet cultural terrorism,' began to admire his essays on Akhmatova, Marina Tsvetaeva, Auden…No, it wasn't just a mere political lie. He knew that he had been judged politically, but he followed the path of his authentic Russian madness and critical talent."

In those autumn-winter months it was said in the yacht club that Andreina had been seen with the red-haired Brodsky in the famous *piazzetta* of Capri and that they were probably in a small hotel in the discreet Anacapri. Gossip usually adds details to feign verisimilitude and appear convincing.

Andreina needed a large dose of freedom to exist and to respond to her gifts beyond obligations or conventional limits. She was her own planet, without predictable orbits. She had a family and children, everything was in its place, except her. She was not willing to survive the erocide of an institutionalized coexistence, nor was she willing to martyr herself between socially declared morality and her will for feminine power. She was too young to forget the body and not yet mature enough to resign herself to companionship and long conjugal friendship, the chrysalis of leaving behind forever the delicious terrors of love in the flesh. As a woman, she was the champion of an era; she embodied the Venetian woman of her time. She was conscious of her power over men; she felt she could enter their lives at will. She knew that she seeped into the dreams or nightmares of many who held her as an unattainable object of desire. Like that rose of the epitaph written by Rilke himself for his tomb in the cemetery of Raron:

> *Rose, oh pure contradiction, desire*
> *to be no one's sleep*
> *beneath so many lids.*

We were at the tables on the Canal, Andreina stretched out on the wicker armchair.

"Summer is ending, I can feel it." A cool breeze was blowing in from the Lido side and she tipped, as a brief gesture of greeting, the brim of her invariable capelina hat. Andreina never exposed herself to the sun and detested the beach and in particular the universe of Proustian gossip. The breeze picked up, raising her summer skirt to mid-thigh. She reached out her hand calmly, without any urgency, and returned the flight of her dress to its obscene task of suggestion. "When autumn comes early, we Venetians know that there will be *acqua alta* in October and November. Let's hope it won't be like that of '66. That would be the end of Venice. Once and for all! We'd be free of this insane marble nightmare that traps us all!"

"Even so, tourists would arrive in guided tours, underwater," I told her.

And then, she stretched out her long, slender legs, that Brodsky connects in his account to their owner's height of one meter eighty, and that, in the opinion of the clever Mario Trejo, are directly related to the skeleton as the essence of natural elegance. That closeness there, in the evening breeze, as if inviting one to a misguided *crack up* and entering the always dangerous dance of life. "Proximity of her tan legs," Fitzgerald wrote without apparent context, almost like a mantra, incomplete, found on a torn parchment.[54] A brief and incomplete sentence. Nothing important but as common and suggestive as what beetles or elephants may feel from time to time.

---

54 The author is referring to F. Scott Fitzgerald's *The Crack-up*, a collection of largely unpublished essays, notes, and letters published posthumously in 1945 by New Directions. Three of the essays, however, "The Crack-up," "Pasting it Together," and "Handle with Care," were previously published in the magazine *Esquire* in 1936.

36

ADA *IN CALORE*. That was announced with strangely swift runs, from the façade to the labyrinthine
and remote back of the palace. At night, disturbing howls.
Calls from the ancestral forest. Lisetta spoke to the woman
who took care of the cats at the gondola station, and they
brought a cat she'd raised, young, healthy, relatively tame,
for a *prova d'amore*. This took place behind closed doors in
what we called the back workshop. The neighborhood cat
lady said she'd attempted several introductions. But Ada's
reaction began to veer violently against the candidate, who
ended up taking refuge at the top of the rickety cupboard
of the famous empanadas.

It was then that the catologist, who handled cures,
deliveries, weddings to go, whispered cautiously to Sabine:

"If signora will allow me, I will tell her that her kitty has
already been *sistemata*."

"Set up, what do you mean?"

The loud caterwauling at night, Lisetta tells me, is
intended for a feline paramour, probably from the mooring
of the *traghetto*. They sense each other, communicate. But if
we take her to the *campiello*, we probably won't be able to
find her again. Better to wait; they know how to manage this.
They communicate, they make use of the water of the canals.

Three days later, when Delia brought breakfast, she said:

"Ada and her friend made a ruckus last night. A battle royal."

"Where?"

"In the back, in the workshop, in the small bathroom. But it appears that the worst happened on your desk. Everything was a mess."

Iván could be heard cackling from the staircase; he ran off to school because it was getting late.

"And Ada?"

"She's in hiding," Delia replied. "She has two or three hiding places that are inaccessible. The cat lady said they have one, the safest, which they use to heal or die. They don't like to die in sight of someone, or reproduce, or give birth."

On the woodworking bench there was a fallen garbage can. But my desk had borne the brunt of the erotic war. It seems that they considered the leather desk cover favorable. Two or three pages of *Daimón*, already typed, lay on the floor next to *Explosion in a Cathedral*, which Carpentier,[55] on a university visit, had given to Sabine. The lover had arrived with wet paws that left marks on the fallen sheets of paper and on the 1917 typewriter I'd bought in Russia.

"The tom cat probably slipped in through the broken transom."

He moved forward at risk of falling into the palazzo's side canal. He skirted the evangelical temple of the Campo Santi Apostoli and left, clinging to the wet bricks. Ada

---

55 Cuban novelist Alejo Carpentier, winner of the Prix Mondial Cino Del Duca, the Prix Médicis, and the Premio Miguel de Cervantes.

signaled the way for him by meowing in the middle of the night under the broken window..." speculated the catologist, pointing to the visitor's presumed erotic path.

"Les jeux sont faits," said Sabine.

"A cat with a bad temper, but with class," I said.

37

A CREATIVE AUTUMN day, with a drizzle and a slow to-and-fro of the barges that unload at the *Pescheria*. "Meters, liters, essences, tomatoes, in succession all the way to the sea." At dawn the astute restaurateurs evaluate the conger eel with distrust and load baskets of vegetables and fruits onto their own boats. Around noon the last *signoras* who argue and joke with the stall vendors they've known all their lives. The voracious seagulls balance on the white plastic boxes where there are always hake heads, an enigmatic octopus eye, small whitings. A faint sprinkle and then a scrim of drizzle, which will last the rest of the day. From my office at the consulate, I saw Sabine with her red umbrella crossing in the *traghetto*, toward the market, to shop in that medieval space of culinary joy.

I continued to sign consular export invoices; death, birth, and divorce certificates; criminal complaints for violence. Dozens of them. Rega consulting with me all the while: *Signor Console*, there's the issue of a family who wants a work visa. Or: an entire family from Rosario was killed near Treviso by a truck; the boy who was driving fell asleep and hit them. And I to Rega: please go to the morgue at Treviso and get the fingerprints of the family. I'll contact Rome and their relatives in Rosario to see if anyone is coming and what they wish to do.

Thanks to the centuries-old cracks in the old Palazzo Mangilli-Valmarana, by one o'clock the irresistible aroma of Argentinean stew begins to waft upstairs, with Canadian corn in a can that Da Mario sells.[56] Winter food on a rainy day; it could have been lentils, roast, sea bass *al prosecco*, rice with fresh seafood. Or Nordic exoticisms, *boeuf bourguignon*, Russian *sudak* with *pirozhki*, *abbacchio*, suckling pig, roulade *mit Spätzle*, every country … Delia's variations and preparations don't always provide a sure result. Corvo Salaparuta, Montepulciano, Tsinandali, Ocucaje, Maison Lafitte, Amarone, Tokay, Gevrey-Chambertin, Vega Sicilia.[57] The expensive ones only occasionally and during important celebrations.

Ada's escapade leads me to tidy up the desk. I gather the chapters of the novel and I see it coming together, born. I feel joy. It will be published in Spain. I believe I'll be able to send the manuscript in two more weeks to Carmen Balcells.[58] Books live (and are born) more by faith than by reason. They arise from unreason; they die of logic. It's necessary to reread them without logical coldness. If possible, adding intuition and risk. If it can be done, delirium.

---

56 Ristorante da Mario alla Fava, specializing in authentic Venetian cuisine.

57 These are all wines, primarily Italian, but also French, Georgian, and Hungarian.

58 The most influential literary agent of Spanish and Latin American authors for more than five decades, until her death in 2015, including six Nobel laureates, among them Gabriel García Márquez and Mario Vargas Llosa.

I go in search of a raincoat and an umbrella. I stop to listen to Delia's and Iván's endless discussions, facing each other at the desk in Iván's room, with their notebooks, notepads, and stacks of textbooks. During these months, Delia's progress is remarkable. The support of Father Michele, a former teacher and assistant at the parish school, is very effective. Blind, he takes care of helping students in the distance learning program. Delia passed the first exams, which were sent by mail, with success. I hear Delia ask Iván: "What about Thales?" "Thales of Miletus," Iván answers. "But what else?" And Iván: "In the beginning there was water. Everything was water. If you went out without boots, you were up a creek." And they both explode with laughter. For a couple of hours every afternoon they go over multiplication tables, declensions in beginning Latin, world capitals, metals, planets, not to throw paper on the street, the forgiveness of Christ, the almost impossible love thy neighbor as thyself.

On my way out, I run into Padre Michele, with his adjustable metal cane, feeling his way up the steps to our *mezzanino*. He senses, imagines me. "*Signor Console.*" "*Padre.*" His last good deed will probably be linked to Delia's adventure. Perhaps he senses in his old age that this help, barely remunerated, takes him back to the passion of teaching, of creating the other and placing them on the threshold of improvement, even spiritual. The passion of teaching. To win the silent battle.

I get lost in narrow *vicoli*, and in one I even hear, as always, the scratching of the umbrella squeezed between walls chipped away by saltpeter. I pass the Calle de la Malvasia, on my way to the Venice without aristocrats, inhabited by artisans, scribes, and sailors before setting sail, who returned from war as invalids, sitting in front of the humble doors, and who will never fear nor distrust the sea, nor the Greek, Syrian, or Nubian whores of the years of ports and wars.

The old, discarded creators of empire. I evoke them; I see them (or they appear to me in the drizzle).

The light of that drizzling afternoon could be the same as the dawn of the summer of 1571. From one of these same doors a quartermaster came out, carrying a coarse seabag made of sackcloth, where he stored the jerky and sweets his wife had prepared for him. He bid her farewell. He kissed his children in the glow of candlelight, to keep them present in his long warrior's memory. The Grand Fleet of Venier and Doria departs.[59] He walks with the exaltation of warriors who meet again amid embraces and jokes. They set out for the feast of courage and danger. War is pagan. I follow him from Tintoretto's house to the gondola carpentry shop, now abandoned. Then we walk by the Jesuit convent from which the seminarian Sorge escaped one night, in my novel, before enlisting for the missions, and found the plaster mask lying outside a brothel, as I recounted to Borges. The drizzle turns into rain, but I resist not following the imaginary sailor with the sea bag on his shoulder. Along the dreary *Fondamente Nove* I head toward the Castello District and the Arsenal. I arrive that desolate autumn afternoon, finally, at the empty space of the main docks, the old one and the one of the galleys. Sea ready,

---

59   Giovanni Andrea Doria, a Genoese admiral and Sebastiano Venier, the doge of Venice. This is a reference to the Battle of Lepanto, in which the Holy League defeated the Ottoman Empire in what was at the time the largest sea battle in history.

the Great Shipyard. My sailor may be called Bembo or
Vercellio or Vianello or Rossi. He looks at the pennants
that I imagine to be spears in the wind.

The fleet of galleys and carracks. They'll depart for
Messina and Vianello. He can't imagine that he'll be the
protagonist of the greatest battle of his time, that of Lepanto,
which would stop Moorish expansion for centuries and in
which the Moors will halt the fierce Christians for centuries.
He'll see an arquebus ball shatter the arm of the Spaniard
Miguel, who confessed to him that he'd have liked to have
been a writer if he returned alive to Castile. I imagine that
he put a tourniquet on his stump, thinking "you'll live, but
say goodbye to those refined ambitions, although for now
you'll only lose your left arm."[60]

Nothing but wind against the sad, decayed walls of the
Arsenal. The same wind that made jungles sail, according
to Quevedo.[61]

A cold wind that makes me quicken my pace until I
reach the Venice-boudoir, that of the pleasure of peace. I
enter through Santa Maria Formosa and have a restorative
coffee in a small Venetian bar. I sit in a corner. They watch
the tourists go by. It's like a flock of exotic birds. Unfortunate
people who don't have a Venice and come from all over the
world to spy on her like on a whore who combs her hair
naked. Not a New Yorker, nor a *Parisien*, nor a *porteño*,
would visit the museums and monuments of their city.

---

60 The author is referencing Miguel de Cervantes, author of *Don
Quixote*, who suffered the complete maiming of his left hand in
the Battle of Lepanto, earning the sobriquet *El manco de Lepanto*
[The maimed hand of Lepanto].
61 Francisco de Quevedo, nobleman, politician, and Golden Age
poet, contemporary of Cervantes.

From my corner, I understand these Venetians in the café. In summer, the tourists arouse ill humor, with their bottles of mineral water, their lurking like disillusioned shoals of fish. In autumn they seem to have confused the calendar, but they're tolerable, they don't take up every space or show their hairy legs in tennis shoes.

38

ICROSS THE Calle del Paradiso and find a small, forgotten movie house where they're showing *Doctor Zhivago*, which I saw years ago. I felt that I'd like to see the landscapes of Russia, the revolutionary horrors, to rediscover something about Moscow where we lived for three years and where Iván was born. The auditorium was empty, and the film was half over. No more than a dozen heads were visible in the semidarkness. Snow glistened on the screen (the protagonist arrives as a refugee to a village in the steppe called Varykino with his family and settles into an old, abandoned property where they used to spend their summers before the Revolution). On the right of the almost empty room, in an area off to the side, the light illuminated two heads and a reddish glow. I was distracted from the film. It occurred to me that it was Andreina and Brodsky. The straight chestnut hair and Brodsky's burnished ginger. The location allowed them to whisper. Brodsky must have expressed a desire to see that celebrated film about the world from which he had been happily expelled. My suspicion was confirmed: when the old Zhivago returns to Moscow, at the end of the Stalinist era, he sees from a tram the figure of someone who could have been Lara, the love of his life lost in the revolutionary slaughter. He struggles to get off and suffers a fatal heart attack.

At that moment, before the end, the tall man left the woman and walked toward the exit.

I also left before the end, in an attempt to avoid bumping into Andreina and making her uncomfortable. She was certainly indifferent by now to the relentlessly conventional Venice. She would take careless risks now. They'd meet again in their hideaway and talk for hours about Pasternak, revolutionaries, and victims. And they would embrace. And they would fall, but not on the snow. I now imagined her myself according to Laurentis's gossip or that of the venomous Alberico d'Alondra, the two biggest gossips from the gatherings at the Gritti.

39

RÓMULO MACCIÓ arrives, with Patricia and the girls, Cayetana and Tristana. They spent a few weeks during the summer in Venice. Rómulo is well along in his career as a famous painter since winning the Di Tella Prize in 1963 and the New Figuration group.[62] I thought he owed a profound debt to Venice. The Venice light dissolved his Buenos Aires fog and that of Francis Bacon's London. Venice returned Rómulo to the Mediterranean of his blood. That happened in the sixties when the beauty of the *Serenissima* freed him from having to "remove the vomit from his soul," in his own words. Bacon, the suicide, was his false aesthetic incubus. Macció took his other figuration to the dark world of "man and his hell," to "the crushed man" and "the lady of sorrows." At that time, they had settled in Venice in the La Calcina Hostel, on the *fondamenta* Zattere in front of the Giudecca. Venice saved him from the anguished *tremendismo* of those years.[63] It freed him from

---

62 A prize awarded by the Torcuato di Tella Institute, a foundation established in honor of the Argentine industrialist and art patron Torcuato di Tella to promote Argentine culture.

63 An aesthetic movement developed in Spain during the mid-twentieth century among writers and visual artists that exaggerated the crudest aspects of reality.

the strident romanticism, from the existential crisis. Venice eradicated Bacon from him and allowed him to face his true demons, to exorcize them freely and to reach the Latin gaiety of his best moments.

We held a meeting with the Baldovinos and with the Tucumán-born Edmundo González del Real, already getting along in years, with a distant and vanquished fame, accompanied by his companion Rosy T. Méndez, a swarthy Ecuadorian he met in Guayaquil when she was twenty years old and had a celebrated body. An employee of the consulate, Milossi, said that once, late at night, he saw her in the vicinity of San Marco. It seemed racist to us, scandal-mongering. Del Real had abandoned his wife and three children for Rosy. He earned money and awards as a painter and bought a catamaran in which he lived with her for a year at the mouth of the Guayas River. He didn't know how to cultivate that moment of his fame; she couldn't stop time. That united them, a great love wounded by "furies and sorrows."[64] (The distrusting Milossi believed to have seen her lurking around San Marco one night.) Macció was already internationally famous, and it was rumored that Leo Castelli, the patron of modern pictorial mythology, had invited him to exhibit in New York. Baldovino was trembling in front of his dismantled easel with his first successes. Edmundo del Real expected nothing. He was drinking a lot and relied on the reliable arm of Rosy, who challenged and insulted him, but who buoyed him so that he could return to the Rialto hostel without falling.

---

64 "Furies and sorrows" is a reference to a poem by Pablo Neruda, who in turn is referencing a sonnet by Francisco de Quevedo.

Perhaps, of the three he was the most artistic. More than Macció and the delicate Baldovino.

I thought it appropriate to invite Federico Vogelius and Lita, who'd rented an apartment on the Grand Canal.

We'd not seen each other since the launch of the magazine *Crisis*, which had become a center of left-wing culture, directed by Galeano.[65] Vogelius was a great collector and what he couldn't collect he copied. His passion was for the works.

The wine flowed. Painters are very much like manual laborers. They provide us respite from reasons and metaphysics. They generally don't try to explain what they do. They bellow like carpenters, bricklayers, or painters (with a broad brush) who celebrate having reached the roof of the building. They end up drunk, insulting each other like *carreros*.[66] Writers-poets all tend to be different; painters have general behaviors, without metaphysical deviations.

It was interesting: Macció was the fulfilled one, the victor, the one who sold and reveled. Fame affirms more than the creative, solitary passion, and everyone wants to dive into this redemptive and borrowed deception. Baldovino, humble, silent, as when he snapped green beans to help his father, had the intimate joy of coming close to the colors of the Venetian palette. The joy of an artist in the sincere enthusiasm of having touched the edge of a successful and genuine creation. The old Del Real and

---

65 Eduardo Galeano, the Uruguayan intellectual and author of the polemical book *Open Veins of Latin America*, founded *Crisis* while in exile in Argentina.

66 *Carreros* [literally cart drivers] refers to horse-drawn trash collectors, which are still in operation in Argentina.

his Rosy, convinced that she still possessed an irresistible sensuality, hit the mark with her tight pants and blouse with tropical colored polka dots. Del Real thought he'd played all his cards and lost. He watched the roulette wheel spin without fear or hope. Twenty years earlier he'd exhibited in the Municipality of Tucumán, to acclaim in *La Gaceta*, increasingly yellowed clippings accompanying his résumé. His friends from his early years in Buenos Aires, Berni, Spilimbergo, and Castagnino.[67] Alcoholic nights at the Royal Keller[68] and in the cantinas of La Boca. He enjoyed a moment of success and sales fostered by the Galería Velásquez. A distant, blessed life, madcap: he'd embarked with Rosy on a dangerous banana freighter to Tripoli and from there they went to Vienna, where they lived in an abandoned bungalow in the Prater.

Empanadas and demijohns of Chianti were circulating. Baldovino prepared a folder and discreetly passed it to the Vogeliuses. Rosy had brought a recording and we played it. She took off her shoes and began to glide on the hall's mosaic tile with provocative glances, like "La Pantera," as she was known in her distant music-hall days of Guayaquil and Quito. She imitated the Silvana Mangano of the famous, long-ago film *Riso Amaro*. *¡Mambo! ¡Mambo! ¡Qué rico el Mambo!* Rosy crossed from one end of the room to the other in her bare feet to the music of Pérez Prado from twenty-five years ago. At first, she made us uncomfortable as she undulated between the *cumbanchero* and corporeal

---

67 Antonio Berni, Lino Enea Spilimbergo, Juan Carlos Castagnino were mid-twentieth-century Argentine artists.
68 A restaurant-café frequented during much of the twentieth century by artists and literati.

eruption.[69] But she proved to be a skilled tightrope walker. What could have plunged into the ridiculous was saved by her grace, by the recondite rhythm of her race. *¡Mambo! ¡Qué rico es es es es!* We applauded her with gusto. Her voluminous, flaccid body had been rejuvenated, saved by her gift for rhythm, her ancestral grace.

The night was teeming with alcohol, and by the time dawn broke with its rosy fingers, Sabine and Lita prepared a delicious broth.

Ada, contrary to her nature, settled in to watch the unusual revelry we were erupting into the silence of the Grand Canal. The three painters, with their glasses in hand, watched the colors slowly descend as they melted down from the sky like waterfalls over the Rialto and the *Pescheria* market. Tones that Giovanni Canal, *il Canaletto*, had certainly captured, perhaps from that very window when he painted there, under the protection of the English Consul Smith, builder of that Mangilli Valmarana Palace, in 1751.

Rómulo had had a lot to drink. In an instant, unexpectedly, he turned to me, on edge, and shouted:

"Venice didn't rescue me from anything! It's a lie. Everything that's said about a painter is a lie, stupidity! No one! No one!" Then he turned to the Canal and finished his drink quietly, then lay on the chaise and fell asleep.

At noon the next day we saw him passing by the Lido beach with Patricia and the girls. Rómulo was walking along the water's edge in his swimming trunks. He smiled at us at a distance. He'd protected his demons. He knew that for an artist they can be the other side of angels. What would

---

69 *Cumbanchero*, from *cumbancha*, refers to the revelry that arises from a love of cumbia music and dancing.

an artist be without the sludge of demons, without disease? When one frees oneself from the demons of imitation, the real ones emerge, which can be even more horrifying.

I add from my memory. I recall the blurred face of Del Real, sallow, like an Indian from the altiplano who's suffered many storms and falls. He died long ago. Above the bar at home is the painting he gave me because, when winter came, I gave him one of those so-called Canadian coats, with a hood and pieces of deer antlers as fastenings. Logger attire, unbearable to Italian good taste. He'd left me his painting at the consulate, as a farewell. Perhaps I underestimated the small oil on plywood as something that's thought of as nothing more than a souvenir, a farewell. But after many moves, the painting was not only not discarded, rather always occupied an ever more important space. It suggests a moonlit night, with geometric lines and a metaphysical atmosphere like that which journalism attributes to De Chirico.[70] Everything passed, but that moment of Del Real's achievement, who thought himself defeated, endures, and retains the gaze of my friends. He went about earning a post through indifference and today occupies a place of unquestionable preference among some whose collections include renowned, top-selling artists. Del Real, an old *criollo*,[71] never understood the words promotion, media, or fashion. Perhaps he couldn't understand them.

---

70 Giorgio de Chirico: Greek-born Italian artist; founder of the Scuola Metafisica art movement.

71 The term *criollo* refers to someone of Spanish stock; in Argentina, this sense of *criollismo* is felt even stronger in rural areas. In the nineteenth century, the term began to acquire negative connotations and was used as an epithet that suggested "backwardness." In the twentieth century, however, the term was reclaimed for nationalist reasons to represent positive virtues.

I was able, from my position as consul, to do something for him: I spoke to Brooks, in the Rome office, and recommended him. They mounted an exhibition of his work at the Casa Argentina and from there he was invited to exhibit in Ferrara and Folgaria.

40

IMPOSING, LIKE A tropical totem, Alejo Carpentier arrives in Venice. He's been invited by the Università Ca' Foscari. He will deliver a lecture and then talk to the professors from the Department of Hispanic American Literature.

My friend Manuel Scorza was one of the few who read Carpentier regularly, that sullen man, quite distant from the fanatical success of the so-called Latin American Boom: García Márquez, Vargas Llosa, Cortázar, Cabrera Infante. Scorza had called me from Paris to tell me that Carpentier would invite me to his conference. We met. He signed for Sabine a copy of the magnificent Cuban edition of *El siglo de las luces*,[72] his most encouraging book, a title that announced nothing less than the arrival of new ideas, the ideas of the French Revolution to the Caribbean and all of America.

Imposing, yes, sullen like all men of character who know the games and impostures in which, out of tact, they were unable to prevail.

He told me, with his slurred Rs, as those of Frankish origin pronounce them, as he and Cortázar were:

---

72 Although the English title is *Explosion in a Cathedral*, translated by John Sturrock, a literal translation of the Spanish would be "The century of lights."

"Look: we were the Boom, those of us who gave something great and without publicity, or triumph, or triumphalism: Rulfo, Guimarães Rosa, José María Arguedas, Borges. The imitator García Márquez is the only good impostor of the bunch. Vargas Llosa is tacky, an unadulterated nineteenth-century huckster. Manuel Scorza and Julio Ramón Ribeyro are the best from Peru. Carlos Fuentes is a dreadful novelist but a seductive lecturer, with facile and rehashed ideas."

"You haven't mentioned Lezama Lima…" I told him. We were walking with Lilia, his wife, and Sabine, dodging the tourist silliness around the Piazza San Marco. Carpentier, who would stay just three days, wanted to see the atmosphere of the Florian and the remarkable church of Vivaldi,[73] the red priest, so called because of his hair.

He was writing *Baroque Concerto* and *The Consecration of Spring*.

"I'd like to stop by the Florian first," he said.

"They made up a whole story suggesting that I was indifferent to alleged persecution by the Cuban government against Lezama and others. I was a literary dissident but never a counterrevolutionary."

I replied:

"In Cuba I was told that they hadn't done anything about the humidity of his little house on Trocadero Street, which was very bad for his asthma."

"It's not true," said Carpentier. "They did everything they could to help him. He died of stubbornness. He was so

---

73 Although the current structure was finished after Vivaldi's death, the Chiesa di Santa Maria della Visitazione, better known as La Pietà, is still referred to as Vivaldi's Church.

fat that they had to take his coffin out through the window. He didn't want to go to the hospital."

I saw that Carpentier was bothered by the conversation. He was perfectly sure of his prominent literary position and made no concessions and sought no facile empathy. Despite his explanation, talking about Lezama Lima was not a pleasant subject for him. Carpentier had used tactics, executed a juggling act, in order not to have to leave Cuba like Sarduy and Cabrera Infante. He had succeeded. At some point during our walk, he said something sincere and harsh:

"A writer in search of art has to accept any situation in order to save his style. Public, political, or personal situations, whatever they may be."

Carpentier was not loved by the Castro brothers and the ideologues of socialist realism, who in the early years of the revolution ruined and distorted many writers. A self-policed freedom was created. He'd been appointed minister-counselor at the embassy in Paris.

"They make me keep a schedule. I arrive at nine o'clock. I write from five to seven in the morning, the best hours really."

When we arrived at San Marco, I invited him for coffee. But he preferred to go in alone and walk the halls where Handel, Scarlatti, and Vivaldi would return to their discussions and conversations, this time within the *Baroque Concerto* he was writing. Without taking notes, he memorized details that I would soon find again when reading the book he sent us.

His lecture in the *aula magna* of the University was a bewildering enumeration of (optimistic) data on Cuba's economic achievements. The philosopher Derrida, who was in the front row and had been invited to participate in another series, looked on in surprise. I, who was part of the panel, saw that he was reading the worn back cover of a Cuban magazine. He had to save himself from informants and honest journalists. As for literature, he limited himself to talking about structuralism, which was in vogue, and quoted Saussure and Chomsky. The professors present applauded with an enthusiasm that revealed a sincere homage to his work. The shrewd Derrida, invited by the Institute of Philosophy, must have been surprised by this Soviet-style report by a creator of "the aesthetics of the marvelous real,"[74] as Carpentier was introduced on the invitation.

Tall, with black hair, a double-breasted suit, dark Creole skin, and an accent of a Frenchman exiled in the tropics, Carpentier seemed to be a living bridge between opposing cultures, like the characters in *El siglo de las luces*.

We had a farewell drink at the consulate. We shared common themes, such as Columbus, the enlightened-trickster-genius-social-climber-sailor, which he had placed in *The Harp and the Shadow*.

He recalled with nostalgia his thirties in Montparnasse, the Café Select, the Dôme. The surrealist painters. His dream of becoming a composer.

"I didn't achieve it. But I believe that my literature must be imbued, percolated with frustrated music, I don't know..."

"A long *andante maestoso*, Alejo," I told him. And he liked that. If I have anything to thank him for, it is *Los pasos*

---

74 The "marvelous real" is the term that Carpentier employed in his 1949 essay "On the Marvelous Real in America," a concept that would later become known as magical realism.

perdidos.[75] *Heart of Darkness*, by a Conrad who knows that the sinister Kurtzes are now in the capitals of America and in the depths of our jungles and rivers. A lost innocence. What wasn't ... *Los pasos perdidos* is a journey through the spiritual genealogy of America. The geography, the tunnel of the Orinoco toward the jungle, goes about laying bare the manhood that one has or does not have. The suit of being in its original jungle.

---

75 Translated as *The Lost Steps* by Harriet de Onís.

41

*A*CQUA ALTA. It must have been seven o'clock in the morning. The siren alerting to the possibility of high water rang out before the alarm clocks. At nine o'clock it sounded again with the shrillness of an ambulance transporting someone who is seriously ill. It was the confirmation. The seriously ill patient was Venice. All businesses mobilize. Employers, employees, children. Everything has to be placed on high shelves (weapons, money, photographic machines, babies, violins, jewelry, pornographic magazines) and the emergency floodgates that protect the entrances from the street have to be adjusted. Water is spirit. A spirit sometimes of revenge, which percolates everywhere. All the radios are tuned to the municipality reporting the magnitude of the flood. The ancestral enemy, the sea, in action. The old fear: the death of Venice. Death by water, of the Empire that rose up and conquered on the seas.

Since there are no classes, the children rejoice. Disasters, even days of war, are remembered forever: the memory of surviving the danger. The feast of fight. Iván, Delia, Luca Bressin, want to go to San Marco. Everyone in rubber boots. In the *piazza* in front of the basilica with its Byzantine Gothic, one can watch the arrival of the enemy. There are large pools. The sea seeps between the stone slabs.

Gently the mirrors of water begin to merge. A serene titanic force ends up covering the entire length of the *piazza*. The Campanile and the basilica seem to emerge from the sea and float. The Venetians' fear is of the titan's fury, as on November 4, 1966, when it nearly breached the retaining walls of the outer islands of the Lido. Its waves, like a cavalry, would have felled the palaces. It was the lowest moment of the century. Will it attempt it today? Venetians ask themselves.

On their way back to the consulate, through the *campo* of San Giovanni Crisostomo, Luca and Iván press their noses against the windows of the elegant luxury shoe store. The water already covers the entire floor, and the shoes float independent of their pairs. A small drain produces a gentle current.

A delicate mauve silk Ferragamo bobs and sways, the slender stiletto is a periscope. Somber, sturdy Church shoes drift like battleships without fuel. Near the drain they twirl and dance a slow minuet. Iván and Luca laugh.

To cross the courtyard of the *palazzo* I had to hold up Iván. His rubber boots had been overtaken.

42

CODOGNATO, THE COLLECTOR of modern painting, or of such famous monstrosities as those of Warhol, Rauschenberg, or Pollock, wanted us to organize a get-together around tango at the Palazzo Mocenigo. I brought two tapes with tangos by De Caro, Fresedo, and Troilo. It was a warm night with the windows erupting into the nocturnal splendor of the Grand Canal.

Carlo Maria Santoro was there, and Sandra, his journalist friend from *Il Giornale*, as well as Gianni de Michelis, the influential socialist deputy, Andreina and her husband, Miranda and Laura Bergamo. After dinner we drank, and with Attilio we played the tango tapes in the dimly lit room. I feared that friends wouldn't be able to withstand De Caro's or Cobián's deep melancholy. No one spoke. We drank in silence, myself included (could tango be explained?). Until the marvelous Sandra and Gabriela Codognato regaled us with a moment we would never forget. When it started, Osvaldo Fresedo's orchestra was singing *Sollozos* and *Vida mía* in the semidarkness. In the silence of the hall, they advanced: Sandra with her open back and a long, provocative cigarette holder, Gabriela in a tight black dress in the half-light. They embraced and glided with long, languid steps, like those born of the genuine intimacy of music, without choreographic improvisation. They turned slowly and advanced, intensifying the reverie of the disturbing couple. They oozed a somber and imperceptibly perverse grace. Sandra exhaled cigarette smoke. They took each other by the waist and began to walk the tango. Carried by the cadence with a certain *canyengue* sway.[76] Then the *Copacabana* tango ended, and they exited the ritual, the art, and headed toward the champagne glasses.

They left us with an intense memory—of tango interpreted with ingenuousness, channeling the suggestion of that strange musical invention. From the azure of memory, that scene remains one of the most intense of my six-year-long day in Venice.

The *acqua alta*: while we were drinking amid the tangos, an unforeseen and rapid swell forced us, amid jokes and laughter, to flee the Palazzo Mocenigo.

The palazzo exit was flooded more than usual due to construction that prevented the drainage. Then we experienced another memorable episode: each gentleman lifted his lady to cross about twenty meters of water at mid-thigh to reach the small street leading to the pier of San Samuele. The women exited atop shoulders, like the gaucho's women riding pillion outside the *pulpería*.[77] It was a moment of surprising intimacy for the couples.

---

76 The *canyengue* is the oldest style of tango, characterized by a close embrace and slight V position, often associated with prostitutes because of its extremely sensual and provocative style.

77 *Pulpería*s were a kind of rural country store, throughout South America, but especially Chile and Argentina, that also doubled as drinking establishments.

43

SARTRE EXITS THE Caffé Florian with a halting step, with feet of lead that drag laboriously. She, Simone de Beauvoir, with her chignon and her purse hanging from her arm, is a disagreeable Latin professor waiting for her valetudinarian colleague. She moves forward on the stone slabs of Piazza San Marco and waits, towering, for the already faltering Sartre to arrive. Then they take two steps together, and she goes ahead and waits for him again. Sartre in a black beret. In 1964 he wrote about Venice, intuiting the elusive spirit, so Byzantine, of the *Serenissima*. He was in the splendor of a blissful society, with its insular empire, her cruelty and her unbridled pleasure to exist, to enjoy, to live in courage, to love, to kill. Sartre noted: "I'll walk all day long between bridges and gondolas, looking for the lost Venice. A kind of mad anxiety. Wherever you are, Venice will be beyond. Unreachable. That feline distance, even if you are caressing it. Even if she is warning us of an imminent earthquake." And I pay for my coffee and chase those two peevish seekers of the Venetian mystery.

Between Judeo-Christianity and the petty-bourgeois paganism of capitalist tourism, Venice stretches out like the mirror of our nothingness. We are a complication without grandeur. We no longer believe in our historical, cultural destiny. For Venice to be achieved, it was necessary to believe and to defy.

Regis Debray rightly calls it "the true laundry of the West."[78] It washes us of moralism, hypocrisy, egalitarian mediocrity. It laughs at our slavery of free men. Today Venice is a desperate sanctuary: it evinces the unattainable, the rabble of the globalized technological society. "If we are the same, why different fingerprints on each of the six billion earthlings?"

Venice gazes at us from her majestic silence interrupted by herds of tourists. Sartre wrote that he became dizzy thinking that the palaces floated and—at the same time— those masses of marble and brick didn't sink into the sludge. He could find no explanation. The *Serenissima* supplanted all existential nausea.

---

78 *Against Venice*, translated by Philip Wohlstetter.

44

MIDDAY IN UNBEARABLE heat, we are under our cabana on the Lido beach and Roque, the bathing attendant for our row, arrives with a message that Rega left for us at Reception at the Excelsior. I'm anxious, as it might be an urgent matter having to do with the Foreign Ministry. Rega says that she's calling me because Patriarch Albino Luciani had moved up his trip to the conclave in Rome and is summoning the consular corps to the sacristy of the cathedral of San Marco at three thirty in the afternoon.

I order a water taxi and go straight to the consulate to give myself time to prepare.

Paul VI, Pope Montini, died just days before. A man of extraordinary intellect, and in some ways a disciple of Pius XII, which is the highest Vatican title one can have. The water taxi is waiting for me at the *rio* Santi Apostoli mooring. I dress in a dark suit, and we head to the cathedral. Instead of waiting at the Caffè Florian or the Quadri, I prefer to visit the crypt and tomb of St. Mark, at that hour deserted even by tourists. It's cool inside the magnificent temple. I identify myself and they lead me to the coffin of the saint and evangelist who died in Alexandria in horrific martyrdom in the first century. For two centuries the body of St. Mark remained lost. It's said that the Christians kept it hidden in a catacomb. It's also said that in the face of the imminent danger of being discovered, they hid the saint's body in the safest, most revered and untouchable place in Alexandria: the Soma, the temple and tomb of the greatest strategist in history, Alexander the Great. Today, on the site of the Soma, razed by the Ottomans, the Rue Nebi Daniel leads to where the Mosque of the Prophet Daniel stands. (I imagine Lawrence Durrell and Justine, meeting at the café on Rue Rosette, after a tedious lecture by Pursewarden at the tumbledown British Council).

But in the ninth century, precisely in the year 828, two Venetian merchants and adventurers uncovered the secret and stole the corpse, which they stowed in a wagon, covered with putrid pork, considered untouchable by the Muslim customs officers. Since then, the body of Alexander the Great, which was a reverential pilgrimage for all the great men of history—Julius Caesar, Mark Antony, Hadrian, Augustus, the Ptolemies—has not been found either.

And if the remains in that crypt I stand here contemplating alone, killing time, are of the warrior hero and not of the saint? How can a DNA analysis be done on dead bodies from two thousand years ago? Besides, would it be worth it? And what if Venice was an empire because of that error of spirit, and it was Alexander the Great whom they venerated in the crypt of the Basilica di San Marco? I recall the words of Patriarch Luciani, the future John Paul I, during my protocolary visit: "One must be willing to recognize that what was sacred fled Venice centuries ago." Perhaps the playful demiurges made them venerate the warrior instead of the evangelist. And it didn't turn out badly for them after all.

It is certainly out of kindness, and in consideration of the exceptional heat of the day, Patriarch Luciani is gathering us thirty consuls in the cool of the sacristy, with its timeworn thousand-year-old gilding and mosaic floor rippled by the passage of millions of visitors. We are placed in order of seniority of presentation of credentials. The Cardinal Patriarch appears, a gesture of meekness as he passes, wearing his usual cassock, like a priest who would enter timidly, on a visit to his small parish of Agordo. However, after an almost inaudible greeting, he took us aback:

"I shall be brief because you must return to your tasks of the day, and I must prepare to travel tonight to Rome. I will share with you all the tenor of the secret cable that you must send to your foreign ministries. It is a very short text, whoever wishes can take note: "Patriarch Albino Luciani requests that we inform you that he knows and that everyone knows that he will never be elected Pope."

We all laughed and so did he. He was saying good-bye with a joke, like a cheerful priest from Caorle.[79]

We lined up and filed by to greet him as protocol required.

As we walked out into the scorching sun of the piazza, we were laughing. Giavi came up to me and said:

"It's true. In England, where they bet on the Popes as if they were horses at the Epsom Derby or those greyhounds at the New York night races, no one lists odds for Albino Luciani. None of them. So, we should send the secret cable as he says.

---

79 A seaside resort in the Veneto Region, home to the Cattedrale di Santo Stefano, built in 1038, which holds the status of titular see.

45

SEPTEMBER 11, Iván's birthday party. Friends from school and the *campiello*. Merriment. Cotillion hats. Cake, laughter, refreshments. They're playing in every corner of the *mezzanino*. I take refuge at my desk in the back where the clatter of voices doesn't reach. Ada comes in two or three times and lashes her tail. Meowing. There's a tremble in the glass of the old windows that announces itself. The clinking of dishware on a train about to derail. Ada jumps up and goes toward the tool and suitcase storeroom. She despairs at my human ineptness to detect cosmic signs. She's in the cosmos. (She never knew if she entered the world or why, nor will she care when she leaves. We live with our backs to the starry night. We know nothing, but we ask ourselves that which will have no answer.)

Earthquake in the Laguna Veneta. The sudden shake is violent. Delia and Sabine urgently gather the boys with their bugles, masks, and little hats, and with admirable speed take them out through the garden to the street, where the frightened neighbors of Cannaregio, our neighborhood, gather. Sabine and others claimed to have seen the bell tower of Santi Apostoli sway.

The cats of the gondola station, Ada's *patria chica*, her birthplace, were visibly restless. Venice imported thousands of cats from Alexandria and the Nile delta to combat the rats. From that moment on, the popularity of these felines began to grow. I thought Ada had drawn my attention to the window, as if to warn me of the danger of being buried by centuries-old debris. Some of the meows that I heard could have been cries from her lover or relatives from the post in response to the telluric disturbance, which was unsettling but ceased, as if to allow the children's party to finish.

Venice fears only the sea. An earthquake could destroy the Campanile di San Marco, as was the case in July 1902, but the mud of the lagoon, the moveable foundation of the palaces' trunks, allow it to absorb the telluric waves. The stone, like in the earthquakes of the Apennines, lacks flexibility, causing it to crack. Silt is plastic, accommodating, foul-smelling, Byzantine.

46

ALONG WEEKEND, when the summer cooled down, we left with our Fiat from the garage of the Piazzale Roma, in search of Rilke's trail in Switzerland.

Happiness to cross the Po Valley. Joy to rediscover *terra firma*, back in Italy, as the Venetians say. Off in the distance, Verona. The irrigation canals and the gentle ascent toward the Alps. Joy for our little family. Iván with maps in hand. Then the highlands, balancing cows, enviable chalets, worthy of the Von Trapp family, presumably smelling of hot chocolate.

The luxuries of Lake Como, until reaching Bellinzona and entering through the Passo del San Gottardo, traversing vineyards with offers of fresh wines on the fences. A sublime and bucolic bourgeois peace. Beyond, the less poetic area: the backbone of ruthless banks, the guarantee of cows, chocolate, cuckoo clocks and that anonymous, anonymizing democracy. That impeccable institutional yawn.

But Rilke in 1921 was not interested in any of that. He sensed he'd entered his time of death. And he returned to Switzerland, to Muzot, because there was nowhere in the world where he could be sufficiently alone to face the work of his life, the *Duino Elegies*. Curiously, Nietzsche too, shortly before going mad, crept up to Switzerland, to Sils Maria, for his greatest confrontation, that of the eternal return.

There's a photo of Rilke from 1926 in the tiny window on the upper floor of the so-called Château de Muzot. A gloomy stone building of some poor but pretentious nobleman who devoted his existence to exploiting a couple of hectares of vineyards. Rilke found this castle ideal for a one-man monastery. From the slope he could see the Rhône Valley which is a stream there but widens when it reaches France, peaceably. Rilke recounted that he'd seen the advertisement for renting the castle in a barbershop window in Sierre. He inquired and found the owner, who asked for an exorbitant sum. Werner Reinhardt, whose family is still the owner, rented and then bought the property for Rilke's stay. No sensible person today would make such an investment. The poet had received, as he used to say, the elegies in Duino, in February 1911, during a winter stay. Ten years later he would have to write what he had intuited. Finally, he was able to make a clean copy, in tiny handwriting, of the text of the ten elegies he sent dedicated to his protectress in Duino, the Countess von Thurn und Taxis.

But we were unable to enter. Someone, a caretaker without opening the door, shouted to us that we had to ask the owners for permission. Sabine's pleas in German went unheeded, Switzerland is Switzerland. (The manuscript of the *Elegies* is rightfully deposited in the treasury of the Credit Suisse in Zurich).

It was to be expected that we would fail. In Switzerland no one is received without prior appointment. Even if it is an abandoned house. We decided to sleep in Sierre at the Bellevue Hotel where Rilke used to receive friends and where he spent some days of his final illness. From there we would go to the cemetery of Raron, to visit his grave.

While driving, I said to Iván and Sabine that Muzot is a cultural turning point. Between 1922 and 1924: the *Duino Elegies*, *The Magic Mountain*, Joyce's *Ulysses*, Proust's *La Recherche*, Kafka's *The Trial*, *Being and Time* by Heidegger. I say:

"Rilke was the poet who went the furthest. He doesn't make anything clear. In Duino, in 1911, he was alone in the enormous castle and in the morning, in the middle of a storm, he went out to admire the furious sea and heard unintelligible voices in the storm. They could be the entities that unite us with the unknown and announce to us that the earth and the cosmos and men and gods may be closer to each other than we thought. The storm brings us closer."

"We're on a cultural trip with a guide," said Sabine ironically. And she recites the poem "The Panther" in German:

> Sein Blick ist vom Vorübergehn der Stäbe
> so müd geworden, dass ihn nichts mehr hält.
> Ihm ist, als ob es tausend Stäbe gäbe
> Und hinter tausend Stäben keine Welt.

Later, lazily, Sabine translates:

> Su mirada, a fuerza de gastar los barrotes
> se agotó al punto que ya no retiene nada.
> Le parece que el mundo está hecho de millares
> de barrotes

y detrás de millares de barrotes, ningún mundo.
Nada.[80]

"Yes. The last cultural trip. When Rilke died, he felt
that the culture of the West was a thing of the past. Let us
take advantage, no, Iván?" He rewrote the elegies during
a week in winter in 1922. He must have been freezing to
death. He had a wooden desk made by the local carpenter, a
four-candle candelabra. Château de Muzot was so neglected
that he had to buy parts for a bath and a stove. With his
intimate companion Baladine Klossovska, he had to block
the rat tunnels with stones and earth. Baladine hired a
frau to cook vegetarian food for him and to clean twice
a week. Rilke, whenever possible, had a pet. This time he
didn't want any distractions and refused the offer of a dog.
Baladine herself, his lover and mother of the now famous
painter Balthus, understood and left Muzot. Rilke was left
with a terrible babbling of words, which are never enough,
and with his own death, or death itself, which came for him
in 1927. "Natural death, which ripens in us like destiny."[81]

When he finished the elegies and sent them to the
Countess von Thurn, he understood that he had nothing
more to do. He traveled to Paris for a few carefree months
in 1926 and then returned to Muzot to die.

We passed through Raron and located Rilke's grave with
his headstone against the church wall. One does not know

---

80 His vision, from the constantly passing bars, / has grown so weary
that it cannot hold / anything else. It seems to him there are /
a thousand bars; and behind the bars, no world. Trans. Stephen
Mitchell.
81 The Spanish, which I have been unable to verify, reads: "La muerte
natural, la que viene madurando en uno como destino."

what to do in a cemetery. One cannot voluntarily grieve, nor truly concentrate. Some people ritually leave a flower, a rose in the case of initiates to Rilke. And one cannot wait to leave with the discomfort of having been too long in the banality of life and without the courage for metaphysical disquisitions.

Back in the Fiat, crossing the rural landscape, strangely un-Swiss, we went to a marvelous inn to eat lamb with the fine, robust wine of the region.

47

A NIGHT OF poets passing through venice. "Why so much Rilke?" the poet Federico Gorbea, asks me. A total poet who, having rejected the world, along with Michèle, his wife, lives a poetic life in the wilderness of the Empordà and eats and subsists on what he grows. He fights against floods, wild boar invasions, Carpetovetonic Catalans who think themselves French, and even against an eagle that two years earlier managed to sneak into the henhouse and decimate its inhabitants.

Why Rilke? And Sabine and I answer: "Because he freed poetry from contemplative nonsense and transformed it into an instrument of existential knowledge in times of resentment and servility to the general ideas of the era. In times of banality and decadence he returned the poetic to its highest destiny, already lost in the frivolity of Western culture."

Gorbea is Basque, one of the surly ones. Requeni is Mediterranean, with Valencian roots. We all want to be Argentines so as not to betray an inexplicable loyalty. Requeni distances us from Rilkean metaphysics and makes us laugh with a poem in which he makes fun of poets who think they have a great work in their hands. He arrived from Naples, and in the museum of Pompeii it occurred to him to imagine a poet ambitious for glory, Sextus Martius, who in the year 79 wrote a poem that he boasted was sublime. Zosima, his wife, was moving pots in the kitchen and, proud and smiling, interrupted him by bringing him a nicely decorated cake. The bard, interrupted in his magnum opus, shouted: "Leave me alone, you and your damned cakes!" and threw her out with a slam of the door. After a while, through the window, he saw that it was getting dark in the middle of the day. They had no time to stop the flaming tongues and red-hot stones from ravaging the city. As his flesh was ignited in flame, the poet sensed that life and glory were leaving him. He burned with the papyri of his poem. Nineteen centuries later Requeni wanders with Virginia, his wife, through the museum of Naples and stops at a shelf with curious, calcified objects. Among them, a cake found at the bottom of an oven. Zosima's cake.

Gorbea extends his last Homeric battles against the coarse nature of the Empordà. Not only against the periodic invasions of hungry wild boars but, especially, against the presence of the eagle that in his own right killed a dozen of his laying hens. He tells how early in the morning he went to fetch the pair of eggs for breakfast and discovered the stunning majesty of the eagle that looked at him with the contempt that every biped deserves, from the roosting bar where his late hens perched. He asked us:

"How do you defeat an eagle?" He managed only to come up with the idea of going in search of a pole. On his way back, he spotted that superior animal against the blue of the sky and in the direction of the freshness of the sea during the early hours.

Poets contest everything. They lead lives of intense solitude. They never agree in their refinements: Requeni,

Gorbea, Tomás Guido, Silvestre, Trejo, or Teuco Castilla limping along without saying that it was the result of a piss-up, attributing it rather to "a motorbike in the Piazza San Marco." They all silently venerate Venice, searching in her for impossible verse and crashing against the silence that is the final destiny for every poet (eagles in their dignity, flying over in all the cities of the world the desert of the decaying culture).

No one is better or worse. Everyone, from all over the world, writes a single book, which is the greatest document of the human condition. To be a poet is to feel life in its deepest human possibility. The written results, poems, are variable, but not the existential result of the poetic: the acceptance of the Universe in its evidence and its mystery, source of all that is religious. And the celebration of the gift of life, with everything, with its celebration and with its death.

No one will ever know why, everywhere and in every time, poets appear.

48

WE RUN INTO our Baucis and Philemon, the Sieverses, who are walking ahead of us as if fleeing from the autumn wind that disrupted the afternoon. We go along the *fondamenta* Zattere, the Venice shore in front of the island of the Giudecca, where the power of the sea enters and the air is heavy with iodine and salt. I was strolling, soliloquizing, and dodging Sabine's angry rebuttals:

"There's no longer any reason to insist on the fate of the human condition, after what's happening in this century. We are a stupid, destructive, harmful animal. Can anyone take sides with hyenas or scorpions? Many of the horrors of the twentieth century are a sign of the desire to put an end to this pedantic, dangerous, and cowardly creature without complacency. Science does nothing but look for an alternative, a robot, a clone, a new homunculus to replace this bipedal destroyer that we are. If after two thousand years of love it has come to this, it is better to try the side of hate … Who can still say that we are made in the image and likeness of God? Of what God? He must be a kind of cosmic Al Capone."

Sabine protests. She accuses me of oversimplifying, wordy hypocrisy, grandiloquent rhetoric. That irritates me. It's a lousy evening, preceded by earlier fights.

Until we see the Sieverses, walking toward the end of the *fondamenta*. It isn't an older couple marching along trying to make it to the supermarket. We understand that those beings who already inhabit the darkest blue of the Blue Age are fighting ferociously. They come closer, as if to hit each other rather than to exchange shouting and invectives. The scene makes our own fight invalid. Sievers is walking with a cane and at times, carried away by rage, approaches her and mutters a shout or insult, his mouth distorted. She, always elegant, stops and confronts him. From afar I glimpse a grimace that reveals teeth like those of Tem, the Mielis' neurotic Chihuahua. To hurl his epithets, Sievers walks a couple of steps as if he didn't need a cane. Then he loses vigor and drags his leg as usual. We follow them from afar, unable to hear the voices carried away by the wind, until they converge toward the entrance of the supermarket famous for its seafood.

"To think that the final, loving hope of Baucis and Philemon is that Zeus grants them the possibility of dying together!"

They prepared to face without sorrow the supreme journey, to the other space. Free from delights, dangers, humiliations, and disappointments. Yet they went about like cat and dog, almost whispering invectives so as not to attract attention, as they were educated, known people. But even in the High Blue Age, we're surprised by the enthusiastic rancor, an important ingredient of life.

Sabine shoots me an ironic, meaningful, almost mocking look. She says:

"What unites them is stronger and more unbearable than love. There is no mistake... The thing is that no one risks Rilke's dangerous phrase.

"Rilke again? What line?" I ask. And Sabine:

"Be ahead of all parting."

49

WE WERE LISTENING to Iván's laughter. Never so loud. Delia was with him. Something exceptional was going on and Sabine and I went in. Delia had told him about a life-threatening moment she'd experienced. Delia said:

"I told him when my employers took me to work at their house in Buenos Aires, on Alvear Avenue. I'd never left Misiones, my province. Everything was strange to me. In that neighborhood I was the only *morocha*.[82] I thought everyone was looking at me. I was fourteen years old, and I was very backward. One day when the bosses went to Mar del Plata, leaving me alone in the house, I filled the bathtub to the top and put in a liter of concentrated bleach, the strong kind. I had time, and I thought that in two or three hours my blackness would wash away."

"Tell them what you were doing with your head!" Iván burst out laughing again.

"I wrapped my hair tightly in one of those shower caps and plunged in. I didn't want my skin to lose its color and my head to stay dark." More laughter, now from everyone.

---

82 An epithet, often pejorative, used in Argentina to refer to a person, a woman in this case, with dark skin and hair.

"A drop of bleach got in my eye. It felt like fire, so I jumped toward the sink to wash myself. I touched my arms and they felt rough, like wood. A strange burning all over my body. I thought that my dark skin would fall off as it dried. I thought that the dark epidermis would give way to another layer, of white skin … which would be a natural color."

We told Iván not to interrupt Delia too much. On the table were her notes and open textbooks. She had to take the European elementary school exam. Twice Sabine found her asleep with her head resting on the kitchen counter, exhausted. She didn't want to give up her job, as we asked her to do. She was having a hard time with English. We promised her that if she passed, we'd pay for a trip in London, a youth exchange trip like the ones advertised on school bulletin boards. But her nerves had gotten the best of her as her exams approached at the school she'd been assigned to as an external candidate and a remedial student.

One night we had some friends over for dinner. She'd prepared a soufflé for the first time. A couple, Professor Salomon and Ana, both famous psychoanalysts, arrived half an hour later and when she opened the door, she scolded them. Delia was being born out of silence. She began to come into being, as she began to better herself. She allowed herself to be humorous, good or bad tempered. She passed the exam successfully and won her twenty-day trip to London. She was beginning to enter another area of her existence. Her good-natured submission, her silent acceptance of the world she believed to be legitimate, was beginning to give way to expressions of her character. Delia was beginning to exist. To say no. To react. She was being born, growing, becoming lost like someone who moves from limbo to consciousness. She would burst out laughing. She looked visitors in the eye, no longer with the evasive submission of a person who considers herself an impostor, a gatecrasher at someone else's party. Always someone else's.

50

PERÓN RETURNS to Argentina. The news fills the papers and newscasts. He arrives in a plane full of loyalists to Ezeiza Airport. Deaths again: several dead and hundreds wounded. Perón smiles. A crowd gathers at Ezeiza. The green spaces are filled with smoke, but it wasn't a Sunday barbeque. It was gunpowder and gas. Torture, castration. The only things missing were scenes of cannibalism. Perón returns after seventeen years of exile. "Now I am a herbivorous lion." The butchers are the others. We see some scenes on Italian television and wait for news on the midnight telecast. *Tender is the night* on the Grand Canal: late-night gondolas like surreptitious violins. The Neapolitan singing of a gondolier egged on by Japanese customers. The sputtering of the vaporetto. Windows open to the faint nighttime breeze.

On TV Perón says "I shall be a peace offering." But war has come to stay, and hatred runs like alcohol spilled in the streets. Cámpora,[83] with admirable thoughtlessness, had assumed the government and freed those who believed that Peronism should be transformed into a violent Marxist

---

83 Héctor José Cámpora: a left-wing Peronist politician and one-time president of Argentina.

socialism. For their part, the military thought that Perón would take the lead in this youthful subversion. The young people felt they were the masters of the country's political destiny. But Perón already knew that Marxism was finished in Russia and that China had used it as a violent ordering discipline in a perverted country. Nor did he believe in democracy, but he'd resigned himself over the years to putting up with it as the form that ultimately corresponded to mediocrity and the bad inclinations of the human condition.

My colleague J.V. would tell me by telephone that Perón, exasperated, slapped Cámpora and fired him loutishly, crossing out the phrase in the decree "thanking him for the important and patriotic services rendered to the State." Cámpora had gray hair, with the look of a notary or a village dentist. After the slap, according to J.V., he smoothed his hair with dignity, stood up, and left with an attempt at a smile. Two days earlier he had declared to a newspaper: "I am not only loyal to the general, I'm also obedient to the general."

That slap would continue to rebound off the cheeks of the beardless youth, who believed that Perón was the Old Man, disoriented in the political jungle they thought they'd tamed.

Bartfeld told me that when the *montoneros* met Perón in Rome, they naïvely brought him three hundred names for public office. The leaders were convinced, Quieto and Firmenich, that they, with their weapons being used in terrorist actions, were the determining force. Perón to them was a flag, a symbol, obsolete prestige. They, the beardless, were the power. Barfteld said that Perón looked at them and asked them as if among comrades: What weapons do you have? Firmenich and Quieto looked at each other and spoke of handmade explosives, of secret factories making long guns, some bazookas. Perón muttered as if looking the other way so as not to annoy them with the ironic look in his eyes. "A force of short guns could only achieve a revolution in short pants," he told them.[84] "How many fighters could they eventually have?" "Seven thousand," the scarcely bearded men answer. Perón looked at them and whispered with veiled sarcasm: "I can add fifteen thousand to that in half an hour," alluding to the Argentine army.

---

84 The Spanish here creates a wordplay, using the word *corto* [short] that cannot be easily rendered in English.

51

THIRTY-THREE DAYS FOLLOWING his investiture, Albino Luciani, the patriarch of Venice,[85] who asked the entire consular body to report "that no one would elect him," dies in his Vatican apartment. The news causes a stupor. On the Lido beach there are whispers of assassination; there's talk about a plot by sinister cardinals. It's a very romantic version. They talk about the IOR,[86] the Vatican banking system, black money. Reality is so boring that people have to weave cinematic fables around it.

I remember him with affection. There are popes of action like Giuliano della Rovere, Julius II, or Alexander Borgia. And there are popes of Franciscan goodness, like John XXIII. There are popes of intellectual brilliance and others of pastoral wisdom. The conclaves elect them without explanation. The Church has navigated twenty centuries now.

It's late at night. I lost track of time making corrections. I stretch out in my armchair and think of John Paul I,

---

85 Known by his papal name, John Paul I, Luciani was born to humble origins in Forno di Canale, Belluno, a province of the Veneto region.

86 *Istituto per le Opere di Religione.*

Albino Luciani, pope, not martyr. I always believed that one must have a great power of indifference not to go mad, or die, if one thinks of the weight of leading a superpower, a country, big finance, or a Church! How did the Kennedys and Khrushchev withstand the missile crisis and that hour when the planes were in the air? How did Pacelli withstand the wave of Germanic paganism? In the newspaper I see the kindly face of the peasant Albino Luciani. They say he died with his glasses on. Anything is possible. It could have been his personal God or his guardian angel who took him in order to save him the anguish of carrying the weight of the world on his back. Implosion due to the anguish of not knowing how to begin, how to begin to empty the sea with a bucket![87]

Immediately the rumor of his possible assassination spread. A week later it was taken for granted. They pointed to a cardinal who had seen in Luciani a wolf that arrived at the Vatican in sheep's clothing. Gelli's P2.[88] The Vatican

---

[87] This metaphor can be traced back to a medieval legend in which St. Augustine, who, while contemplating the mystery of the Holy Trinity, has a vision in which he happens upon the Christ-child on the seashore, using a seashell to spoon the water of the sea into a hole on the beach. When Augustine asks the boy what he is doing, the boy answers that he is trying to bring all the sea into a hole. According to the legend, Augustine tells the boy that such a feat is impossible, to which the boy replies that it is no more impossible than trying to understand the immensity of the mystery of the Holy Trinity.

[88] Licio Gelli was an Italian financier who in 1981 was revealed to be the Venerable Master of the *Propaganda Due*, a pseudo-Masonic lodge, whose charter had been removed in 1976 by the Grand Orient of Italy.

Bank. Calvi and Sindona.[89] Three weeks later the details "became known," the last cup of tea that Sister XX takes to his bed. At six o'clock in the morning he's found leaning on the back of the bed, with his glasses on. Martyr for his courage?

Martyr for believing with his Church and the great popes of the century that European Western civilization could not accept the destiny of being subjected to the pincers of the two imperialist powers that had taken over the world to the dismay of Western culture? (Did he foreshadow the assassination of Aldo Moro?)[90]

---

89 Roberto Calvi, an Italian banker dubbed "God's Banker;" Michele Sindona, an Italian banker, known as "The Shark," member of *Propaganda Due.*

90 Twice prime minister of Italy (1963-1968; 1974-1976); in 1978 he was kidnapped and executed by the far-left terrorist group *Brigate Rosse.*

52

ADA DELIVERS. TEM dies. Just a couple of days apart. Tem, the Mielis' hysterical Chihuahua, had distemper, which triggered pneumonia. For two agonizing days the family watched him die. Renato returned from Rome when Bianca informed him that the vet saw no chance of recovery; he broke down. His daughter passed Sabine on the Strada Nuova and told her that she'd found her father lying on the floor, holding the feverish little paw of a Tem that was agonizing inside a box with a linen napkin. He sobbed at times. Renato Mieli, the Jew from Alexandria, polyglot, anti-fascist fighter who'd come to Rome as part of the intelligence team of the Allied army. He negotiated in Monte Cassino at risk to his life, reorganized the Communist Party with Togliatti, founded *l'Unità* and was retiring from the editorship of *Il Corriere della Sera*.[91] His friends were Montanelli, Enzo Bettiza, Jean Daniel, Raymond Aron.[92]

---

91 A major Italian daily newspaper.
92 Indro Montanelli, renowned Italian journalist; Vincenzo Bettiza, Italian novelist, journalist, and politician; Jean Daniel Bensaid, French journalist and executive editor of *Le Nouvel Observateur*; Raymond Aron, French philosopher, political scientist, and journalist.

Fifteen years before the rest, he understood the economic defeat of imperial Marxism. This was the man who at times sobbed while holding the tiny paw of Tem, the unbearable Chihuahua. Dogs die like humans, infected with humanity. Cats hide to die because they know they are replaceable. They know they are eternal.

Two days later, Delia, who was carrying laundry to the back, is led by Ada to a hiding place under the woodworking bench where there are three kittens, offspring of the furious tryst on my desk. Ada had thoroughly washed her offspring. It seems there was a fourth, certainly defective, that was eaten with the placenta. Indispensable proteins that she'd transform into nourishing milk. We all ran to the back with Iván in the lead. Ada was unenthusiastically reclining on the cleanest dishtowel she'd found, and the three newcomers, sojourners in this mystery, were jostling for position to nurse.

53

OCCASIONALLY ON SUNDAY mornings Venetians walk along the longest *fondamenta* in Venice, from the *Punta della Dogana*,[93] facing San Marco, to the distant maritime station, a long route, where horse races used to be held in the time of the doges. A real boardwalk in front of the island of the Giudecca, with bars and restaurants. Since the end of the war, the *Trattoria da Gianni* has been a Sunday meeting place for the gratin, between eleven and one o'clock: chic young people, artists, snobs, journalists. On cool spring mornings, before beach time, the tables would fill up, and Giovanni would come and go with pizzas and plates, aided by his wife. The guests drank beer or wine from Friuli or an *ombretta*, the quintessential Venetian aperitif. They sat in aluminum chairs emblazoned with the Cinzano brand on the seatback as they watched the boats go by, rowers who were defying the waves left in the wake of some melancholy Greek or Panamanian tramp steamer, one of those imagined by Álvaro Mutis.[94]

---

93 The *Punta della Dogana* refers to Venice's old customs house, as well as a triangular area where the Grand Canal and the Giudecca Canal meet.

94 The author is referring to a novella by the Colombian novelist Álvaro Mutis, titled *La última escala del Tramp Steamer* (*The Tramp Steamer's Last Port of Call*, trans. by Edith Grossman).

It had been a couple of weeks since I'd seen Andreina. She was sitting there with the engineer Balder, her husband, who had two huge Alsatian Shepherds on a short chain. They invited me to sit with them; I took a seat beside those monsters with tight leather muzzles who were watching me with serious and perhaps unpredictable attention. Balder explained to me that he enjoyed making them run along the long *fondamenta* Zattere.

"It's mutual: I take them out for a walk, and they walk me."

"You stay in shape," I told him.

Balder is an elegant athlete, always generous, reserved, sociable. He's also rich, enterprising, and very well positioned within the caviar-communism of Northern Italy. We talked about politics, Argentina, the driving force of Berlinguer, head of non-Stalinist communism, which was open to dialogue.[95] With his usual kindness, Balder told me he was "very interested" in Perón's return to Argentina. Andreina struggled to keep her hair in place against the breeze that floated in from the open sea into the sprawling Giudecca Canal at its widest and deepest point. She holds her hair with one hand and her wide, flouncy skirt with the other. She greets acquaintances with a fleeting gesture. In a city where everyone frequently crosses paths, out of centuries-old experience, no one looks anyone in the eye, or approaches tables to say hello. It would be unheard of. A brief gesture of politeness is made, and they continue on their way.

---

95 The author here uses a term *comunismo dialogante*, which was coined in the Italian press to refer to Berlinguer's willingness to engage in dialogue with opponents of communism, in particular the Catholic Church.

Balder left us talking, not unlike on other occasions, and departed with the canine monsters for their keep-fit walk. Andreina had brought a book by her friend Nadezhda Mandelstam. The subject of Russia was always coming up between us. What's more, *Il Gazzettino* announced a lecture by "the official dissident," the poet Yevgeny Yevtushenko, in Padua.

Although Andreina didn't seem to be in the best of moods, it occurred to me to say:

"A few days ago, I was walking around aimlessly and happened upon a movie theater on Paradiso Street, where they were showing a movie: *Doctor Zhivago*. I went in to see it. It's a tremendous frieze. Did you see it?"

"There's a theater on Paradiso Street?" She looked at me with a special glint that was either honey or mustard, according to the categories with which Brodsky described her in his ambiguous Venetian memoirs (or desires).

"A small movie theater. I think its name is Arcobaleno," I added.

"I've never heard of that theater. *Mai sentito*," she said. "What a funny thing that sappy tearjerker! Pasternak was a good poet. The best part of that never-ending story is Zhivago's death, when he thinks he sees her from a streetcar, twenty years later, and dies of a heart attack. Pasternak kills him. What could a novelist do after the horrors of the Revolution and of love?"

"Then you saw the film."

"It would never occur to me, but I read the novel." And she gives me a look that bordered on mocking. "Nadezhda's account is the most frightening and accurate. What a country of wretches and cowards! Brodsky, so mad and intractable, was lucky to get out alive into the Western trap.

Otherwise, they would have killed him. He and I have long exchanges."

"He's a stray dog… No, that's not right, he deserves to be called a stray wolf. Somehow, I try to dissuade him from the idealized West in the steppes. At the same time, he tells me incredible things about the infamous cruelty of Russia to its writers: Akhmatova lived in Leningrad in a wretched little room, even after Russia's victory in the war. No one dared to tell Stalin (who read poetry) that the greatest poet had been living since 1946 in a kitchen of an apartment from Raskolnikov's times, with stacks of books and a rickety bed under a tiny window that opened onto a ventilation shaft. Akhmatova, who begged in the snow for the life of Gumilyov, her husband, who was ultimately shot! She made a pilgrimage to Vladimir's prison to pray for her son as well. She survived and laughed at Brodsky's youthful madness. 'My friend the redhead,' she used to say. He also made me laugh with stories of his conviction at the age of twenty-four. Akhmatova said: 'They condemned the redhead to what he wanted most. What a curious turn by the KGB toward kindness!' As it turned out, he was banished to Norenskaya, a village in Arkhangelsk, in the Arctic Circle. After prison and unbearable confinements in clinics for social misfits, Joseph found himself amid forests of mysterious blue mist. 'I've managed to keep my head from ending up in the basket. I lived the best two years of my life in a place worse than Siberia,' Brodsky always says. 'But I was alone with plenty of books!' There wasn't anyone else. Just wolves, trees, and Eskimo-like peasants."

Andreina laughs with relish, as she must have laughed when Brodsky told them that, when he was there, he was horrified to learn that Sartre, Shostakovich, the Russell

Tribunal and many well-known people in the world had asked for clemency for him. It was customary humanism during the Cold War.

"But what happened?" And Andreina:

"Imagine the frozen desert of the White Sea and its savage forests. That's where the village was. They gave him a small bungalow, with no electric light and no heating other than the firewood he was able to collect. The villagers looked after him. He had hundreds of books sent to him, anthologies of English and German poetry, novels, essays of all kinds. During those couple of years, he was visited by Basmanova, the mother of his son, and even Bobyshev, the person who betrayed him out of jealousy. Very deeply Russian: the three of them must have embraced each other on some floe and cried and forgiven each other, exchanging horns for orthodox forgiveness. There he read Auden closely, Frost. And it was precisely Auden who recommended him as a poet-in-residence in Michigan when he was expelled from Russia."

"How did he survive?"

"The people of Norenskaya gave him a kerosene lamp and firewood until he learned to chop it like a man. They taught him to turn ice into water and to shit in 40 below zero. It's not easy; a person can die in the course of such a banal function. There he adopted a wild, naturist culture. Like Thoreau, but Russian style. 'I read for two years in a row,' he says, 'and the idiots of the KGB thought they were punishing me!' He made himself an indispensable vegetable garden because the only sure things there were cabbage, potatoes, and horsemeat. He loaded the wheelbarrow with manure from the wild horses he was able to track in the forest. He was the happiest condemned man in all of Siberia!"

Marina Ligabue walked up to say hello and said something in her ear; they were very buddy-buddy. "Are you leaving tomorrow?" she asked her. Several people looked at her in an attempt to say hello, but Andreina knew how to avoid silly conversations. Marina told me that she'd heard on the radio that something had happened in Argentina, but she didn't know exactly what. Mieli and his friend Jean-François Revel sat at a table. They both thought they could still Europeanize liberalism and lead the economic boom of those decades. They saw each other periodically, and I believe they were writing a book or coordinating articles in major European newspapers. I ordered another *ombretta* and a glass of champagne for Andreina. We were marooned in silence, after the tale and laughter about Brodsky's years of archangelical gold.

Andreina pointed out to me, at the end of the Giudecca coast, the enormous, abandoned building, known as the *Molino Stucky*. A great failed enterprise, which left an abominable architectural eyesore, overrun by rats that, in a Homeric-style battle, prevailed over the cats.[96]

"Anti-Venice," Andreina observed. Then she looked at me intently, and her lips pursed ironically. She said with alarming nonchalance: "Brodsky wanted to see *Doctor Zhivago*, that's the truth. He thought it was wonderful and fell in love with the actress who played the role of Lara." Andreina put the ball in my court, as a possible recipient of her confidences, a role that did not interest me. She added: "Now I must escape. Disappear. Brodsky, that crazed wolf

---

96 Today a Hilton luxury hotel, the Molino Stucky is a large neo-Gothic structure, built by the Swiss businessman Giovanni Stucky, as a flour mill and pasta factory.

trampling the garden of the West, is harmless. A scandal that doesn't involve two Venetians is a distraction of minor consequence. Venice is a humanly insignificant village. A hamlet that was once an empire. There is an inner voice that tells you, you're just a woman, and the moment you become free, you must escape so as not to be forced to enter the godless convent of the bourgeoisie. You see: I'm a total communist, of the future." And she laughed. "Brodsky escaped from his gulag. I must do the same from mine, the gulag of marble and Tiepolos.[97] Brodsky doesn't understand that he's in another society just as cruel and condemnable as the Soviet. He was useful to the CIA as an object of global propaganda and dissidence. He exists now as a literary figure of resistance. He still doesn't realize that poets in this final West are now living in catacombs. Brodsky comes from another era, from a world in which literature and art still had prestige. He believes that spiritual decadence existed only there, in the Leningrad of the last Stalinists…"

And we left it there. I paid Gianni for the drinks because Balder's dogs were by then running toward us, as he was coming back from the Stazione Marittima. I took the opportunity to ask Andreina:

"I heard Marina say something about your traveling."

"Yes, early tomorrow morning. I've been invited by the Lomonosov University again. I'm a Slavicist, am I not?"

I waved goodbye to Balder as he muzzled his fearsome Alsatians. We stood up to say goodbye and Andreina kissed me on the cheeks, and I smelled that perfume that Brodsky

---

97 Giovanni Battista (Giambattista) Tiepolo, an eighteenth-century Venetian painter and member of the Venetian School.

thought was called Shalimar. As I dodged the horrible aluminum Cinzano chair, I stretched to kiss the top of her cheek and for an instant my thigh rested against hers.

Sometime later the rumor mill circulated that the trip to Russia as a Slavicist was a ruse for Venetians and her husband. In reality, did she travel to Rome to meet Brodsky? The versions from the marble village were numerous. It seems that Valeri Manera and Liselotte, the tapestry designer, saw them in the *piazzetta* of Capri, before dinner, during the indiscreet hour of the aperitif that delights and inspires love. (Others were inclined toward Florence and Siena).

I began to think that Andreina enjoys having a bad reputation. She would suffer from being a proper and predictable bourgeois. Flirtation includes the boastfulness of sin. The unforgettable abysses hidden in the attic of every soul.

54

SABINE AND IVÁN were probably enjoying the Lido beach on that cool, bright summer morning. I walked slowly back from the *fondamenta*, still wrapped in Andreina's aura: spontaneity, subtlety, verbal grace, a certain malevolence, administered delicately. Almost all of these were metaphors. In the end, a sense of unattainable distance prevailed. Her ambiguity wasn't irritating, rather it was a weapon of her charm. Andreina was one of those women who should be satisfied with the power of her body, an inescapable object of desire. Nonetheless, a daemon led her to challenges and crises such as the one she was causing for herself with her misbehavior. Every Venetian woman hated or defamed her, not without reason. Brodsky wrote that she "keeps married men's dreams wet." The last straw for the aristocratic bourgeoisie of Venice was the enthusiasm with which she betrayed her class. She mocked with irony the dying embers of the lost Empire, which they'd rented out as a museum and a bedroom for tourists in sneakers. The pedestrian shoal begging for a glimpse of what was once a great culture, a *savoir vivre*, a way of moving fleets by dint of adventure and celebration of war.

Those surnames of the Venetian Gotha,[98] the Foscaris, Corners, Marcellos, Albrizzis, Dorias, Grimanis, that once meant conquest, courage to kill and die, now decorated lists of directories of banks and international corporations managed by implacable Milanese. Andreina, in the European renaissance of the fifties, barely a teenager, chose to insult them with Stalinist communism. Her friendship with the *Il Manifesto* group, Rossana Rossanda, Nilde Iotti, resented by millions, like Feltrinelli[99]—a terrorist aficionado—and Inge, his heiress. Even the *Brigate Rosse*, her limit on the left and, on the right, Berlinguer or Europe's ultimate failure in social-democratic progressivism. Minor, *costumbrista* politics.[100]

I was hungry and wandered toward the Castello District. I sat down, with a sense of calm, in a pizzeria. The encounter with Andreina, the engineer Balder and his dogs, forced me to postpone my solitary lunch.

At some point in our long chat, Andreina began to rail against the legendary vulgarity of the Biennale, and we recalled the meal at the Mielis, when Marina Lante dipped the silver cigarette case in the frozen dessert. Andreina asked me:

"Who is this Borges really? He seemed to be somewhere else, though not too far. The other day I read that Nabokov

---

98 Reference to the *Almanach de Gotha*, a directory of Europe's royalty and higher nobility.

99 Giangiacomo Feltrinelli was an Italian businessman, publisher, and member of the Italian Socialist Party. He was responsible for publishing *Doctor Zhivago*, Boris Pasternak's censored novel, based on a manuscript that had been smuggled out of the Soviet Union.

100 The term *costumbrista* in Spanish refers to a literary or artistic representation of everyday life or "customs."

had said in an interview that Borges was "a façade without a house."[101] You read him; you're a friend … Is there a house? I've only just glanced at something on a table in the Toletta bookstore."

"Yes, there is a house. No narrative or novel structure. His is a great language. He's a poet. He rejects excess, which seems vulgar to him."

"A person without excess or lust," Andreina whispered. "You seem to be talking more about whitewash than a house. A house is a pillar, cement and mud bricks, marble, a garden, a cellar, a roof. However, I can't forget his head raised in the middle of our chatter that night at the Mielis. That statuesque but inert head. Eyes like the blind; one has to know he's blind, because he doesn't have eyes like the blind … As if he were floating above the table like those little men with canes and bowlers by Magritte."

"Yes, there is a house. Nabokov was wrong," I repeated.

"A house is Dostoyevsky, Tolstoy. Proust himself is a Venice of palaces built by an obstinate, perverse architect. But a house, and more: a mansion," Andreina insisted.

Borges had awaken in her the feminine attraction to ambiguity. I knew that she wouldn't stop reading him when she got her hands on him.

As I cut the joy of a solitary pizza, I laughed, imagining Andreina at that very moment, grappling with good-byes before her "Slavicist's trip" to Moscow, but preoccupied with the light clothing of her escape with Brodsky, no doubt to Sardinia or Positano, or Amalfi.

---

101 The closest quote I was able to find of this kind was one in which Nabokov referred to Borges as "an interesting porch, but a porch without a house."

55

OVER TIME, reading Brodsky's memoirs, written after his Nobel Prize and the hurricane called Andreina, I was able to understand that after the secret meeting with Brodsky in the Arcobaleno movie house, each of them walking together through the snows of *Doctor Zhivago*, they'd picked up again after breaking up during the poet's visit over Christmas the year before. Brodsky had arrived from the bitter cold of Michigan. Where he was teaching the courses his friend Auden had arranged for him. He was ready for a month of solitary creation and total Andreina. He had the idea of renting the apartment of a retiree in a dreary and necessarily discreet side street in the Campo San Vio, not far from the consulate.

According to Brodsky, the apartment was impregnated with the humidity of a cave, which is how they baptized it in their lovers' argot. "What time will you be in the cave?" "I'll be at the cave at seven."

The retiree, accustomed to renting to foreigners, had taken the electric stove with him. The poet had dreamt of writing his essays and lectures during the day and waiting until the evening for visits by the delightful Andreina. But that heaven was transformed into hell as if by revenge of the treacherous Soviet cold. They failed in their first meeting:

Andreina shivered, and he began to drink vodka and Scotch; things warmed up in the Russian style but drifted toward violent or pathetic ravings. "To embrace her was like trying to embrace a statue of Venus in a Novosibirsk municipal garden in January,"[102] he wrote as if to justify himself.

The demonic circle was closing in on the lovers. Since he was there as a clandestine conspirator, he continued to drink and relapsed into aggressive alcoholism. Brodsky recounts that she would crawl into bed wearing colored woolen stockings, two sweaters, and a Bolivian-style knitted cap.[103] The poet would light the two gas burners on the stove, but he wasn't able to resolve the impossibility of the lovers' skins touching. The attempt ended in fierce clashes, and on December 24th, while the poet wrote, waiting for Andreina, a memorable Christmas poem, he suffered a heart attack. (Brodsky nearly starved to death during the siege of Leningrad, for which he paid with a coronary problem that occasionally reappeared.) Andreina was surprised that Joseph didn't open the cave door. She opened with her key and found a pale Brodsky, reeking of vodka and gasping for breath.

Andreina sensed that this could end in public disaster. She called for help, and a boat arrived at the nearest *pontile*. Two paramedics took Brodsky to the hospital of San Giovanni e Paolo, the largest in Venice. She introduced herself as a member of the Italo-Soviet Cultural Institute

---

102 I have been unable to find the origin of this quote as it does not appear in Brodsky's previously cited Venetian memoir *Watermark*.
103 Brodsky writes, "She would bundle up for the night—pink woolen jersey, scarf, stockings, long socks—and, having counted *uno, due, tre!* Jump into the bed as though it were a dark river."

and the doctors assured her that it was a decompensation resulting from a pre-infarction. There was, according to the poet's account, only one young doctor on duty.

Christmas Eve is a sacred family holiday, and Andreina was expected by her husband and children to celebrate at her brother's house near Treviso. She felt she was on the verge of scandal.

Brodsky recounts verbatim: "The cardiac cripple in me panicked and she somehow shoved me onto the train for Paris, as we both were unsure of the local hospitals [...]. The carriage was warm, my head was splitting from nitro pills, a bunch of *bersaglieri*[104] in the compartment were celebrating their home leave with Chianti and a ghetto blaster."

It was true that the doctor who treated him inspired little confidence. Andreina assured him that her friend, a famous cardiologist, who was in Paris, would admit him to Hôpital Cochin. He could travel on the night train. Brodsky is sincere in his assertion that he suspected nothing bad in his lover's behavior. In France they gave no importance to the cardiac episode. In his account, in fact, he leaves no room for any other interpretation. Still, it must be asked: If they were lovers, how could she have put him on a train to Paris on Christmas night? Would doing so not be the last straw, an irreparable affront? Or did she merely attend to him with a sense of urgency, with a pretense of humanitarian concern, only to arrive at her family Christmas Eve party, sensing that she was already under suspicion?

Is everything by Brodsky a lie and the inveterate slander of the Venetians? Brodsky's chronicle seems to

---

104 Members of the Italian Army's Infantry corps.

invoke his desire for reality, more than once. I wrote this all down about the harsh December in Venice during which Andreina hid or traveled, without the poet being offended. "I don't believe that I, or, for that matter, anyone, can be mesmerized or blinded by romantic tragedy. The latter aspect, however, is of advantage to you if you go out on a short errand, say, to get a pack of cigarettes, for you can find your way back via the tunnel your body has burrowed in the fog; the tunnel is likely to stay open for half an hour. This is a time for reading, for burning electricity all day long, for going easy on self-deprecating thoughts or coffee, for listening to the BBC World Service, for going to bed early. I set out for the place I was staying, to collect my bags and catch a vaporetto. I walked a quarter of a mile along the *Fondamente Nuove* I remember one day—the day I had to leave after a month here alone. I had just had lunch in some small trattoria on the remotest part of the *Fondamente Nuove*, grilled fish and half a bottle of wine. With that inside, I set out for the place I was staying, to collect my bags and catch a vaporetto. I walked a quarter of a mile along the *Fondamente Nuove*, a small moving dot in that gigantic watercolor, and then turned right by the hospital of Giovanni e Paolo. The day was warm, sunny, the sky blue, all lovely. And with my back to the *Fondamente* and San Michele, hugging the wall of the hospital, almost rubbing it with my left shoulder and squinting at the sun, I suddenly felt: I am a cat. A cat that has just had fish. Had anyone addressed me at that moment, I would have meowed."[105]

---

105 This quote, taken directly from Brodsky's English text, does not coincide in every respect with the author's quotes.

56

THEN CAME ANDY Warhol, inventor and manager of his own fame. Reveler of the sales of his journalistic glory. Attilio Codognato organized the dinner of the season in the Palazzo Mocenigo, with more than three hundred guests. With some delay suggestive of a head of state, Warhol crossed the great hall of the Palazzo Mocenigo surrounded by half a dozen beautiful, ethereal, Nordic girls and a boring group of silent ephebes. Gabriella Codognato, Ripa di Meana, Gregotti, Leo Castellani, Solomon; and the great speculative gallery owners from New York and Milan welcomed him. On the staircase leading to the *piano nobile* there was one of those quadriptych portraits of Marilyn Monroe, in this case owned by Codognato. Against the main wall, illuminated by spotlights, a commercial metallic bed frame. From a boarding house. A decisive work in the career of Rauschenberg, founder of technological art. Also a Pollock, one of those that swallowed several tubes of oil squeezed with rage and alcoholic circularity. An old door, with a high transom, without walls, alone, opening and closing toward nothingness, a revolutionary work, after the 1931 "Urinal,"[106]

---

106 Titled *Fountain*, Duchamp's urinal sculpture was originally exhibited in 1917, in New York, after which several replicas were made.

by Marcel Duchamp, which Attilio showed with invariable pride to the guests.

The banquet's organizers, the New Yorkers, had intended to place a large reproduction of Warhol's foundational painting: the *Campbell's Soup Cans*, a work that, in reality, inaugurated the Pop Art period.

Pop! But Warhol refused the possibility. He certainly believed that he'd eclipsed Rauschenberg and Pollock too much to share a wall.

Warhol had immobile, opaque eyes. He carried himself with gravity, concealing his fear of exposing himself outside his own myth. He feared letting go, looking wild. His hair and face displayed a great deal of hairdressing and cosmetics. He was as artificial as his fame. Ontologically, he was the Campbell's soup can that made him world famous.

Stripped of his solemnity and cosmetics, he betrayed a glimpse of the suburban hustler, from Brooklyn. In the music room, where Monteverdi premiered a series of his musically revolutionary madrigals, Warhol greeted the VIPs. We were all living a farce of subjugation. The perpetrators of the scheme looked on complacently. A legion of waiters lit the chandeliers atop the rows of tables. The head table was in front of the windows facing the Grand Canal, in that same space consecrated by Sandra and Gabriella, carried away by the mystery of tangos in the twilight, *Vida mía*, *Boedo*, *Flores negras*. There, on that night, the epiphany of an instant of art, of grace, of nostalgia had taken place. Scarcely an instant, like the pass of the cape of the bullfighter who manages to deliver forever the mystery of the silent music to his audience who explodes with excitement.

Valeri Manera, the Countess Volpi di Misurata, the Prefect of Venice, the young philosopher Cacciari, Vittore

Branca, the Resniks, the Count Corner, the Albrizzis, the Tornabuonis of Florence, Tomás Maldonado of the Bauhaus,[107] and Inge Feltrinelli. Their presence at this already unusual banquet represented a social event. Warhol shook hands, understanding neither names, positions, nor the why. Valeri Manera went closer to Liselotte Hoerst, a renowned tapestry designer who wanted to be photographed with Warhol. Stefanutti, the poet. Renato Mieli, unmistakably bored.

At the head table were seated Warhol and some of his youthful entourage, Madame Couvreux-Rouché, France's powerful cultural representative, the New York and Milanese mafia, creators of false fame and shameful exclusions, the engrossed Codognatos, the director of *Il Gazzettino*. The critics of the Biennale and the new management, Ripa di Meana and Gregotti. Pierre Restany, Bonito Oliva, and the critics of the major newspapers. They all gladly welcomed the dose of nihilism promoted by the mercantilism of global visual arts. As in all such outlandish banquets, one must find a friend with whom to talk, amid so many eccentrics with no other way out than conventional chitchat. Carlo Maria Santoro and I changed the order at the table of consuls and official to be able to sit together. The electric lights were dimmed so that the grand chandeliers could provide the light of another Venice, with hundreds of candles burning. A spectacle of ancient grandeur in times of arrogant technolatric misery. From the upper box of the

---

107 Although not directly affiliated with the Bauhaus (1919-1933), Argentine artist, designer, and academic Tomás Maldonado was professor and rector, from 1954-1967, at the Ulm School of Design, whose co-founder, Max Bill, was a student at the Bauhaus.

ballroom, Claudio Scimone's Solisti Veneti started with the melancholic subtlety of the Venetian masters, so admired by Carpentier: Albinoni, Benedetto Marcello, the infinite Vivaldi. Codognato's aestheticism was rewarded with the greatest admiration: silence at all the tables. Codognato and the Yankee gallery owners gave Venice a moment of its lost eighteenth-century aesthetics. The ducal Venice, to increase Warhol's value in commercial art markets.

In the delicious and discreet glow of the candles, I saw Mujica Láinez at the art critics' table. He was passing through Venice, and at my suggestion Codognato allowed me to invite him. For many years Manucho was the visual art critic of the newspaper *La Nación*. At the table of gray-suited journalism, Mujica Láinez was an infiltrator, a spy from the eighteenth century. He was wearing the regalia of a Porteño lord, as he was wont to dress when he celebrated his birthday in Buenos Aires. Black coat, brocade vest with white piqué trim, a shirt with cufflinks and black tie, between a bowtie and a cravat. In the half-light the flickering flames of the candelabra glimmered in his monocle hanging from a black silk ribbon. Warhol must have seen it too, and it must have seemed to him like a ghost of the Impressionists from the turn of the century, much more a collector of Braque and Cézanne, now interested in Warhol. The art critic of *Il Gazzetino* wrote that Warhol was the bravest representative of the countercultural movement. It must have been easy for him to achieve that distinction.

Manucho had gladly accepted the opportunity to attend. He was always telling stories of the last great Venetian ball in 1951, amid the frescoes of the Palazzo Labia that the multimillionaire Carlos de Beistegui had bought. After the Berlin crisis, that great tycoon thought that Europe would be reborn from its own navel, the omphalos of its culture, Venice. He wanted to give Europe, and in Venice, an act of faith and enthusiasm, a symbol of the necessary European revival, with a colossal party. The celebration of the renaissance (but with European snobbery) after the Second World War. Mujica knew a few Argentines who were invited, but his stories were based on the anecdotes told to him by the ineffable Leonor Fini, the painter of cats, as she was called in France. It was dubbed the party of the century. The anti-war, the anti-death, imagined by a brilliant eccentric. Following the theme of Cleopatra, as illustrated in Tiepolo's frescoes, Beistegui hired his friend Salvador Dalí as set designer and, for the guests' costumes, Christian Dior, who was assisted by two talented newcomers, Pierre Cardin and Nina Ricci. Cecil Beaton, the photographer, took pictures, in the early morning light, of Leonor Fini in her spectacular Egyptian princess costume with Fabrizio Clerici, also a painter, boarding the gondola to return to their hotel rooms, to the twentieth century. The orchestras were putting away their instruments. Proust's last friends were leaving. The Princess Ghislaine de Polignac, the Princess Gabrielle d'Arenberg, the Princess Colonna, the Duke and Duchess of Kent, Anthony Eden, the Princess Natalia Pavlovna Paley, Jean Cocteau and his Jean Marais, Ira Kostelitz.[108]

At the direction of Gabriella and Attilio Codognato the salmon from Ireland was sliced and the turkey and roast carved at each table. A heavenly river of Amarone from Friuli and Veuve Clicquot flowed for the thirsty. Halfway through the second course, the clamor released by the

---

108 I have corrected name spellings and titles of nobility.

imbibing grew, and Claudio Simone realized that Benedetto Marcello's *adagio* was not worthy of the surroundings.

Andy Warhol drank orange juice and looked around with his hard, dark, opaque little eyes. He was casting quick sideways glances like someone who fears being detained at any moment.

We walked back along the Calle Merceria, with the stores conveniently closed. I thought of Baldovino's aesthetic happiness, without gimmicks, on a very early Sunday, in front of the gondola boatyard of the Squero di San Trovaso, his wife serving him *mate* and he searching for the ineffable mystery of Canaletto's skies. And Macció, in Medinaceli, with the light of Venice erasing the perverse influence of Bacon from his palette. The hard, dark, powerful gaze of Picasso in Vallauris, in 1952.[109] The happiness of the village master, an autistic genius. But art—wild, new, mysteriously, inexplicably, true, and necessary. Not Campbell soup.

---

109 The author is referring to a photograph, titled "Les Pains de Picasso," taken by French photographer Roberto Doisneau.

57

WE HEARD WHINING and an alarming cry in the perfect, spherical, silent night of the Grand Canal. In between dreams I imagined it was one of Ada's extemporaneous heats or her rakish cat with whom she'd been *sistemata*. But it was Iván; Sabine rushed to his room. Iván was having a nightmare. His covers in a mess, his face perspiring, his hair soaked in sweat. He wouldn't open his eyes. Sobbing, he hugged his mother. It was something strong, inexplicable, something more than a bad dream: an anxiety attack. He kept repeating:

"I don't want to grow up! I don't want to grow up!"

I sensed that it was akin to the anguish of the newborn, confronted by the light of the operating room and the masked faces of the doctors and nurses.

"I don't want to grow up! I don't want to!"

Sabine wiped his forehead. I took his tiny wet hand. Slowly, but with difficulty, he emerged from his anguish. He found himself between his parents, saved from a shipwreck, a fire, back in his mother's safe harbor.

Iván had been saved from a shadow of horror. What had he seen? We were approaching the end of six years in Venice. Where in his DNA was this unwillingness to grow up?

What darkness had he glimpsed, what jaws, what abyss? What happened to Iván was not mere fear, the transitory fear of nightmares filled with beasts. Vision, prophecy, revelation, warning? Delia, another intuitive, walked up to him in her robe and leaned down without understanding, to take Iván's hands.

I thought about the happiness and the strange explosion of fear of growing up, of being, of a happy child, of his age, a student in the Istituto San Giuseppe and of the gang of friends from the Campo dei Santi Apostoli.

Sabine lay down, hugging Iván as he returned to the womb of sleep. Iván was becoming soothed. Was he forgetting?

Something ineffable had emerged, from the labyrinth of their intimacy, from the mystery of their oneness, like a sign that can't be deciphered.

The next morning, at breakfast, Iván spoke of Napoli, his soccer team, and his singsong voice was so fresh and crystalline that it put us completely at ease. Sabine said to him:

"Last night you woke up crying, very agitated."

"Did I?" Iván asked. "I don't remember anything."

I called our friends Salomon Resnik and Ana, very respected psychoanalysts who practice in Venice and Paris. They listened to me intently.

"A first impression would be something like an intoxication from happiness, of the life he leads in Venice, without the shadow of school violence or classroom demands that happen elsewhere. Yes, an intoxication from the experience of happiness and the sudden shadow that in the future it might change," said Solomon. But it seemed to me that Ana doubted that interpretation.

"But why should he feel or sense that in the future it might change? It's strange: no boy doesn't want to grow up," said Ana.

A boy screams during the night. Intoxicated with a mysterious anguish. What's wrong with the world? What could the boy have seen?

What could he not have seen or already glimpsed?

58

I ACCOMPANY MUJICA Láinez to the Galleria 1, in Campo Santo Stefano. Manucho walks with decision more than agility, but he keeps a brisk pace at this almost siesta time when there are not so many people in the streets. He wears an elegant and wrinkled white linen jacket, his flying tie and a Panamanian straw hat. He leans on his walking stick.

"It helps me on the steps of the bridges," he tells me. He read in *Il Gazzettino* that Giorgio de Chirico was passing through Venice and that he would be greeting people at Galleria 1, where some of the master's recent sketches were on display.

The quite old De Chirico is seated in an armchair and next to him there's a man with sallow skin with whom he converses. De Chirico's body is leaning forward and he barely murmurs. Behind him, the poster of the oil painting of the mannequin in the moonlight, and a floor of black and white flagstones, perfectly delineated, but giving a sense of unreality.

We introduce ourselves to the great painter who makes an attempt to sit up. Mujica tells him that he's a critic for *La Nación* of Buenos Aires. The man stands up. He's tall, once athletic and now timeless, beyond the body. His hair is shaggy, thick, straight, darkened.

"I am Serge Lifar," he says.

Manucho surprises us. He stares at him with a glint of irony:

"I danced for you…"

"Well, what a surprise, the dancer was almost always me."

"We laugh."

"You came to Argentina in the fifties. You danced at the Colón, and we went to eat with a group of friends at the home of the poet Oliverio Girondo; we improvised something from the ballet *Don Quixote*." Lifar laughs.

"I always met people whom I had danced for!" He has the grace of the gypsies.

Lifar travels almost every year and visits the tombs of Stravinsky and Diaghilev, in the cemetery of San Michele Island. It is the memory of, and homage to, the renewal of ballet in Paris. The famous Ballets Russes at the Théâtre des Champs-Elysées, glory of Nijinski; Lifar's revelation with his interpretation of Icarus. The genius of Stravinsky: Diaghilev had died in Venice in 1929, and since then, that love and respect for his master was expressed in his homage at his tomb in San Michele. Mujica and Lifar converse. De Chirico seems to doze off in his armchair. His head bowed, as if it were already too heavy for him. He was thinking. Maybe he was saying goodbye to Venice forever. That may explain why the great metaphysician, as Braque called him, had insisted to the gallery owner to be present at an exhibition of sketches "to greet some friends." His great friend was Venice and all the colors of Carpaccio, Tintoretto, Bellini. He died months later. And Lifar laughingly asked Manucho:

"Do you still dance?"

"I do what I can..." and he showed him his walking stick. In that half hour no one had come in to greet De Chirico. None of those who'd gathered around Warhol. De Chirico, perhaps the last of a great few, had closed with delicate suggestions and metaphysical settings what since Cézanne, including Braque and Picasso, had been released in form and color. A perfect cycle until the atrocious Venice Biennale.

59

MUJICA LÁINEZ STAYS with us for a few days. We usually have breakfast facing the Canal. It's a time for laughter, for anecdotes. In public he's rather catty, with biting ironies. At home he's fresh, amusing, and at times melancholic.

"I must confess that I always wanted to be a consul in Venice. This is the only city I would leave Buenos Aires for. I'd even plot to have you kicked out and me appointed."

Then he tells me that at the beginning of Lanusse's administration he met General Denicola at the October 12th cocktail party at the Spanish Embassy,[110] and he was very influential then. The general told him straight out that he'd not read him, but that his wife was crazy about his articles. He invited him to visit him at the 1st Regiment in Palermo, which he commanded. Manucho told me that he dressed in the most conventional way, in an old gray suit and blue tie. The general's aide was waiting for him with a jeep at the barracks gate and took him to the main corps, where the host was waiting. He told him that he'd like him to get to know that historical unit well, the Patricians'

---

110 October 12th is known in Hispanic America as the Día de la Raza [Day of the Race], known elsewhere as Columbus Day.

Regiment.[111] He explained everything to him, as the guards of each platoon stood at attention as Manucho walked past, amid the strident sounds of regulation heel-clicking. The general recalled with fondness the historical battles, the old commanders, whose names were now streets. He was moved by his command. It lasted almost a full hour. "I got out of the jeep with as much agility as possible, and we went to the commander's dining room, with spartan wooden furniture where small labels with the inventory number were visible. Two place settings faced each other at opposite ends of a long table, with individual placemats. Then General Denicola said to me, 'Since I became commander, all the officers eat the same thing as the troops; it's a matter of principle.' Next a fine young man appeared, wearing a tailcoat and white gloves, to wait on the table. He brought a plate of cold meats and served red wine and water. 'It's common table wine, doctor. An indulgence I allow myself when I have guests.' The aide came in and served two plates. I tried to look at him as little as possible. He was a product of the Argentinean immigration miracle: a veritable Germanic hussar, probably the regiment's standard bearer, given his height. The spectacular boy managed to lend a contour to the service tailcoat. I was able to withdraw my admiring gaze upon the arrival of the main course, which the general called 'Creole stew': three huge potatoes and two pieces of stew meat, covered by a dense, invasive sauce. I understood that I must pay, in any way possible,

---

111 The Regimiento de Infantería 1 "Los Patricios" is one of the oldest and most prestigious Army regiments in Argentina. Located in the Palermo neighborhood of Buenos Aires, it serves as the honor guard for visiting dignitaries.

for the democratizing principles of the general! Luckily, he broached the subject that interests me, as I was going for the first potato. I told him that for a while I'd been director of cultural relations with the rank of ambassador. 'I was thinking it was something like that!' he said. It was clear that he found my work as a journalist and writer laudable, although somewhat adjectival to the seriousness of life." Manucho continued.

"'You've never thought about diplomacy? I have excellent relationships with the Foreign Ministry, in particular with Costa Méndez. Would you be interested in any particular embassy?' he asked me with absolute good will. Then I dared to tell him what I'd never said before: if anything might interest me, it would be to be consul in Venice. 'In Venice?' he asked with astonishment. Venice, yes... and I believe beyond the potato mountain range, I saw the Grand Canal, this marvelous although somewhat rundown *palazzina,* and, for a second, I even identified the tailcoat aide with my Prince Orsini of Bomarzo. Yes, Venice, I told him. The truth is he called Costa Méndez to pass on the request. The Chancellor told him that it wasn't a very important post and that the consulate staff had specific professional tasks, and that an embassy would suit me better. The only one available was the one in Ankara. Because a few days later the general called me elated: 'The Chancellor is agreeable, but not Venice, which isn't a good fit for you according to what he explained to me, but Ankara is free, now that relations with Turkey are beginning to become important.' Of course, I had to disappoint him. I had to tell him that Venice was something very special to me. And I was left without Venice, as you can see!"

60

I HAVE TO go upstairs to the consulate. I pass in front of Manucho's room, whose door is open. He's lying on the bed in a silk robe. His thin, white legs are hanging motionless. Next to him, the young biochemist who's traveling with him and wants to be a novelist squeezes the black rubber pump of the professional device to measure Manucho's risk index; the latter is looking at me with opaque fear and sadness.

"Last night it was 170 / 80. That's high."

I should have offered some words of encouragement, but I laughed and Manucho said:

"How can you laugh? To top it off I wanted to visit the Palazzo Labia, considering I wasn't at Charles de Beistegui's infamous party."

I laughed because seeing the biochemist pumping the rubber bulb reminded me of one of Manucho's famous anecdotes.

Two or three years ago at his birthday party, one of his friends from the "race of men-women," as Proust wrote,[112] came up to greet him and in doing so introduced him to an ephebe. "I dared to bring my nephew without telling you,

---

112 *Sodom and Gomorrah.* Vol. 7, *In Search of Lost Time.*

he admires you and wants to meet you," to which Manucho replied: "Yes, I know him very well. Two years ago, he was my nephew."

After two hours, Manucho reappears, dressed for his departure. He says he feels better.

"Although I got tired with the four steps in the corridor," he murmurs. He stands at the window and talks as if he were alone: the announcements. 170 / 80 which then dropped to 160 / 60. "Who comes up with these announcements? What for? Like on Italian ships: 'Final announcement! Visitors are requested to disembark, *La nave è in partenza!*' The clocks are terrible; when your blood pressure is 180 / 70, the ticking sounds like a warning cry. And everything: the suit hanging in the closet, but without your body. Everything you see and feel at 170 / 80 turns into rejections, even the mirrors seem to expel you. Now, for example, the water of the Grand Canal … Heraclitus and his *no man bathe twice in the same river*. The water passes by, but sometimes you feel it carries you away … " Delia brings him a tea sweetened with honey, just as he asked: "This must be my lunch. If I'd been feeling well, I'd have gone to the Palazzo Labia to see Tiepolo's frescoes and invoke the characters of the feast of the century, so that they might welcome me on the other side with their costumes! I'm closer to their side … Soon I'll see them … "

Manucho was evoking the party he missed that morning when he awoke beset with health issues. The eternal threat of his hypertension.

"A minor annoyance, blood pressure … as you can see."

"What tiny annoyance could you have had in Venice?"

"I was annoyed that Borges didn't send me the prologue, an introduction, for *Bomarzo*[113] in French translation. The book sold very well in Spain, but I don't want to present it in France without a little push from Georgie! You see, my pressure's already 170 / 80, and I wasn't translated into French! Kodama is very kind, but the weeks go by ... "

"I know he appreciates you. Right here, in Venice, he included you among the sixty-four books in his Personal Library ... "

"Kodama must have suggested it to him. They included *Los ídolos*.[114] But he has yet to send me the prologue. Borges is like that; he never truly considered me a good writer. He's emotionally broken. Notice that on the back of that anthology (the absurd omissions and inclusions) he didn't include Bioy, whom in the prologue to *The Invention of Morel* he called an author as important as Kafka; nor did he include his much-admired verbal genius, Macedonio Fernández, which seems hard to believe ... I accept that someone else's hand could have been in. But Borges can surprise you. By playing a joke or a good *boutade*, he's capable of mixing it up with anyone he wants. Not long ago María herself was seriously upset by a literary invitation to Mexico and Georgie's idea of being accompanied by the daughter of the bookseller of the Galería de la Ciudad. I witnessed it. What a hullabaloo! The girl was very pretty, that's for sure."

---

113 *Bomarzo* is a historic novel, authored by Láinez, about the life of Italian nobleman Pier Francesco Orsini, Duke of Bomarzo, published in 1962, and which later becomes the basis for an opera by Argentine composer Alberto Ginestera.

114 *The Idols*, published in 1952, is Láinez's first novel, often referred to as a "saga of Buenos Aires's aristocracy."

I recalled what Borges told me about *Bomarzo*: "It is full of characters, and one doesn't understand what they do. It's a sort of telephone directory of Tuscany in the fifteenth century. An unbearably *overcrowded* book." Manucho went on about Borges:

"That nitwit Bioy did a lot of harm to Borges. When Borges arrived in the center, we all thought he was a neighborhood kid who'd been educated Borgesianly between Geneva and France. He'd written verses to Lenin and later, with Petit de Murat[115] and the bums from *Crítica*,[116] he even became a fervent Yrigoyenist.[117] That lasted only a few years, until he ran into Bioy, in the 30s, a kind of stupid snobbery infected or awakened in him. He thought the Casareses were the pinnacle, top drawer. They were the owners of La Martona: Basque dairy owners who'd managed to become astonishingly refined in a single generation; some becoming outstanding jurists. But Bioy involved Borges in campaigns of mockery, discrediting, Buenos Aires aristocratism, what was in and what was out. Pure snobbery, and Borges allowed himself to get carried away in that circle of after-dinner slander! Which the devious Bioy wrote down patiently, day after day, like a eunuch at the court of China."

---

115 Ulyses Petit de Murat was an Argentine poet and screenwriter.

116 *Crítica* was a daily newspaper published in Buenos Aires from 1913–1962; its weekly cultural supplement, *Revista Multicolor de los Sábados*, was edited by Borges and Petit de Murat between 12 August 1933 and 6 October 1934.

117 A follower or supporter of Hipólito Yrigoyen, twice president of Argentina (1916–1922 and 1928–1930) of the Radical Civic Union party.

The water taxi that would take Manucho to the airport was arriving. He said goodbye to us with great emotion and gave Iván a print he'd drawn of a cat with whiskers like his own. The young biochemist had taken the valises down to the palazzo's pier and said goodbye to us warmly. From the window I saw the novelist on the last flight of stairs, with his Panama hat and his walking stick, now overwhelmed by his feebleness. The biochemist was one step below, and Manucho was leaning firmly on the young shoulder.

It would be my last image of that friend who'd turned himself and his life into a more vivid and memorable character. A character from Buenos Aires.

That was the last Venice for Manucho.

61

DOES ADA INTUITIVELY sense evil? I wondered after a curious incident, when we saw her laboriously bringing in her three kittens, one by one, clutching them with her teeth. Iván discovered this chore that was forcing the cat to travel from the back of the house, where she normally stayed, to the front room and hide them under a cupboard in the dining room, an almost unreachable place. What could have happened? The cat was struggling to sneak toward the litter and suckling them under that protective cupboard. The scene betrayed a temporary decision in the face of danger. Iván and Delia searched the storage room in the back. Only two days later did they find the culprit: a scorpion, a rare species in Venice, black, with a shiny tail, with its dreaded poisonous stinger at the end. It was hidden behind some wood.

How had the scorpion gotten there, and from where? There are no scorpions in Venice.

Did Ada sense its poisonous nature? How could she, having no previous experience with these pests?

For Álvaro Mutis it would be obvious: cats sense evil. They were sacred and even deified in Egypt, but they were secular victims of human perversity when it was fashionable, throughout the Middle Ages, to link them with the devil.

They were burned alive. Children stoned them to death. They were thrown into the very flames of the bonfires of those condemned for witchcraft.

Delia, having spent her childhood in the jungle, knew about such pests. With an inverted glass, she quickly caught the scorpion. She slid a piece of cardboard underneath. No one dared to kill it. They brought it to me, and I released it in the bathroom with the door closed and squashed it medievally with the sole of my shoe, trying not to hear the crunching noise. Could scorpions really be demonic? (If a pest can be killed with such "artlessness," it shouldn't be strange that God would do the same to us.)

During the night, Ada transported her brood one at a time back to the home where she would raise them.

62

PHILEMON AND BAUCIS, the Sieverses, even if they are inexorably approaching their joint end for which they pray to Zeus and the most current gods, are surprised by what remains of life and love.

Giovanna, the psychoanalyst who, because they are neighbors, is always nearby, told us what happened. At times with her ironic skepticism, at times with a brow wrinkled from worry. She told us:

"It's not the first time I saw them arguing with vigorous determination, shall we say, considering they are residing in the Great Anteroom. With no turning back... The nurse from emergency services told me that Philemon argued with Amalia because she'd left the gas on for the umpteenth time. As a psychologist, I believe that a deep-seated hatred emerged, that secret hatred like a cesspool acid that can reappear in people who've lived together for more than sixty years. She began to scream in a customary fit of hysteria for him not to hit her anymore: 'Don't hit me anymore!' And she threw herself to the floor without his touching her, screaming in a voice loud enough to alert the neighbors in the nearby apartments. Amalia protected her head from imaginary blows. Sievers closed the doors because of the dreadful screams. Because they didn't stop, the discomfited captain, perhaps as desperate as when the Andrea Doria sank, opened the door to explain himself to some concerned neighbors."

The situation was alarming. I told Giovanna that some time ago we'd once seen them arguing harshly near the *fondamenta* Zattere.

"Hatreds never die; they accumulate like geological layers and explode volcanically and ridiculously," says Giovanna. "Out of guilt for a forgetfulness caused by senility, she feels that the captain is right to become fed up, which makes the righteous blows she imagines become reality. To this you must add the notion of hysteria as an evasive explosion: the attack of tremors and cries brings everything to an end and ends with the injection given by the paramedics from emergency services."

Sabine recalls the Goethean theme of Philemon and Baucis, and says:

"Now Zeus will be forced to alter his decision to have them die at the same time and transform her into a linden tree and him into an elm. They'd scandalize the whole forest! Not even Zeus can handle the human condition!"

And Giovanna:

"It's not a joke. Old age weakens hatred but doesn't extinguish it. The hatred of sixty years of coexistence accumulates in the deepest levels of being. It remains latent, until it explodes like a volcano, as happened to the poor Sieverses."

"So ... " Sabine asks. "How do they go on?"

"Well, they will readjust to tenderness, to complicity, to mutual nursing," says Giovanna.

"Zeus will grant them the vegetable eternity to which they aspire. Although he has no hint of Christian piety, he's moved by the indestructible perpetuity of the human couple," I remarked.

And Giovanna:

"Nothing is more enduring than love. I'll tell you a little professional secret: Amalia comes to see me; she asks me for advice regarding the clashes that end in violent insults. She tells me: 'However, the other night I woke up and I thought he was no longer breathing; he was lying on his back next to me. I touched him and he turned toward the wall. I fell asleep happy, at ease.' Two days later Sievers came to get a prescription for pills for insomnia. He says to me: 'Sometimes I wake up thinking she's not breathing enough or that she's not moving. I reach out my arm, and when I see that she's alive, I fall asleep peacefully as if I'd taken three of these pills!'"

63

A S USUAL, WE put on the evening news. They
killed Rucci, the pillar of the CGT.[118] He was shot
with unusual excess, as if the assassins had just finished
watching the movie *Bonnie and Clyde*. Because of the exaggeration of lead, a testament more to the fear of the
executioners than to hatred for Rucci, they themselves
christened it Operation Traviata, after the popular brand
of crackers with symmetrical rows of little holes. Hours
earlier Perón had won his third presidential term by 62
percent of the vote. Iván called Delia, and we watched
from seven thousand miles away the red car with the
smoldering upholstery and the beat-up doors. We saw
the woman crying, the failed escorts, the delayed policemen, the flurry of stunned journalists. Ambulance sirens.
Hugs from weeping supporters. We didn't notice that Delia was falling apart. She fell and rolled on the carpet.
She stretched out and contracted her legs, trembling. Her
eyes were lost as if in the confusion of another dimension.
We held her ice-cold hands. She was making faces. Iván

---

118 José Ignacio Rucci was an Argentine politician and general secretary
of the Confederación General del Trabajo [General Confederation
of Labor].

was frightened and hugged her as if to stop the incredible trembling. Sabine dries the carpet and soothes her fever-ish forehead with cologne. Delia reacts. She murmurs and repeats that we not call the emergency services. I hang up the phone. Her opaque, disoriented gaze begins to be-come lucid and connects with our gaze.

"Please don't call; it's happened to me several times; it's nothing. Nothing…" Iván looks back at the ambulance where they loaded what's left of Rucci. Sabine and I lift Delia, who proudly attempts to stand up, and we take her to her room.

"I can't take it anymore," murmurs Delia exhausted. It's as if she'd climbed Monte Bianco. She closes her eyes and dozes off. Sabine checks her pulse. It's stable.

I stay awake, alone, watching Spanish television. It's an unsuccessful challenge from the terrorists against Perón, who's just been overwhelmingly elected. Spanish and Argentine commentators describe it as a long-planned premeditated event. The assassins rented a house near Rucci's several weeks before.

It's late, I turn off the TV. The *palazzo* is filled with silence. I sense that death has been unleashed with unusual force. Everyone is asleep, even Delia, calm. The vaporetti pass by every hour or more. The sea enters at a cat's pace and purifies the lagoon with salt and iodine. On the marble steps, the sea murmurs as if disguising its power. Venice will forever leave me with two sounds: the sputtering of the vaporetti at night as they pull away from the dock, and the dulcet splash of the water on the decaying marble steps of the palazzo. Faint taps, audible only to the insomniac who's resigned himself to sleepless nights.

Young idealists dive into a pool of blood, with the glee of suburban strategists. They believe that Perón, *el Viejo*,[119] as they call him, will give in. Estefanich, Perdía, Kunkel[120] believe they will regenerate a world on the horizon of the West, following that brave misguided Ernesto Guevara de la Serna, who was going in the direction opposite the sun: they march enthusiastically toward the East, when the two Marxist empires are already beginning to turn toward the West, toward the resounding, smiling, and unbridled Western capitalism, in brilliant technolatric agony.

Perón won't forgive the arrogant beardless youths. The news arrives about the pack that believed itself untouchable and ideologically holy because of its humanitarian redemption through terrorism. After the bloody attack on the Azul barracks,[121] Perón established the doctrine of defense of the State. "The fight against violence and subversion is left to the entire population, the police and security forces and, if necessary, the Armed Forces... The small number that remains will be exterminated for the good of the Republic." In those days Perón reiterated the word "annihilation" for the first time from the presidential podium. He imitated Roca[122] when he recommended the

---

119 "The Old Man."

120 All members of the Montaneros, a left-wing Peronist guerilla organization, which took its name from the nineteenth-century paramilitary groups during the wars of independence.

121 An attack in January 1974 against the Azul military garrison by People's Revolutionary Army (ERP) against the government of Juan Perón.

122 Julio Argentino Roca, general and statesman who served as president of Argentina from 1880 to 1886 and again from 1898 to 1904, known for his military campaigns of annihilation against the indigenous populations of Argentina.

"*malón* against *malón*."[123] He settled on the hypocritical indecision of the Argentines and, in fact, while saluting, as the military man he was, in a storm in Paraguay, he contracted the pneumonia that would kill him.

The telegram of the leader's death was brought to me by Rega, who acted scandalized. We organized a mass and the book of condolences in our neighborhood basilica in Cannaregio. There was little repercussion. Italian newspapers begrudgingly acknowledged a "former Mussolini supporter." The Italians were so sincerely fascist that they accused others of being so, like cheating schoolboys.

He was succeeded by his wife, Isabelita, and a cabinet of Justicialist[124] caciques who obeyed the general's doctrine and signed the decree of annihilation, a sort of final solution. Impotent and mediocre, they yielded, with almost unconcealed complacency, to the relief of the military coup of March 24. Videla, Agosti and Massera,[125] the leaders, implemented and won a battle of annihilation that was widely supported by the middle class, the active forces, and the unions.

---

123 *Malón* refers to raids by indigenous, mostly Mapuche, warriors during the 17th to 19th centuries, both against rival indigenous groups and European settlers. As a result, Roca implemented a policy of occupation of all indigenous lands as a means to "extinguish, subdue, or expel" the indigenous peoples who lived there.

124 Reference to the Justicialist Party, a major political party in Argentina and largest branch of Peronism.

125 The three-man military junta that ruled Argentina during the period known as the "Dirty War," from 1976 to 1983.

64

DELIA BEGINS TO fall into existence. She was getting closer to life. She came round to reason and emotion, and their inevitable dangers. She transforms, her self grows. She gives her opinion, interrupts, laughs. She develops a taste for being and gets drunk on mere existence. Venice and Iván push her toward self-esteem. She's now using Iván's schoolbooks. Sometimes they debate. Together they support each other. They often study across from each other at the desk in Delia's room. We bought them a blackboard at the Standa department store. They share classroom tricks. They hurl flecks of incipient bad faith at each other, in their arguments. They're advancing within the forest of adulthood. Delia possesses the—somewhat naïve—joy of someone who wins the first chips at roulette.

Delia asked Iván to take a picture of her by the cistern in the palazzo courtyard. She carefully dressed in her apron and her servant uniform. She had the photo blown up in sepia and told Iván that from now on she would be working in black pants and a white blouse. The photo was like a certificate of farewell for a stage of her life. It didn't seem very coherent. Delia was existence in motion. And that gesture did her a lot of good because no one suggested it to her. Her self-esteem was born.

Another unexpected step was her friendship with a male employee of the communal school where she took her monthly exams. Giancesare Scocchimanni was a young lawyer who'd come from Catanzaro to try his luck in the North. Delia had taken Sabine into her confidence. They walked many Sundays, dined in picturesque *trattorie,* and eventually traveled ten days to Florence and Rome. The only thing I could learn was a few sentences from Sabine's Germanic parsimony:

"It seems that the trip didn't go very well. Delia complains about Silvio's continuous aggressive remarks against the Venetians. He seems to be quite resentful."

I thought Scocchimanni would make common cause with a third-world "refugee." I later learned that Delia had returned to Sundays with her Peruvian friend, Carmen, and that she was still teaching everything she learned in her courses to her friend's son, a boy of about fifteen. It seems that Silvio's definitive distancing was due to an immensely brash phrase from Scocchimanni: "How can you love that country where people are dying of hunger?" he said in reference to Argentina. After a while, Sabine told me that Scocchimanni, according to some of Delia's comments, soon adopted a posture of European racial paternalism, protective in appearance, almost preachy. Sabine added:

"If she'd liked him, she would have put up with it. But I don't think Delia will be able to fall in love with any man," she said as if she knew a mystery or a secret.

"But if she'd fallen in love, normally?" And Sabine:

"She would have left him anyway...Her wonder at having a normal life ended, as happens to everyone."

As Sabine returns from a meeting, she crosses Piazza San Marco and sees a group of people talking, laughing, and commenting around two tables at the Florian on the square. They are Delia's classmates from the exams.

"Then I understood that Delia exists, that she's now soaring outside of the shadow that was her lot as a child ... "

She was dressed in her black pants, white blouse, and vest. She tells them things about her country. They pay attention. She's the exotic one. They are girls who come from Conegliano, from Treviso, from Mestre, from Caorle.[126] And Delia is already the famous one of the group that very likely meets after all the monthly exams.

"I felt that Delia was enjoying her popularity. I was thrilled," Sabine said. "She was the one who raised her hand to call the waiter and who divided the bill among all of them. La Delia, la Delia, they called her ... The pants and the short vest give her a good figure. And she is certainly the leader of her group."

---

126 These are all towns in the Veneto region or boroughs of Venice. The suggestion here is that they are all local girls.

65

THE REORGANIZING MILITARY coup arrives in Venice "for me," on a sizzling Bastille Day, July 14, celebrating the French Revolution. I receive a message from my colleague Mazzini, in New York:

"I've been told to warn you. You're not seen in a good light. Apparently because of your books and because you resigned from your professorship with Fayt, related to the Night of the Long Batons... [127] That's the message."

"Thank you."

A functional cowardice invades me, darkens the day. I feel like Adam on that morning of serpent and whoredom, when Jehovah drives him out of Eden. You will till the earth. By the sweat of your brow... That calling could be the beginning of our best stage, perhaps unequaled. That threat would disturb me in my responsibilities for months. *The Dogs of Paradise*, my novel, was still a puppy. My profession could be over.

---

[127] La Noche de los Largos Bastones was the violent removal on July 29, 1966, by the Federal Argentine Police of students and faculty at the University of Buenos Aires who opposed the attempt by the military dictator General Juan Carlos Onganía to revoke the academic freedoms established in the Argentine University Reform of 1918.

Ada was sitting on the doorway's cool marble, her ears perked up, as if to remind me of her species' tradition of vulnerability and risk that we humans can no longer even imagine.

Sabine entered with Iván, protesting. They had to leave the beach early. We had to go to the fresh and genuine champagne reception of my colleague André Tronc, who was celebrating France's national holiday.

How would I fight? I was considered a good professional, trained in France, professor and diplomat by competitive examination.

The military would exercise reorganizing distrust,[128] without distrusting. They would enter singing with the social redeemers, in an Argentina transformed into a suburban slaughterhouse.

As Sabine and I walked toward the pier, I whispered to her, as if not to alarm her, that a friend had warned me to be careful regarding my professional career.

"I thought something was going to happen... It was because of your novel *Los bogavantes*,[129] you were censored in the Planeta Prize, you made fun of Franco's military..."

We were all placed on standby, civil servants, judges, and diplomats. They did not want malicious infiltrators,

---

128 This is a reference to the National Reorganization Process, a euphemism for the military dictatorship that ruled Argentina from 1976 to 1983, which seized power from President Isabel Perón, the widow and second wife of former President Juan Perón.

129 Although never translated into English, the title translates roughly to *The First Oarsmen*. This was the author's first novel and presumptive winner of the Planeta Prize in Spain until disqualified by Franco's censors.

especially ideological ones. Commissions were formed. The Ministry of Foreign Affairs had been given to the Navy. To a group of happy-go-lucky officers and two dour admirals. While we were on our way to the consulate, I told myself that I had the obligation to preserve what was superficial but essential: my profession as a diplomat, my family. I had to preserve what I understood, already with two published books, my destiny as a writer after nine years of service between the embassy in Moscow, then in Peru during the revolution of Velasco Alvarado.[130]

I must fight for my prestige, I thought on the vaporetto, without telling Sabine. I'd have to defend myself with cunning, to shamelessly plead for my freedom as a writer and my rights and prestige as a professional. I was running the risk of losing my career; I would soon learn that others were losing their lives between the two prongs of the pincer of violence: the terrorism of the revolution and the death executed by power with an easy trigger. Until the end of our six-year term, friends would arrive in Venice, witnesses to irreparable and misguided violence: Hipólito Paz,[131] Holver Martínez Borelli, the lawyer and poet who'd been tortured and stripped of all will to live. And Antonio di Benedetto, the extraordinary writer, on whom they practiced torture and pretend executions that didn't end up in the roar of rifles but in something worse: the henchmen's heinous laughter.

---

130 Juan Francisco Velasco Alvarado, a Peruvian General and dictator from 1968 to 1975 who was declared by coupists as the "First President of the Revolutionary Government of the Armed Forces."

131 Argentine writer, politician, diplomat, musician; also, ambassador to the United States and minister of Foreign Affairs during the presidency of Juan Perón.

The French Consulate with its open gates and its kepi-clad gendarmes. The usual greetings. It seems that I'm giving in to a feeling of farewell. I always found cocktail parties unbearable. Fellow consuls, high-ranking officials. Gianni de Michelis, Napolitano. André Tronc, the host, with his bow tie, accompanies Peggy Guggenheim to the pier, where her gondola awaits her with its two gondoliers dressed in the heraldic colors of the Palazzo Venier. With her Brancusis, Giacomettis, Max Ernsts, Calders, a Picasso and Juan Gris, the millionaire Peggy of the roaring twenties thought herself more important than Venice itself. She was rejected for her arrogance. It is known that she hired Consul Tronc, an amateur writer, to write her biography, listing her loves and lovers of both sexes. At the end of the book, she attacks her relatives and controversial acquaintances and, above all, tries to impose the—desperate—notion that her much-adored daughter had not committed suicide. It was discovered that Peggy had left early that July 14 because she decided to cancel the agreement with Tronc to write her memoir. We later learned that she considered Tronc's work dull; he thought it inconvenient to include Peggy's lesbian relationships.

Tronc was not a career diplomat. His incautious freedom made that obvious. We spoke a great deal; he wanted to know about Che Guevara and Cuba where I'd traveled as a guest. After the failure of the bestseller project about the then octogenarian Peggy Guggenheim and her insouciant memories of an eroticism *tous azimuts*, he went on to write about the heroic Argentinean, who lived in the wrong century.

A feeling of farewell? I had three glasses of champagne in a row, Sabine four. And this time I plunged with a certain joy into the party. An effusive embrace with Tronc, Giavi, the *cavaliere* D'Aloja, the taciturn Lake. I thought we'd no longer go to the monthly dinners on the floating terrace of the Gritti Hotel. The Venetian counts and countesses, Corner, Loredan, Albrizzi, the Volpis, and the head of the historical aristocracy, Vendramina Marcello. The intelligentsia: Massimo Cacciari, communist in his secular life and angelologist in the esoteric vein of Henry Corbin. Professor Aimonino, Vittore Branca, Tomás Maldonado, who has arrived from Milan with Inge Feltrinelli, his partner. Hugo Pratt, imposing, ironic, less famous than his universal Corto Maltese,[132] reminding me of his Buenos Aires, that also mythological city. Mieli and his friend François Revel. Our extra-consular gang: Sandra and Carlo Santoro, with the Codognatos laughing at Guggenheim's nobiliary gondola. The Mielis, Lieselotte, the tapestry designer, and her husband Giorgio. They spread in derisive whispers that they'd seen Brodsky and Andreina seated in one of the crowded bars in Capri's central square. The sarcastic Giorgio said:

"There is nothing wrong with it. They probably met by coincidence. She returning from her conference in Moscow and he from the University of Michigan. Although Capri doesn't have an international airport ... "

Tomás Maldonado had walked up and led me away from the group I was in:

---

132 An Italian comic book series that recounts the adventures of a character of the same name, created by Italian comic book creator Hugo Pratt.

"They ransacked the house of Federico Vogelius.[133] The country home in San Miguel. They beat him viciously. They stole his paintings and incunabula from his library he'd designed to protect them from humidity and temperature variations, how ironic! They smashed to pieces a totem by Sesostris Vitullo. It was all because of the magazine *Crisis*, which had become a mouthpiece for the guerrillas."

"We should call Sabato; he's the only one who can do something … " I said.

"They're arresting people in droves. They're disappearing. They're hauling them off. They're killing them."

---

133 An Argentine businessman, newspaperman, art collector, and founder of the liberal political and cultural magazine *Crisis*.

66

UPON RETURNING I mention to Sabine that I'd always believed myself to be above the routine cocktail parties of diplomacy. But my career had allowed me to go to Moscow and meet, precisely at a July 14 celebration, the detestable Ilya Ehrenburg, who'd written *The Thaw*, recalling those fellow writers who'd died during the Stalinist cultural regime in the face of their complicit silence. And I was in the box next to the commander of the "Red Cavalry," from the battles of 1925, Marshal Budyonny and Alexandrov, the camera assistant to the great Eisenstein, who told me about the filming of *Ivan the Terrible*.[134] And the poet friends of Yuri Datskievich.[135] If I am not confirmed to my rightful post, I will miss my career. Budyonny with his mustache of a patriotic poster general. Venice is sinking in time for me. I would like to never leave. Ever.

Sabine interrupts my thoughts:

---

134 This is a reference to the 1944 Soviet film directed by Sergei Eisenstein.

135 According to the author, a Russian functionary whom he met in Moscow whose duties involved cultural relations with artists from Latin America.

"Don't worry. Let's go live in Seville, as we discussed before, you'll write for Spanish newspapers; I'll work in some German company. We'll go to the Real Maestranza[136] to see Curro Romero!"[137] She laughed and remained pensive. "At the end of the day, wouldn't that be better?" And like always she quotes her beloved Rilke: "Be ahead of all parting." "To be invulnerable leads always to a stagnant life. One is always born vulnerable."[138]

"Or one dies of hunger," I said sinisterly. I didn't want to tell her the terrible news about Vogelius. The boys were friends of Iván. Everything was tinged with death.

I felt that reality was preparing me to say farewell. That cocktail party was excluded from the happiness of our life in Venice. The faces of that sea of acquaintances and friends would vanish into oblivion, according to a secret inner law that we will never decipher.

Venice was slipping away from us, as if drifting away in the calm night.

But the political crisis passed. I was confirmed in my post and with my rank. Two years later, at the end of the six-year term, we would have an anodyne, melancholic farewell, but without the taste of the anguish of being victims to stupid military repression.

Our professional exile in the *Serenissima* continued. I met again with my Wednesday colleagues at the Gritti,

---

136 Plaza de toros de la Real Maestranza de Caballería de Sevilla (a 12,000-capacity bullring in Seville).

137 Francisco Romero López, a Spanish bullfighter known by the nickname Curro.

138 Although Rilke writes at length about vulnerability and defenselessness, I have been unable to locate these lines. I suspect that the quote may be a synthesis of Rilke's writing.

with their newest gossip, with their predictions about the corruption of the officials and this month's extraordinarily high water. It was as if these November floods had magically brought Venice back to us.

67

ANOTHER HOT SUMMER comes to an end: the sunset brings a cool breeze. I work on my books during the siesta. I half-close the shutters; the Canal languishes in the heat. On the shore of the market and the Nuove Fabbriche, from 1709, the exhausted tourists lie down in the shade of the arches. They take off their burning tennis shoes, weary from their pedestrian homage to the Venetian labyrinth they don't understand. They drink water with the thirst of explorers. They doze. Some embrace.

I persisted in the search for my voice. *Daimón* has left for Spain, carrying the madness of Lope de Aguirre, with his dream of taming the monkeys of the Amazon to create a liberation brigade against the king of Spain. What is this impulse that takes so many hours away from a creator's life? Days of drought. Moments of enthusiasm. Almost puerile ambitions. Doubts as a betrayal of feelings or truths.

The rows of letters like a caravan of ants going down the sheets of aged paper of the old forms from the daily ledger ripened in the most lost orlop of the *palazzo*.

When Sabine and Iván return from the Lido beach, I review what I've written in the café in Piazza Santi Apostoli.

And I generally think it holds up. I correct mistakes and await the next siesta.

One morning my agent calls me from Spain with the joyful news that *Daimón* is under contract and will appear in three months. I look at the time, the space, and I sense the flattering timbre of his voice, such an important impulse for the lone navigator. Then I know that I will finish the wager of a more rigorous, more insane, freer language of *The Dogs of Paradise*.

But what is this wager that accompanies (or carries) us all our lives? What's it all about, I ask myself again. Not even the victims of this useless passion know it.

68

THE BIMONTHLY DINNERS and luncheons of the consular corps were seductive, almost unmissable. Richard Hurny, our dean, would open the session and propose a topic of administrative interest to the consuls. Later everything devolved into gossip, stories, anecdotes, and protests about the blatant corruption in the famous Moses plan to defend Venice from the fury of the sea. Days of laughter or political bickering among the honorary consuls (the Italians in the group). Decisive times were approaching for the politics of the Historic Compromise.[139] A real transformation of a Europe that hadn't yet decided whether to exist. Unarmed, dependent, squeezed between Berlinguer's communism, which sought independence from Soviet Stalinism, and Moro's wing of Christian Democracy, which wanted to break with the tutelage of the United States. With the aspiration that the Common Market could establish itself as an autonomous power in the face of the US-USSR grip. In other words, to relaunch in some way de Gaulle's failed project. But with no De Gaulle in sight.

---

139 The *Compromesso storico* was a political accommodation between the Democrazia Cristiana and Partito Comunista Italiano.

I understood that something serious and great was at stake in Italy, despite the apparent mediocrity of parliamentarism turned toward everything small, alien to Nietzsche's Great Politics, which predicted that "the real Europe will be born again as it approaches its grave."

At these meetings the master of ceremonies was often Alberico D'Alondra, a Neapolitan nobleman exiled in Venice, as he was fond of saying. He was similar to Totò: thin, angular, with very lively eyes and that restrained yet sarcastic spirit typical of the age-old Neapolitan character.[140]

He recounted, mimed, and interpreted Casanova's escape from the Leads,[141] a prison famous for its cruelty and connected to the Ponte dei Sospiri of the Doge's Palace, where trials were held. The condemned went from legal sentence to torture and death, including nobles.

Casanova went to the Doge's Palace for a certificate and learned that he was condemned in absentia to five years for "occultism, lust, sexual corruption" and, worst of all, for "Cabalism." Death in the prison came in two or three years—for those who went to the dungeons on the roof, who roasted beneath their 140-degree lead plates, as well as those who went to the underground dungeons, the *pozzi*, the wells, where they died of pneumonia, from spending hours under floodwater, or simply drowning. The ineffable D'Alondra recounts:

---

140 Antonio de Curtis, or Totò, was an Italian actor and comedian, dubbed the *Principe della risata* (Prince of laughter).

141 Called "the Leads" (*Piombi* in Italian) because of the lead plates that covered the roof, the cells were located on the top floor of the east wing of the Doge's Palace and were reserved for prisoners of high social, political, or religious status.

"Casanova, desperate, knew that the only thing to do was to flee, and soon. He climbed up the ridge beam, barely leaning on a brace, and began to unhook a lead sheet with a piece of iron. Always by a single hand."

D'Alondra jutted out his lower chin, and with a fixed gaze he made pathetic gestures as if to unhook the plate and not fall. "He felt a sort of inspiration as he looked through the slit at the cool blue night and stars. A cellmate, the portly friar Balbi, who'd tagged along during the escape, thought Casanova would abandon him. He stretched as best he could and clung to the waistband of Casanova's pants. The priest was also carrying a bag of papers he'd stolen from the ducal archive and thought he could sell for a large sum of money. He wore the bundle hanging from his neck. Casanova endured that dead weight as he clung with one hand." And D'Alondra scrunches up his face, and with his left hand pretending to hold on, he even looks like he's about to sweat. We almost applaud him for his histrionic ability. He tells us what Casanova wrote: "My first impulse was to give him a kick and send him after his bundle; but God be praised, I had enough self-command not to do this, for the punishment would have been too severe for both of us, since I alone could never have escaped, but also by the prick of Christian piety. Killing a priest would bring us bad luck..."[142] "With considerable effort he manages to get past the friar, but the latter loses the bundle he'd tied around his neck, which rolls and falls without making much noise on the side of the building. The rope they'd

---

142 The author's quote seems to be a composite of quotes taken from Casanova's memoir. In an attempt at historical accuracy, I have included as much of the quote from the memoir as possible.

fashioned disappears with the lost bundle. This signals failure. Casanova despairs. Any attempt to escape is met with the *garrote*,[143] immediate strangulation. At midnight on the first of November the bells of San Marco shake the night air, greeting All Saints' Day. The sinner Casanova's courage was restored; he knows that among the multitude of saints is his heavenly protector. He writes that upon hearing the bells he felt, without self-importance, that God was giving him a push toward life, which can only be conquered with boldness and courage, the same as with a woman. Without a rope, he reenters the sinister building through a small window with the friar clinging to his waistband, and they begin their descent through the granary and storeroom of the building along the side canal. They break down a pair of doors. Casanova fixes his torn white stockings and his morning coat as best he can and incredibly, they enter the Scala dei Giganti, that is, the main exit door of the Ducal Palace. They've fallen into the tiger's mouth!" exclaims D'Alondra, well along into his story. "Some of the guards see a shadow come out with the obvious gait of a gentleman with hints of official jargon, followed by a possible buffoon in a red waistcoat and ridiculous violet-colored culottes and no stockings. It seems logical to them. At this point Casanova rids himself of the friar. He finds a gondolier working at night and orders him to take him to Fusina,[144] to seek refuge from Venice on the mainland.

---

143 The *garrote* is an instrument of execution that dates to Ancient Rome and involves strangulation or breaking the neck of the condemned person by means of some sort of ligature, often an iron collar, fixed to a chair.

144 A locality of the municipality of Venice, located on the mainland and included in the municipality of Marghera.

But D'Alondra tells us that Casanova is lying. That he ordered the gondolier to take him to the Campo Santi Giovanni e Paolo, to bid farewell in his classic way to Venice where he would return some twenty years later. He knew that he would find M.M., the novice Marina Morosini, his mistress during his hours of greatest lust, whom he shared with mutual, discreet, and silent tolerance, with the French ambassador in Venice, Cardinal de Bernis. Everyone smiled, looking at Pierre Dron who could not conceal a look of national satisfaction. And D'Alondra concluded:

"We will never know if she was free from the cardinal or if Casanova had to continue worse for wear toward Fusina beyond the rigor of the *Serenissima*. Out of harm's way but leaving Venice without the taste of his great nights in his mouth ... "

We applauded him with fervor and laughter. His implications and his poignant gestures were those of a consummate actor.

And then a wonderful fish and seafood frittata. Prosecco, Negronis, scotch or Amarone del Friuli. All for 15 dollars, as agreed by the deft and influential Giavi, permanent secretary of the "Club of 13."

When everyone said goodbye, Lake, Hurny, and I stayed behind for another coffee.

"Our Italian friends are hiding political unrest from us."

"After the outrageousness of the invasion of Czechoslovakia, global communism entered into crisis, and the ideological and electoral rise of Berlinguer shatters the Stalinist obedience of the Togliatti era," said Hurny, who throughout the meetings seemed to me the most informed on international affairs.

Lake explained that Aldo Moro's Christian Democratic wing proposed a great alliance, the Compromesso Storico, to break with the US-USSR dominance, which was consolidated worldwide after 1945.

"So important was the matter in secret diplomacy that it seems that Henry Kissinger had a meeting with Moro to almost threaten him with such a move, which for Nixon was tantamount to reissuing De Gaulle's policy: a united Europe from the Atlantic to the Urals."

It occurred to me to tell them that Aldo Moro was a reincarnation of Casanova, breaking his hand to lift the lead sheet, as our friend D'Alondra had so amusingly recounted.

A few months after that meeting, on another fateful Ides of March, Moro was kidnapped and held for two months. His "companions" after so many years in power proceeded like those of Julius Caesar. Moro's body was found in the trunk of an abandoned car. No one had defended him. Everyone imagined who'd had the power to assassinate him.

Europe remained mired in happy consumerism and its cultural and political decadence. A kind of NGO full of traditions, but afraid to assume the destiny of being the cultural center of the West, not as a memory, but as a power.

Splendid Venice was the reflection of the courage of its history and responsible for History, as in the times of the Holy League of Lepanto.

69

EL PORTAZO, not just the closing, but the slamming of a door. That's what we call Delia's final phase before our departure. Restlessness, turbulent silences. Weeping. What Iván called a "concert of pots and pans" to show her crankiness from the kitchen. It was not directed at us. We were beginning to realize that we knew nothing about her. Who was Delia really? One believes he knows the other's— his fellow man's—intimate self, but it's merely gestures, almost nothing.

Something was breaking inside her. We'd gone to Rome for two days and would return the afternoon of her birthday. We were delayed and called her to say we'd arrive late in the evening. But we made a mistake. We didn't wish her a happy birthday. She would experience this venial omission in a call from the road as a disappointment, almost an affront. She threw the laborious *coq au vin* she was preparing for the celebration into the trash can and then suffered an attack with tremors that was similar to the one she'd had when we saw Rucci's assassination on television. Lisetta, the caretaker of the *palazzo*, discovered her fallen, moaning. She called the emergency services and they loaded Delia into the water ambulance through the side gate. They kept her under observation for a week, unable to make a diagnosis. Who was Delia? What ghosts was she carrying?

During our last year, she trained for her life alone in Venice, where she would continue her adventure. She and her Peruvian friend, Carmen, rented a small apartment and began to cook, with great success, meals for the receptions held by our Venetian friends.

Carmen, years later, told us about the day Delia returned from medical school, when she'd already successfully passed more than two years of medical school, and told her with determination:

"I am not going back to school. I don't want to be a doctor." Carmen said she couldn't believe it. As it turned out, that afternoon, during the surgical rotation, she was asked to make an incision on a line on the abdomen of an anonymous cadaver, embalmed for dissection.

"The line became blurry. I inserted the scalpel, and thick, black blood spurted out. It was the blood of death. It wasn't the living blood we know. It wasn't blood either. It was death. Pure death."

Carmen tells us that the teaching assistant and a group of classmates traveled from Padua to make her change her mind. It seemed incredible to them that she would abandon everything after so many years of effort. They loved and even admired her. But Delia left the apartment without saying anything to them before they arrived. That's the way she is. She ran away. She couldn't explain what she felt …

She got the idea, Carmen recalls, to raise money. As much as possible. She began working in a *trattoria* in Campo Santa Margherita. She spent hours preparing special dishes. After six months, the owner of the place, who saw his business growing, offered her a share as a partner. Professor Giovanna Contro lent her the necessary money, which Delia paid back unfailingly in installments. But then came the endpoint. For Giovanna, a process that was already underway reached its completion when she learned of Iván's death years later.

On a freezing January day, when I was already working at the embassy in Paris. We were devastated, expelled from the garden, yet there seemed to be no hell for us. The phone rang late in the never-ending night. Sabine heard only a groan and then: "What can I do now in life? Now that Iván is dead, what am I to do in life!" And Delia just hung up. Without saying anything more.

We know from Giovanna Contro and Carmen that Delia wanted to go to the mass for Iván that was celebrated at the Istituto San Giuseppe, with his teachers, his former classmates, their parents, and the grieving Mother Lucrezia.

"We went with her; she seemed to be in a calm sleepiness," Giovanna told us.

But Delia fell apart before the third chord of the organ in the requiem mass. She fainted and again the water ambulance took her to the Santi Giovanni e Paolo Hospital.

For Carmen that was the endpoint. Without Iván, in the midst of a crisis of not wanting to be what she'd longed to be and for which she'd fought to win.

Her hidden demons had kidnapped her. They seemed to want to return her to the space of colored mud, of solemn toucans and of those flocks of joyful, screaming, thieving magpies. To the space where her parents had given her to a family of Ukrainians.

Delia had overcome the temptation to exist. She was crumbling into her misty past. Those pasts that one wants to push beyond oblivion, to recover one's own life and death line. The dangerous authenticity.

She said to Giovanna:

"In reality I'd never have been a real doctor. Always "*la morettina*," the *morochita*.[145] I tried at being. But being for nothing. You can only leave through the only door you have, not through the doors you invent."

She ended up earning good money that year. Her share in the *trattoria* had increased significantly because of the quality of the food. Venetians with a good palate flocked there in a city culinarily degraded by shameless tourism that invaded every space.

Giovanna, a psychologist, provided her with talk support therapy more or less every two weeks. She told us that Delia had recurring dreams, which became obsessive because of the frequency. She saw herself at the Santa Lucia station, on the night train to Rome. She felt an extraordinary feeling of peace, as if she were freeing herself of an enormous burden, when she stretched out in the train's berth and covered herself with a blanket. Then she dreamed of herself on an Alitalia plane, free of pain, in a continuum of pleasurable escape. From the seat of the plane, she transferred to the night bus of the Chevalier line, without abandoning the placidness or the warm somnolence of the train she'd left behind in Venice. The route along the Argentine coast. It was very strange. She only seemed to open her eyes when we reached the coast of the Paraná River.

---

145 Each of these are epithets, the first Italian, the second Spanish, both in the diminutive form, which here can be interpreted as condescending, roughly translated as "the little dark girl."

The herons awaking, the flock of birds in Corrientes Province, the yerba mate fields, and the forest of the town of Esquina. And that huge river and the banks muddied with reddish silt.

The motherland, destroyed, difficult, the missionary jungle, from childhood and now in their reunion.

Already from that bend of the great river in Esquina, it was as if she'd awakened from the drowsiness of the whole trip. She lay her head against the bus window, and I saw her relaxed face looking at the landscape that unfolded before her. She emerged from a very long sleep. She was looking at the golden *pacús* and huge *suruvíes* offered for sale by children on the roadside.[146]

"She told me words unknown to me: *coatí, caraus, patos naranjeros, tijeretas, camoatís, carpinchos.*[147] As if she were showing me the other side of the moon and recognized all the little animals that calmed her childhood."

For her part, overcoming some discomfort, the kind-hearted Carmen explained to us:

"Professor Contro knows this, but I think you should know it too, given that Delia chose her jungle. Before you hired her in Buenos Aires to come to Venice, she had a son. A son by that miserable *machista*, rather defiler, of our life of misery. A son who, just as they did to her, she "gave" to a family. It's understandable that Iván, who was five years old when you left Buenos Aires, was the son she helped raise as mother and sister. To laugh, to play, and to recover

---

146 Two species of fish common to the Paraná River.

147 *Caotí* (a long-tailed mammal), *caraus* (large heron-like bird), *patos naranjeros* (a species of duck common to Argentine coast), *tijeretas* (earwigs), *camoatís* (a kind of wasp), *carpinchos* (capybara)

her childhood, and even to catch up and surpass him with her demanding studies. A blond, happy boy. Maybe so happy that she preferred to leave before the party went sour.

"I thought you should know Delia's biggest secret. I myself found out too late, never imagining anything so usual that she felt like she had to hide it like a crime. A son, no less. I accompanied her on that dream-trip to Misiones. With her bag full of dollars, to buy land for some brothers and sisters, all from different fathers, of course. She'd made out a bank draft with all the proceeds from the *trattoria* to a bank in Posadas, the capital of her province. But none of them remembered where Delia's son had gone. I myself went with her to put notices in the local newspaper and on the radio in the region. The son appeared straightaway. He was doing odd jobs, living in a shack in an abandoned cattle ranch. Living with a prostitute, unspeakably rude and violent like him, both of them always drunk. On the very night of our arrival the violent boy gave the woman a thrashing; he was drinking *grapa* straight out of the bottle.[148] He hurled foul insults and even shoved Delia, his own mother, when she tried to intervene."

The cycle had come to an end.

"But I won't forget that when we arrived, as we approached her son's rundown house with our bags, sinking ankle-deep in the reddish muck, she took off her elegant Hugo Boss sandals, which she'd bought in Venice, tied the laces together in order to hang them around her neck, and sank her bare feet just for the pleasure of feeling it, as if it were the fresh sands of the Lido in Venice.

---

148 A very inexpensive grape liquor

70

I RECEIVED NEWS of my likely transfer. My, or rather our, happy six-year term was coming to an end. I didn't discuss the rumor with the family. Delia would stay. We would not be there to celebrate her doctor's degree.

My walks in the rainy autumn afternoons were losing their flavor. Venice was receding as if Canaletto had stolen its colors. Even Delia's casseroles seemed to lose their aroma. A cycle of happiness was beginning to close.

I walked along Venice's undistinguished *fondamente* and moorings. The poor Venice of pensioners and laborers. For the first time I understood the journalists who insisted on the alarming depopulation of Venice. It had lost 30 percent of its permanent inhabitants. There were no more than fifty thousand. The palaces were being subdivided, and the interiors were modernized with white walls, armchairs of modern design, and Swedish or Danish lamps. Venice was losing its own life, its people in love, defiant, indifferent to dry land and even to the rest of Italy. The glitter of imperial pride was becoming lost.

I strolled along the poor part of the Castello and Arsenale neighborhoods, as I had done before. But even I had already hocked my poetic lens.

I'd just read the sociologist Salvatore Settis who speaks of "the agony" of Venice. His book is entitled *If Venice Dies*. It is dying because its people no longer believe in it. Settis says that countries and empires die when they lose their memory, when they are unaware of their former glories. When, without realizing it, people lose the identity of homeland, of pride, of shared passion. He writes: "Since the 1966 sea flood, Venetians received twenty billion dollars of national and international aid to 'save Venice,' including the Moses plan. It all went to corruption and political spending. The most undignified form of death for a historical glory, a creative adventure or unicum like Venice, is when young people consider abandoning it for a better life. Everything collapses when they believe that Venice is a limiting ornament, a city-museum that they abandon because they don't know how to rescue it according to the codes of present times."[149]

I lived it when I saw those three and four centuries-old houses eaten away by the saltpeter, the unpainted barges moored along the Fondamenta Nuova. One begins to write down the telephone numbers of friends. Everything becomes a long goodbye, that morbid feeling of farewell. That *ciao* Venezia, *ciao* Giovanna, *ciao* Attilio, *ciao* Andreina.

The drizzle intensifies. There was a melancholy café on the melancholy *fondamenta*. A table of retirees playing cards, shouting like old sailors in that Vèneto dialect where the Spanish of the sixteenth century still resounds, when our language was, like English today, the language, the lingua franca of all the ports of the Mediterranean.

---

149 I was unable to locate this quote anywhere in the English translation of Settis's text.

I drank the hard, bitter coffee; through the window I could see the sea and the pines and cypresses of San Michele, the cemetery island. But no longer visible were the proud masts of the imperial fleet, the origin of the marvelous "made jungles sail," or as the brilliant Góngora wrote "sailing forest, populated by trees / that wear leaves of restless flax."[150]

I returned by way of Santa Maria Formosa. I thought about Argentina: we'd reached decadence before triumph, which seemed inevitable to us! When André Malraux visited Buenos Aires for the first time, he was amazed and said to his Argentine friends: "This is the capital of an empire! But where is the empire ?"[151]

We Argentines have lost the zeal of country. We are a well-molded ceramic, but it was taken out of the oven too soon, and it remained unavoidably crude. I'll return, I'll continue on that always foreign path, which in life (always built by someone as a path for others), we nevertheless follow with the obedience of a sleepwalker.

As Cioran would say, Iván didn't want to fall in time, and Delia fled from the temptation to exist, when she was at the summit of her incredible journey. Both in their own way slammed the door.

---

150 Like his contemporary and lifelong rival Francisco de Quevedo, Luis de Góngora y Argote (1580-1645) was one of the leading poets of Spain's Golden Age.

151 The quote in French is believed to be: "Buenos Aires est la capitale d'un empire qui n'a jamais existé" [Buenos Aires is the capital of an empire that never existed].

71

THE FORMALITIES OF departure. Nothing will change in Venice. It just happens to be our turn on the *pontile di uscita*, the exit pier. During our years here we arrived as tourists, and we leave as now nostalgic residents. We're leaving its salon, "the most elegant salon in Europe," as Napoleon said of the Piazza San Marco, after attacking and bringing Venice to its knees.

The very British Lake used to say that we diplomats die several times, in pieces. Because leaving a country, a capital, after four or six years was like preparing to die. The *hasta pronto* is in reality a "never again." For the friend to whom we say it and for ourselves. These unfulfillable promises sound bad, almost unseemly. "We'll see each other in Buenos Aires; I'll leave you my number." "Whenever we're in Venice, we'll make sure to see each other."

We all have unique emotions: we greet others as one does the dead who'll continue to walk through the *campielli* and the *palazzi*. And, in reality, they embrace us with the affection of a wake. We are the dearly departed, those who leave.

But the reward is to be reborn in another city, good or bad, underdeveloped or very modern, Eastern or Western, or eccentric and surprising like Moscow or Buenos Aires.

Happiness is generally achieved in the city with the most contemptible reputation, sent by a chief of staff who hates us for a reason we'll never know, or for a simple mistake.

Lake would laugh at the profession and say:

"It's also true that one of the possible luxuries of being a diplomat is not having to move again. I retire in December. I bought a three-room apartment on the Grand Canal, it's true, with a wooden terrace on the roof, so I can go up and read the *Times* and the *Observer* in shorts on my canvas lounge chair. I can't imagine a better future than a terrace with no phone or keypad. I'll stick with retirement and Venice. Perhaps the best solution. The rooftop terrace will be my happiness!"

But when we know that we'll soon find out the departure date, everything becomes a fog. The house begins to seem empty. We look differently at the furniture and objects that will remain or that we'll give away. The rooms lose their aroma and temperature. In short, the house itself dies as boxes of books accumulate, pictures are taken down, curtains are abandoned.

A cruel literary retrospective is executed, and works are lovingly thrown into the bags that the employees from charities or the City Hall will collect. Poets, novelists, whose written voice will remain in Venice like abandoned cats.

Some have a hard time with their lovers, male and female. There are intensely professional wives, accomplices in the drama, who, without a hint of jealousy, support their husbands in the difficult task of leaving their local mistress, the intern or the young typist who's finishing a doctoral thesis on Emily Dickinson or Grazia Deledda, Nobel Prize laureate of 1926. They behave with reserve and efficiency, as if complying with an instruction from the secret rules of the chancelleries.

We are shutting down the house. We give away the mediocre wines from the cellar.

Until the day the employees from the moving company come and check all the furniture and decorations that haven't been discarded. They bring the boxes for various purposes. They collect the furniture in some spacious out-of-the way place suitable for packing. The prepared bundles will be taken by boat to dry land to be put into the container for the trip to a new destination.

The consulate employees organized an "Argentinian lunch" in the house of Mabel Vilela, the new official. They reminisced about their years there, the important people the consulate assisted. We laughed, toasted with champagne, and they gave me a medal that read *Al nostro caro console*,[152] and the traditional image of the lion of San Marco. I walked back. It was a particularly nice moment.

Andreina and I said goodbye a few days before my final departure from Venice at the café on the *Ponte dell'Accademia*. She told me that she and her ex-husband had filed for a mutual consent divorce because not even hatred bound them any longer.

"We avoided a hearing with insults and courtroom dramas. Venice is a one-horse town filled with palaces that no longer correspond to people who have nothing to do with its great past. I'm fed up with their stupidity and gossip that my husband always believed. At least we saved him from having to prove he was a cuckold, and I didn't

152 "To our dear consul."

have to prove my disgust for adultery. Justice is absurd. I finally need to get out of that cage of resentment and distrust. It's broken, unfixable. As for you and me, we'll meet again, here or somewhere else. Ritual goodbyes or feigning sadness is unbearable. We've had our laughs. We've seen eye to eye on issues of politics and life. We're almost like schoolmates. And comradeship is indestructible. Love and sex are ephemeral; what's permanent is friendship, that complicity that awakens in others the fiercest jealousy." And she laughed.

"Only lust is remembered, and with horror!"

"Are you really leaving? To Buenos Aires, so far away?"

"Where do you want me to go, to Albania, to enjoy the grandeur and austerity of the underdeveloped socialism we like?"

"That wouldn't be bad at all," says Andreina. "But you won't stop coming to Venice; it's contagious. Couldn't they make you ambassador to Italy?"

"I'll always come back, even if Venice is underwater, and you're on top of the roof of your palace."

We heard the bump of the vaporetto as it moored. Andreina had to go to the cocktail party at the Ca' Foscari University.

"Come on, ciao, come on. No Casablanca-style farewells." She gave me a kiss and ran off. "*Merde, bon voyage!*" she shouted.

"*Bon divorce!*" I replied, while waiting for the change from our coffees.

72

ADA DIVINES THE end of the consul's term in Venice. Cats don't tolerate the lack of routine in homes. She sniffed out every change. Delia only came for a few hours. The blond boy no longer left at a quarter to eight with his school bag and the black uniform with a white collar and school crest. The Consul himself came and went, dressed in dark clothes, to say goodbye to officials and friends. In the house upstairs, the consulate, proceedings were prepared after hours, beyond four o'clock in the afternoon. The inventory was being taken.

The house was being stripped bare. Ada undoubtedly sensed it. Cats know that empty houses are dangerous; they smell hollow. They're occupied by rats instead of affectionate and mischievous mice. And rats act in invincible packs. Ada's obvious anxiety was understandable. Everything was changing and her young, although already grown, would be in danger like that time when the scorpion appeared.

When the moving company began to drop off the large cardboard boxes for packing, Ada became anxious enough to lead her three offspring to the consul's literary desk. There was the table that she perhaps remembered as the scene of the night of passionate lovemaking with that brown, stray cat that arrived balancing on the ledges, only to frolic with her on my pages of *The Dogs of Paradise*.

Ada knocks down three empty cardboard boxes. She evaluates the scant danger of those cubes and insists. With a precision leap she latches on the edge and drops inside.

I'm sorting notes when Ada climbs onto the desk of her nostalgia. We look at each other. Not for the first time. She keeps her eyes on mine. We try to delve deeper, fall into each other. Her green pupils have that dark center rhombus that adjusts according to the amount of light. We seem to be about to bridge the divide. As if attempting an apprehension of that living other, of similar survival functions, of variable and reiterative eroticism. I gently place my hands, as if holding her head, without looking away. But as other times, I don't pass the barrier: she remains in the universe and in eternity. I am still outside the origin. I remain before the world. With all the humanity of my useless and even anguished conscience. In Ada there are no goodbyes, her dimension is eternity.

That would be the last encounter with Ada, with no solution to the biological-existential mystery. That afternoon, the cat lady would return her and her young offspring to her tribe at the gondola station, next to the Ca' d'Oro.

The Venetians say that when one moves in autumn, Venice takes revenge with a fierce cold. The house slowly peels away; my library is already half packed with the signs I write in marker to indicate the position of my three thousand books, which will alight again in another country.

What's certain is that we're taking turns catching colds. It is a customary psychosomatic retaliation. It's certainly the drafts that run from the Grand Canal through the open windows of the Strada Nuova and the Piazzetta Santi Apostoli.

Add to this the inhuman exercise of cordial goodbyes, professional in most cases. Even the fatigue of false effusiveness. But above all the heaviness of those almost perfect years that are ending with the two books I wrote, in which I believe I was able to achieve something, the most important thing.

73

THEN THE ALBANIA affair. Something rather unusual, almost unthinkable. Those experiences that interrupt reality and become tenaciously anchored in memory as the inexplicable, but indispensable. Albania would never have occurred to me. It seems that the last time we mentioned it with a smile was when Hipólito Paz traveled to Venice for a few days because the military coupists had threatened him. In the evening I invited him to a *trattoria* near the house called Aquila Nera.[153] Paz told me:

"Coincidentally, when I was ambassador to Greece, I had to visit Tirana, the capital of Albania. They call their country Shqipëri, land of eagles, and everywhere there's a black eagle like the one on this menu. And the coat of arms is more attractive than the country."

What's certain is that I had to board at Marco Polo Airport with a voucher from Altours, the Albanian state-owned company, which is the equivalent of a visa. It was a small, rickety Tupolev with sixteen seats, most of them empty. Once a week it made the Trieste-Venice-Tirana route. You boarded on foot by crossing a secluded landing to a plane that was the color of a shiny pair of pants. It was

---

153 Black Eagle.

298

one of those planes that were part of Soviet military aid before the Albanian dictator, Enver Hoxha, broke with the Soviets. I plopped down into a seat that was more cushiony than springy and felt settled in. My drowsiness helped me to doze off. It was a two-and-a-half-hour flight. Tirana was on the other side of the Adriatic, around the same latitude as Bari. There were eight of us: a pair of Japanese, two Belgian students, and three Albanians in suits, most likely civil servants. We approached from the sea over the port of Durazzo and hit the runway hard, with the energy of a military pilot.

A civil servant in a suit and tie, but with some kind of uniform cap, showed us where to go.

In the airport lobby, there was an imposing shield with a black eagle on a red background. Four soldiers with light machine guns were guarding a long counter. Three little girls with bows and traditional costumes offered us candies from their baskets and greeted us in their language.

I looked over and through the glass partition of the immigration line, I finally saw my friend who made a discreet nod to me. She was dressed in a long, bell-shaped white dress.

"Welcome to the future!" she said laughing. "I rented a car from Altours; we'll stop by the hotel, the Stalingrad, it's the best, maybe the only one. Luckily, it's sunny; we should leave your things and go to the sea, to the beach."

I nodded, barely moving my head and observing the strange surroundings of that motionless airport. It had a sought-after, remarkably disheartening effect. It was an abandoned village railroad station.

"Nothing like the horrendous Cancun or Portofino! No matter, let's go to Stalingrad and the beach; fortunately, there's plenty of sunshine! The little car from Altours is lovely," my friend said.

It was alone and sad in the deserted parking lot. It was a distant Volkswagen Beetle, with several coats of rabid yellow paint. Atop the gray it shone like a provocative jewel with the blue Altours insignia.

'It's a lovely ride, you'll see," she said. And she took advantage of the opportunity to ask the soldier on duty the way to the beach. The man, in halting Italian, showed her the road to Durazzo, toward the sea and then more precisely to the resort. We passed some cargo trucks heading for the port, then turned toward the beaches with names written in the pre-Indo-European language that distinguished, even silently, the Albanian tribe. It was an asphalt road with deep potholes but visible from afar. She was driving.

"You see, this is what the world will be like after the third war. There'll be time to read, to contemplate. A general socialism. Healthy austerity. A return to nature."

Each entrance to the sea was marked with a cheerful, unpainted beach umbrella.

"One mustn't confuse the natural with the sad," my friend said. "Do you feel better?"

"Yes, the worst part was on the plane. Fatigue and drowsiness."

We could see the serene waves with their foam edge. They rolled over the rather grayish sand and broke with a low, mournful bass drum sound that could be heard from the road.

There was a boy struggling to pull an old dapple nag to the water's edge, to wash the mud off its legs. The horse wasn't having it and was backing away with his wide haunches like Paolo Uccello's horses.[154] We decided to continue to the next beach. We brought the car as close as the dune floor would allow. There was no one there. I preferred to take advantage of my drowsiness to remain reclined and to recover without running the risk of the coast's fresh air. Andreina took off her white dress and with bathing suit and sandals in hand ran along the dune. I watched her enjoy herself from afar. She motioned at me, and there on the hard, wet sand she performed exotic dance steps, stretching her arms as if to climb Jacob's ladder toward the joy of the world, the sea, the void.

The autumn wind brought clouds. I'd fallen asleep when she arrived and put on her dress.

The Stalingrad Hotel belonged to the Stalinist Gothic trend that produced Moscow's great hotel or ministerial towers from the 1930s. Above Skanderbeg Avenue—named for Albania's national hero of the fifteenth century—near the hotel, one could see the enormous monument to Stalin, signaling to the *rigor mundis* from his bronze mustache.[155]

The reception was underwhelming. We were given the Skanderbeg suite.

"Does it have two beds?" I asked.

"No. But it's king size."

"Do they take reservations for the dining room?"

A tie was required for dinner. Women, no pants, said the "chairman" in an affected Italian.

---

154 A fifteenth-century Florentine painter; in his tryptic *Battaglia di San Romano* horses rearing in battle figure prominently.

155 This statue to Stalin was removed from the square in 1991 and replaced with a statue of Skanderbeg.

I would have an aperitif. I was wearing a tie. I'd wait for her to get dressed. The dining room opened at seven.

The adjoining bar displayed a few bottles of indecipherable local drinks and Amaretto di Saronno, Martini, and several brands of vodka ... I ordered a vodka and was served with a couple of appetizing slices of country salami with a slice of extremely white bread, warmed by the bartender in an infrared oven – a delicacy.

A dining room with the infeasibility of Soviet luxury. My friend, dressed to the nines, is the center of attention. We chose a table along the side, near the garden used as an outside dining room.

The menu began with a starter of some disappointingly small *sardelki*,[156] which I'd become familiar with in my Russian days. Then tagliatelle, somewhat thicker than normal, so much so that they resisted being rolled up with a fork. An impressively thick and pure olive oil and wine from the hills. A quite robust red.

An octet came in, dressed in very drab morning suits with wrinkled silk lapels. Viennese waltzes. Khachaturian.[157] When dessert arrived, the table of officers with their wives began to dance. A Japanese couple also. The dark-suited officials, who paid with vouchers, continued to talk, or rather whisper.

We talked about Moro's death, as the end of a possibility of freeing Europe from American and Soviet colonialism. It was the night's main topic.

After dessert the music turned sentimental.

---

156 A kind of knackwurst sausage.
157 A Soviet Armenian composer and conductor.

I thought I heard the bars, the beginnings, of *Hay humo en tus ojos, Laura,* and of the restless *Siboney*.[158] The dance floor became lively and two more couples, who were at the bar, joined in.

I handed the maître d' the two dinner tickets. He asked me if he should send champagne to the suite, 'It's included,' he clarified.

Everything was prepared so as not to interrupt. As we walked up the Skanderbeg suite, a young waiter passed us, climbing two steps at a time and carrying a silver bucket with a bottle of champagne, overwhelmed by chunks of ice, evidently cut with a hammer and punch.

They turned down the bed and delicately placed a soft candy on each pillow.

The lights were bright white. The setting was decidedly marital. My friend tried to soften them, and then with a certain ill humor locked herself in the bathroom for those twenty minutes that are routine for women and inexplicable.

The Albanian protosocialism, the *ur-sozialismus*, as the future of the world desired by chic antimodernism, was hitting us more than our fair share. I crawled onto the side of that bed. I rummaged in the bedside table drawer and at the back I found an intact copy, in English and on India paper, of Mao's *Red Book*. The Stalingrad Hotel was apparently five stars. Red.

---

158 "Smoke Gets in Your Eyes"; "Laura," also known by the title "Cuando tú no estás" (When you're not here), sung by 60s Spanish pop icon Raphael; "Siboney," a Cuban song in cut time, originally sung by Rita Montaner, which symbolizes nostalgia and homesickness.

When my friend arrived *en déshabillé*, I made her laugh with a line from Fitzgerald: "What's a girl going to do with herself on a boat—fish?"

I collapsed from the drowsiness caused by my flu-like state. Without speaking we understood that we'd entered a vault. But we also knew how long, and even tender, the night can be and that bodies find the right time, that they know perfectly when it is not the time to fish. They find inspiration on their own time; they know what they have to do and do not listen to reasons of esteemed spiritual dimensions (ethics, respect, love, hate, sin, etc.). They do not bear in mind or even know what they are doing; they are like blind beasts. But it is they who engender life. The spirit is sterile.

I thought it was she who'd touched my forehead as if to take my temperature. When I opened my eyes, I was surprised by the brightness of the day and the laughter of Iván who shouted: "He woke up, he woke up!"

Dr. Graziani spoke to me with his usual kindness:

"The signora was worried. You took the two *Dormidryl* tablets that I told you to take. Rather than a cold, yours was a case of *esaurimento nervoso*."

"You fell asleep at nine o'clock; it's now twelve noon. I was worried and the doctor was kind enough to come to see you."

"Are you feeling better, *Signor Console?*"

"Yes, perfectly fine."

"*Dormidryl's* long, deep sleep is purifying," added Graziani.

"You seemed to be in the best of all worlds," said Sabine.

"I think I dreamt about Albania, odd, isn't it?"

"Albania?"

Iván's shrieks of laughter started up again, and even Ada came over to check on the curious disorder of schedules.

74

REDEEMING SCANDAL. DEFENESTRATION of a poet. As in the case of Delia, it was about three years after our departure that we learned of the scandal—absolute, resounding—with ridiculous but redeeming particulars for Andreina. With that episode, rumors are consecrated and confirmed, as a totality of gossip, a pack of lies about a woman who, as Brodsky wrote in *Acqua alta* (or *Fondamenta degli Incurabili*),[159] "could have no other destiny than to be cursed in a city where sooner or later all men will have wet dreams about her."[160]

We were already stationed in Paris when I received some calls that indicated to what extent a scandal can be

---

159 *Fondamenta degli Incurabili* (Foundation of the incurables) is the Italian title of *Watermark*, Brodsky's autobiographical essay on Venice. The name is derived from the sixteenth-century Ospedale degli Incurabili (Hospital of the Incurables), located in the Fondamenta delle Zattere. Commissioned by the Consorzio Venezia Nuova (a consortium of the Ministry of Infrastructure and Transport whose mission is to carry out studies, experimental activities, designs, and works to safeguard the Venetian Lagoon), the text was written in English and then translated into Italian by Gilberto Forti.

160 As mentioned before, the author seems to have taken some liberties while citing Brodsky. Neither the Spanish nor the English versions contain this exact verbiage.

distorted in the most opposite directions. Some of the most unusual details of the episode had the ingredient of a comedy so far-fetched, that in and of itself, beyond whether there had been an amorous encounter or not, it was worth recounting as cocktail party banter. And there is returning from ridicule. But when the surreal is surpassed, it becomes invalid. It enters the dimension of exaggeration, the fantastic, and it no longer has any worth as reality.

When the scandal occurred, Andreina was already divorced from the engineer Balder. (The fantasists imagine that Brodsky found out from one of his Venetian buddies.) Brodsky hadn't returned since that December when she'd sent him away on Christmas night, despite the poet's suspected heart attack, by train to Paris, shoddily.

My telephone informants, Ana Taquini, the eminent psychologist, and Giovanna herself, differed in the basic elements about what had happened, which the whole of Venice took as a joke.

Andreina had already been living for a couple of weeks in the apartment that was granted to her for her exclusive use according to the court decree. In the early afternoon that December, she's said to have received an unexpected call from Brodsky in London. He told her that he'd traveled from Michigan for a conference on the great poet Auden, by then deceased. He added, according to some versions, that if he had time, he'd like to see her, have a coffee, since his itinerary included Italy. Probably driven by guilt, but with the need to avoid scandal, Andreina told him to call her when he was in Venice, believing that the call was indeed from London.

This is what Ana reconstructed: at mid-afternoon the doorbell rang, and Brodsky was at the door telling her that he was just stopping by to say hello and that he was leaving for the airport to fly to Rome and from there to the United States. Brodsky was carrying his usual nonsensical equipment, an overstuffed duffel bag and, attached by a hook, the portable Olivetti typewriter with a Cyrillic keyboard. He had the beanie with a pom-pom that he wore in winter and the Soviet jacket he'd worn ten years before, when the KGB had shoved him aboard the plane that took him to the perverse West of his dreams.

Perhaps as a guilt reflex, Andreina could not bring herself to send him away. It would have been unpleasant but feasible due to the presence of the building's caretaker, who was busy cleaning the entryway stairs.

The apartment was partially unfurnished. There were packages of books and documents that hadn't been removed yet by the Engineer Balder, who'd acquired a luxurious penthouse, one of the few in Venice. He was remodeling it, a mania of every architect, and was building a large room for his drawing boards and a suitably large kennel for his beloved Alsatian Shepherds.

One often invents in order to defame someone, but what's most unacceptable is to add precise, collateral details to create verisimilitude. It's not difficult to presume that Brodsky left his horrid luggage of a steppe traveler and that he poured himself one or more whiskies from the open bottle that husbands abandon after they've taken the best wines. It's not illogical to presume that he expressed to her, with despair accentuated by the alcohol, his physical and metaphysical love that had taken him to Venice on his university leave almost every December. This blameworthy version supposes that they were in the bedroom and already *in flagrante delicto* when they heard the first explosion. The other version is that Brodsky was just passing through and they were listening to Mahler's music, so dear to Andreina, on the HiFi, which Balder had abandoned because he'd acquired a more sophisticated one. Giovanna's innocent version is that Andreina was alone and indeed listening to Mahler because the person who disconnected the Bang & Olufsen was the caretaker. He'd already locked the Alsatian Shepherds in the apartment's empty utility room. But he took pity on them during the cold night and brought them up from the basement.

There was a narrow hallway leading to the living room and bedrooms from the kitchen and the service area. The animals had broken free in a rage, burst through a flimsy door and ran down the hallway until they crashed into the bottom half of the hardwood entrance of beveled glass with family coats of arms at the top.

They thought it was an explosion when the two beasts bounced against another not very sturdy door. Again and again, they took off running and crashed against it with terrifying barks, and howls of pain and rage.

How could they bear it in any of the imaginative hypotheses? Brodsky, from his youthful fears, felt the return of the wolves of every Russian childhood. He must have thought it the ultimate revenge of the KGB against a traitor of the Soviet motherland. If Andreina were alone, Giovanna hypothesized, did she perhaps think of those characterological metaphors that could interpret the hatred of the engineer Balder?

The blows continued. Probably, if they were together, they took refuge behind the bedroom wall and watched with horror those fanged animals that could easily tear them apart. Did they only perceive Brodsky as the target, the intruder to be exterminated? Was Brodsky feeling the Jewish agenbite in the face of universal persecution? Did he think that those beasts the engineer used to walk along the Fondamenta Zattere were bastards of the wolves of the snow-covered tundra and the frozen nights of his exile in Arkhangelsk?

The glass trembled but withstood the onslaught. The Alsatian Shepherds continued to butt the bottom of the door; had they leapt at the end of the charge, the crystals would have burst in an indescribable tragedy. At whom was so much fury directed?

Andreina managed to use the bathroom intercom to call the caretaker, who'd heard the noise and called the police, thinking of rookie assailants smashing the door of Mr. Ferrari on the fourth floor.

From the outside door the caretaker, who had been hired to attend to the engineer's dogs, whistled twice in a certain way and the bloodied assassins froze, exhausted and defeated. The police helped the caretaker take the dogs, using the service elevator to the basement storage rooms where they should never have left.

The whole thing lasted no more than five minutes. The caretaker apologized and even begged for mercy. The policemen wrote out a fine for the lack of muzzles on the dogs and the neighbors closed the windows.

Perhaps Andreina put on the interrupted Mahler symphony again. Nobody saw Brodsky. If he'd been there, he could have vanished down the staircase while the caretaker and the police returned the dogs to the basement.

From then on, the scandal was the subject of every kind of unfounded lie and possible truths. The stories canceled each other out. What had happened was too extraordinary.

There was no shortage of people who claimed with authority that "the engineer had unleashed the dogs on that Russian vagabond."

The engineer Balder, indignant, removed his dogs and took them to a veterinary boarding house until the kennel in his luxurious apartment was built.

I found this story hilarious. But all that reached me from afar was laughter and irony at what was essentially a mysterious or frankly unbelievable act. Just one more element to the myth of the marvelous Andreina Vernier. "A Renaissance goddess in Venice with the body of Raquel Welch," according to Brodsky.

Years later, I'd traveled to Caracas because my novel *The Dogs of Paradise*, product of the happy and enthusiastic work of so many Venetian siestas, had been published. I traveled in early August 1987. I stayed at the Ávila Hotel and there I heard on the radio that Joseph Brodsky had been awarded the Nobel Prize for his poetic work and his talent as a critic. Nine years later, he died in New York of a heart attack surrounded by his last wife and the son he had in Russia with the poet Marina Basmanova.

Nadezhda Mandelstam, an extraordinary literary figure of the hard Soviet times, predicted in her famous *Hope Abandoned*: "Brodsky is a remarkable young man who will come to a bad end, I fear."[161] He never forgot this sentence. According to his last will he was buried on San Michele, the island of the dead in Venice.

On a visit with Sabine to the cemetery (we go to Venice at least every two years), we saw Brodsky's headstone, which

---

161 Translated by Max Hayward.

is a few steps away from Ezra Pound's. In that part of the cemetery there are spaces for the dead. In that part of the cemetery there are empty spaces, "futures." Brodsky and perhaps Pound himself will be waiting for the Venetian Anna Akhmatova. But they will have to wait a long time to see her in San Michele.

Andreina, the seductress, married, at the age of forty-six, the most powerful industrialist in Italy. She lived with him in Milan; they divorced three years later.

She returned to Venice with an existential door slam, not unlike Delia's when she plunged into her ancestral jungle, in Misiones. But Andreina lives in a magnificent three-story *palazzina* in Campo San Vio. As for Delia, it was impossible for us to find her, but we know that she generously distributed lots of land to her siblings, or rather half-siblings. I hope to go to Misiones when I retire and find her in the green sea of her jungle.

75

*N*OW IT'S TIME *in blue. A precious, unexpected adolescence: there is nothing to restart. Guilt and sorrow are extinguished in the mist. Irresponsibility is the belated prize, a wisdom of pardoned offenders.*

In the blue of the days nothing can worry and nothing is expected. Nuisances are avoided and a sense of the ridiculous restrains utilitarian endeavors. One learns, with Cicero, that it is incomprehensible for those who are well to pretend to be better.

Lax living, limbo, affections without tortures of love. A long threshold without clocks.

Dead friends—so many!—are in their boxes, with their prestige and pain. They're lined up like in a library. A library-universe, like Borges dreamt. They attempted to create a destiny for themselves, and one imagines them on their horizontal shelves. The squawk of the gravel. All with their arms crossed over their chests. In a peacefulness of closed eyelids of people who fell asleep as if listening to Chopin's delicateness, although they all have their own personal, nontransferable song, usually some nostalgia of love, in any rhythm from anywhere in the world, from As Time Goes By *to* Himno a la alegría.[162]

---

162 Translated into English as "A Song of Joy," a popular rock song performed by the Spanish singer Miguel Ríos and recorded in 1970, set to the tune of Beethoven's Ninth Symphony.

In the blue hours, an imaginative freedom allows us to enter and leave Venice, Moscow, Buenos Aires, or Añatuya at will.[163] *But when I recall Venice and return to my* sestiere *of Cannaregio, there I am still* il Signor Console. *And I still sense that it is the city I would relish revisiting and rediscovering over time.*

---

163 A city in the Argentine province of Santiago del Estero.

GLOSSARY OF ITALICIZED WORDS

(la) abnorme: extraordinary

l'acqua alta (literally "high water") refers to the periods of high tide that occur in the Venetian Lagoon that cause the city to flood

altane wooden terraces built on rooftops in Venice

Arsenale (arsenal) a complex of former shipyards and armories that were once home to Venice's naval fleet; it has been repurposed and serves as the operations center for the MOSE project

Biennale (plural *biennali*) Founded in 1895, Venice's Biennale is a contemporary visual art exhibition held biannually in the Giardini dell'Arsenale, also referred to as the Giardini della Biennale

Bricole (singular *bricola*) are groups of two or three wooden poles, usually oak, that dot the lagoon, indicating the limits of navigable water

Ca' abbreviation for casa (home), also used to refer to a palace, e.g., Ca' d'Oro

calamaretti squid

calle (plural *calli*) is a narrow street, e.g., Calle Merceria

campo (plural *campi*) is the equivalent of "square," often attendant to a church, e.g., Campo dei Santi Apostoli *campiello* a "small square." Like "campo," often attendant to a church

canal the city of Venice is built on 118 small islands that are connected by a series of 177 canals of varying sizes and linked by more than 400 bridges (*ponti*)

Canal Grande The S-shaped *Canal Grande,* also called *il Canalazzo,* is the city's largest canal and divides the city into two parts

canaletto a small canal

cancelliere registrar or clerk

chiesa church

console consul (*il nuovo console* = the new consul)

esaurimento nervoso nervous breakdown

Ferrovia the public water bus stop for the Santa Lucia train station

fondamenta (literally "foundation"; plural *fondamente*) the street or dock that runs along a canal (with the exception of the Canal Grande)

Fondamente nove (Venetian for *Fondamenta Nuove*) is the departure point for ferries to the northern lagoon islands of Murano, San Michele, Burano, Torcello, Vignole, and Sant'Erasmo

foschia a haze or mist

Lido The seven-mile-long barrier island in the Venetian Lagoon that is home to some 20,000 residents

mezzanino an intermediate floor in a building or palace, often between the *piano nobile* (main floor) and the *piano terra* (ground floor)

motoscafo literally a "motorboat"; in Venice, the narrow and fast motorboats that operate as private water taxis

murazzi sea walls built with Istrian stone to defend the banks of the lagoon from sea erosion *paline,* not to be confused with *bricole,* are single posts used for mooring boats

Pescheria formally the *Pescheria del Mercato di Rialto,* Venice's main fish market located adjacent to the Rialto bridge, facing the Grand Canal

piano nobile literally the "noble floor," so called because it was where the palace residents, who were often members of the nobility, resided; located above the *piano terra* (ground floor), which was used by servants or staff, the *piano nobile* corresponds to what is the second floor of buildings in the United States

piazza, the Italian word for "plaza" or "square," but Venice only has a single piazza, that of San Marco; all other squares are *campos* or *campielli*

piazzetta is that which follows the Palace of the Doges until it reaches the San Marco basin, where, in a more gruesome way, capital executions took place between the two columns

ponte (plural *ponti*) bridge

pontile is a landing stage or floating dock where passengers are able to board various watercraft such as vaporetti

rio (plural *rii*) is a small canal, the most numerous, and are permanently crossed by using one of the 420 bridges of Venice (or more … the "experts" argue on the number)

ristretto like an *espresso,* but shorter and stronger

salizada from the word *selciata,* meaning "cobblestone," these are streets that due to their importance were the first streets to be paved in Venice

(la) Serenissima once a sovereign state and independent republic known as *la Serenissima Repubblica di Venezia* (The Most Serene Republic of Venice), the now city of

Venice (*Venezia* in Italian and *Venèsia* in Venetian) is often referred to by this sobriquet

sestiere (plural *sestieri*) district, a section of Venice, not unlike the boroughs of New York or the *arrondissements* of Paris

stil nuovo new style

strada standard Italian for street; there is only a single *strada* in Venice, the Strada Nova in Cannaregio

tartina canapé

traghetto, also called a *gondola parada,* is a large gondola, which can carry up to ten passengers, piloted by two gondoliers

trattoria (plural *trattorie*) an eating establishment that is generally more casual than a ristorante

vaporetto (literally "little steamer") water bus; unlike gondolas, which are largely private, the *vaporetti* are operated by Venice's public transportation system

vicolo an alley

www.ingramcontent.com/pod-product-compliance
Lightning Source LLC
Chambersburg PA
CBHW030818090426
42737CB00009B/781